EXCHANGE RATE POLICIES, PRICES AND SUPPLY-SIDE RESPONSE

Also by Eric J. Pentecost

EXCHANGE RATE DYNAMICS
THE MACROECONOMICS OF INTERNATIONAL CURRENCIES
   (*with Paul Mizen*)
REGIONAL ECONOMIC PERFORMANCE WITHIN THE EUROPEAN
   UNION (*with K.J. Button*)
MACROECONOMICS: An Open Economy Approach

Exchange Rate Policies, Prices and Supply-Side Response

A Study of Transitional Economies

Edited by
Christos Papazoglou
and
Eric J. Pentecost

palgrave

First published 2001 by
PALGRAVE
Houndmills, Basingstoke, Hampshire RG21 6XS and
175 Fifth Avenue, New York, N.Y. 10010
Companies and representatives throughout the world

PALGRAVE is the new global academic imprint of
St. Martin's Press LLC Scholarly and Reference Division and
Palgrave Publishers Ltd (formerly Macmillan Press Ltd).

ISBN 0–333–79457–5

This book is printed on paper suitable for recycling and
made from fully managed and sustained forest sources.

A catalogue record for this book is available
from the British Library.

Library of Congress Cataloging-in-Publication Data
Exchange rate policies, prices, and supply-side response : a study of
transitional economies/edited by Christos Papazoglou and Eric J. Pentecost.
    p. cm
    Includes bibliographical references and index.
    ISBN 0-333-79457-5 (cloth)
    1. Foreign exchange rates–Europe, Eastern. 2. Foreign exchange
rates–Europe, Central. 3. Foreign exchange adminstration–Europe,
Eastern. 4. Foreign exchange adminstration–Europe, Central.
    I. Papazoglou, Christos. II. Pentecost, Eric J.

HG3942.9 .E943 2001
332.4'5647—dc21   2001027368

10   9   8   7   6   5   4   3   2   1
10 09 08 07 06 05 04 03 02 01

Printed and bound in Great Britain by
Antony Rowe Ltd, Chippenham, Wiltshire

Contents

List of Tables

List of Figures

Acknowledgements

The papers in this volume are a selection of the research output from ACE/Phare research project No. P96-6176-R, 'Exchange Rate Policies, Prices and the Supply Response under Transition'. We are grateful to the European Commission for funding this research and for the hospitality provided by the hosts of the four workshop meetings held in Athens, Ljubljana, Rethymno and Prague. The editors also wish to thank Mrs Denise Simpson for secretarial and administrative support.

CHRISTOS PAPAZOGLOU
ERIC J. PENTECOST

List of Contributors

Vladimir Benacek is Associate Professor, Charles University, Prague, Czech Republic.

George Chobanov is Dean of the Faculty of Economics and Business, St Kliment Ohridski University, Sofia, Bulgaria.

Urszula Ciesluk is a member of the Department of Econometrics, University of Lodz, Lodz, Poland.

Aleš Delakorda works at the Bank of Slovenia, Ljubljana, Slovenia.

Alexis Derviz works at the Czech National Bank, Prague, Czech Republic.

Jan Hošek works for CERGE, Charles University, Prague, Czech Republic.

Boštjan Jazbec is a member of the Institute for Economic Research, Ljubljana, Solvenia.

Pavlos Karadeloglou works at the European Central Bank, Frankfurt, Germany.

Vladimir Lavrac is a member of the Institute for Economic Research, Ljubljana, Solvenia.

Wladyslaw Milo is a member of the Department of Econometrics, University of Lodz, Lodz, Poland.

Aleda Mitchell was a member of the Department of Economics, Loughborough University, Loughborough, England.

Christos Papazoglou is a member of the University of Crete, Rethymno and the Central Bank of Greece, Athens, Greece.

Eric J. Pentecost is a member of the Department of Economics and the Centre for International and Financial Economics Research (CIFER), Loughborough University, Loughborough, England.

Bas van Aarle is a member of the Centre for Economic Studies, University of Munich, Munich, Germany.

Piotr Wdowinski is a member of the Department of Econometrics, University of Lodz, Lodz, Poland.

Aneta Zglinska-Pietrzak is a member of the Department of Econometrics, University of Lodz, Lodz, Poland.

1 Introduction: Issues, Structure and Policy Recommendations

Christos Papazoglou and Eric J. Pentecost

INTRODUCTION

The significant fall in output was a common experience of all transition economies of Central and Eastern Europe in the early 1990s. This fall in output was to a large extent unavoidable due to the destruction of the existing structure of production as these economies moved to new, market-guided activities. While the output decline has been a common event in all these countries, the extent of output recovery, as the transition process has progressed, has not been the same. That is, while most countries have followed qualitatively the same steps, their growth paths have deviated significantly. There are countries with quite impressive growth performance, while others have lagged significantly behind.

There are specific reasons behind these differences in output performance among the transition economies. These reasons primarily reflect the importance of the initial conditions within these countries at the start of the transition process, the speed of the structural reform process and the effectiveness of the stabilization policies adopted. While the initial conditions largely explain the initial output decline, the subsequent deviations in growth mostly reflect differences in structural reforms and macroeconomic stabilization. It is a fact that the transition economies neither proceeded with the same eagerness to liberalization and privatization measures nor showed the same commitment or adopted the same policies with respect to macroeconomic stabilization.

With regard to macroeconomic policies, the removal of the large macroeconomic imbalances and the improvement of conditions for private sector activity constitute major tasks, with important implications for output growth. A fundamental component of these policies, which has been vital to growth prospects as well as to the stabilization effort of these countries, refers to the role of exchange rate policy. A critical issue regarding the role of exchange rate policy on the growth of output concerns the relative importance of the various channels through which exchange rate changes are transmitted to output in the case of the transition economies.

1

Following the traditional literature there appears to be two major channels through which exchange rate policy can affect output. The first channel operates through the demand-side and represents an external channel of influence, since it captures the impact of real exchange rate changes on external competitiveness. With respect to the demand-side channel, real exchange rate depreciation, for instance, is expected to lead to a gain in competitiveness, which in turn leads to a rise in the demand for domestic output as the current-account balance improves. The increase in output comes as the real depreciation alters the relative price and profitability of domestically produced goods relative to foreign production. It is, however, also necessary, but not sufficient, for the sum of the import and export price elasticities of demand to exceed unity for the external balance on current account to improve.

The second channel operates through the supply-side by affecting labour-market behaviour and thus wage determination as well as the prices of imported inputs. The supply-side channel constitutes an internal channel of influence operating through the cost of production since it primarily captures the effect of exchange rate policy on wage-setting behaviour and imported raw materials. The effect on wage determination, as well as that on imported intermediate goods, could exert significant influence on production costs generating a supply-side shock to the economy.

The two channels described above differ in importance across the market economies. In most industrial countries the demand-side channel appears more significant while the supply-side channel gains in importance in the case of developing countries. In the case of the transition economies, the relative importance of these two channels is conditional upon a number of factors, which reflect the specific features of these countries. Some of these features may be common while others may differ from country to country and this in turn explains some of the differences in output growth. These factors may include the degree of wage indexation, the different nature of shocks affecting the economy, the degree of discipline in fiscal and monetary policy, the availability of alternative policy instruments, the existence of an initial competitive edge, and other structural and institutional reforms.

Furthermore, across the transition economies, exchange rate policy may affect output through a third channel particularly relevant to the situation of these countries. During transition the exchange rate may also affect the growth of output indirectly through its contribution to both liberalization as well as stabilization efforts which are vital for improving economic performance. Liberalization involves freeing prices and trade from state controls, while stabilization refers to the reduction of domestic and external imbalances. Exchange rate policy influences the liberalization process by exposing domestic markets to world prices and competition and the stabilization process through its contribution to the achievement and maintenance of external balance.

THE STRUCTURE OF THIS VOLUME

This volume is made up of studies that are concerned with the effects of exchange rate policy on the supply-side response – defined as the response of output and the price level – in four transition economies of Central and Eastern Europe: Bulgaria, the Czech Republic, Poland and Slovenia. This involves the development of appropriate theoretical models in addition to empirical research that is concerned with modelling the principal transmission mechanisms through which the exchange rate may affect output in these transition economies.

The text is divided into three parts. Part I outlines a theoretical framework within which to conceptualize the transmission mechanism and the final effects of exchange rate changes on the supply-side of the economies. Part II provides a comparative perspective of the direction, speed and size of the supply-side response to exchange rate changes in the four transition economies. Finally, Part III consists of six country-specific studies.

Part I consists of two chapters offering a theoretical analysis of the effect of exchange rate policy on the supply-side response. Chapter 2 presents a general macroeconomic framework for analysing output adjustment in economies in transition. It examines the dynamic output behaviour considering liberalization shocks to the demand and supply of output and to the demand function for financial assets under fixed as well as flexible exchange rate regimes. The model captures some of the basic characteristics of the transition economies – namely the thinness of financial markets, the potentially low degree of capital mobility and the endogeneity of output, which adjusts not only to the level of demand but also to the progress of the transformation process. The model is able to explain the stylized fact that the progress of transition from a command to a market-based economy may be characterized by a fluctuating level output and by real exchange rate appreciation. In the case of a supply-side shock, for instance, which represents efficiency gains from the transformation process, the resulting positive output growth may be partly crowded out by real exchange rate appreciation.

In contrast, Chapter 3 examines the consequences of an exchange rate regime shift from a target-zone system to a free float through the introduction of a dynamic general equilibrium model of production, trade and consumption in a small open economy under conditions of uncertainty. That is, it analyses the impact of the loss of credibility and the subsequent depreciation of the exchange rate because of the effect of the regime shift on the behaviour of exporters, international investors and domestic households. The analysis demonstrates that exchange rate changes do not affect the demand and supply functions for import or exports, although this result only holds if the currency is fully convertible. In particular, it is shown that the demand for imports gradually rises and, with the presence of currency options,

the supply response on the import side will leave households to consume more imported goods than what they would without the options.

Part II consists of three chapters that offer a comparative, primarily empirical perspective on the supply-side response of real exchange rate changes. These three chapters identify two major channels through which the exchange rate affects output. The first one refers to the direct effect, particularly important to industrial countries, which operates on output through its impact on international price competitiveness. The second channel, which is the indirect one and is especially relevant to the case of the transition economies, relies on the close association between disinflation and growth in these countries. This means that to the extent that exchange rate policy has led to lower inflation in these countries it has indirectly contributed to higher economic growth. Chapter 4 strongly suggests that the exchange rate has significantly affected output indirectly, through its contribution to lower inflation, as well as directly through its impact on competitiveness. Finally, the analysis concludes that a fixed exchange rate regime to the extent that it appears to be more effective in reducing inflation, particularly during the early stages of transition, may have a greater impact on output growth.

Chapter 5 estimates the response of output to changes in the real exchange rate in the four transition economies. The theoretical section shows that the effect of a real exchange rate change on output is ambiguous since the demand-side effect works against the supply-side effect. On the demand-side, a depreciation of the real exchange rate should improve competitiveness and enhance the demand for output, whereas the supply-side effect suggests that output may fall as competitiveness improves since this makes imported inputs more expensive thereby raising the cost of production. The empirical analysis, using panel data-estimation techniques, shows that the output response following real exchange rate changes is similar in the four economies. In all cases the most important influence on output growth is the real exchange rate, and a 1 per cent rise in the real exchange rate (depreciation) gives rise to a 1 per cent fall in the level of output in the long run. That is, the effect of devaluation on domestic output is shown to be contractionary, which in turn means that in the case of the transition economies, the supply effect of a real exchange rate depreciation on output prevails over the demand-side effect.

Chapter 6 is a comparative simulation study that attempts to assess the contribution to output growth of exchange rate policy in Bulgaria, Poland and Slovenia. A multi-equation structural model is used for each of the three countries and compares the results with respect to output following real exchange rate changes. The analysis is based on a traditional wage–price–GDP model in which the main explanatory variables of economic activity are factor prices, competitiveness and the exogenous policy variables. The results show that the effectiveness of the exchange rate in boosting output growth is limited. In particular, the high pass-through of exchange rate changes and the negative impact on output of real wage

increases, appear to be the main reasons that make the impact of an exchange rate depreciation on output either contractionary (Poland) or insignificant (Bulgaria, and to a lesser extent Slovenia where it appears marginally expansionary). This result is fully consistent with that obtained from the use of panel data estimation in Chapter 5.

Part III of this text presents six country-specific studies, one chapter on each of Bulgaria and Slovenia and two chapters on each of the Czech Republic and Poland. This section serves to highlight specific features of the output or price-level response that have been overlooked in the comparative studies due either to the need to employ a common framework or possibly to data inconsistencies. In particular, Bulgaria, for instance, moved from a floating exchange rate to a currency board, while the Czech Republic followed the opposite route moving from a fixed to a more flexible exchange rate regime.

Bulgaria is the only country in this sample to have a currency board, introduced in July 1997. Chapter 7 on Bulgaria, therefore, describes the operation of this specific currency board and attempts to compare the supply response before and after the currency board. It shows that under floating exchange rates there was a positive correlation between real exchange rate appreciation and economic growth, whereas under the currency board the correlation is negative: with exchange rate appreciation associated with lower economic growth. It seems therefore that with a currency board the standard demand-side mechanism dominates the supply-side channel. The problem with this is that to reduce inflation by appreciation also involves lower real output growth. The chapter also develops a simple macroeconomic model to illustrate how this demand-side channel operates under a currency board.

Chapters 8 and 9 are devoted to the experience of the Czech Republic. Chapter 8 examines the Czech experience concerning the impact of the real exchange rate on trade flows in order to argue that Purchasing Power Parity (PPP) is an inappropriate concept for economies under transition since the technologies, endowments and tastes are very different. As a result, for a country undergoing transformation, the real territorial structure of trade does not respond to the relative price-level differential. That is, exports, imports and domestically produced commodities for local usage are not perfect substitutes and therefore their relative price differentials are not relevant indicators for the allocation of trade. Consequently, it is argued that the real exchange rate becomes a concept that gives elusive conclusions for economic policy. Moreover, it is asserted that the real exchange rate has a significant impact, but only in cases of massive devaluation during the early stages of transition. In the Czech case, the 113 per cent devaluation of the koruna in 1990 had a large impact on the volumes of exports of Czech textiles and clothing products to the EU members giving a sharp rise in volume. Chapter 9 assesses the influence of the main macro- and microeconomic factors that affect the price

level in the Czech Republic in the short and medium run. The analysis finds a pass-through from the exchange rate to (non-food) tradable goods prices of 0.06 per cent, while food prices exhibit a much higher degree of pass-through (0.6 per cent). Overall, a 1 per cent change in the exchange rate will raise the domestic price level by about 0.15 per cent in six months. It is also demonstrated that exchange rate changes are not the only channels for inflation even in a small open economy. The level of disposable income, price deregulation in the non-traded sector, interest-rate policy and the level of unemployment are the other determining factors which, along with the exchange rate, define the space for the inflationary potential.

Chapters 10 and 11 examine the supply-side response to monetary and fiscal policy in Poland. Chapter 10 examines the economic performance of Poland in relation to its accession into the European Union (EU) under fixed as well as flexible exchange rate regimes. The analysis introduces a stylized macroeconomic model that captures some basic characteristics of the Polish economy and considers the effects of exchange rate policy together with monetary as well as fiscal policy. A simulation exercise shows that a flexible exchange rate regime may be more preferable during the transition period until the accession of Poland into the EU, since this kind of policy has important advantages in terms of monetary policy independence, flexibility and insulation from foreign disturbances. With respect to the effect of a real exchange rate change on economic performance, the results of the analysis suggest that there is a small supply response in that Polish competitiveness improves following a foreign price increase, but that this improvement is confined to the short and medium run. Chapter 11 examines the strength of the effect of fiscal and monetary policy instruments (including the exchange rate) on Polish inflation, output and unemployment using a partial equilibrium framework. It establishes a strong positive correlation between the nominal exchange rate and the rate of inflation and economic growth in Poland. In addition, the money supply is negatively correlated with the level of unemployment.

Finally, Chapter 12 examines the determinants of the real exchange rate in Slovenia and the exchange rate impact on prices and output. More specifically, in the first part of the study, the main empirical determinants of the real exchange rate, resulting from the use of an error correction model, are the real wage, the terms of trade, interest rate margins and inflation. The second section of the chapter models the price and output response to real exchange rate changes. In particular, simulation results indicate that the exchange rate has a significant impact on the price level and economic activity, but not on the volume of exports. It is argued, therefore, that factors such as foreign demand and competition improving economic policies, are vital in enabling exporters to invest in new technologies and introduce new products to promote export activity in Slovenia.

SOME POLICY RECOMMENDATIONS

The principal policy recommendation that comes out of the studies in this volume refers to the fact that the effect of a real exchange rate appreciation on output is not necessarily contractionary. This suggests that policy-makers should not be skeptical in using exchange rate policy as a primary stabilization tool because of potential output losses. As a matter of fact, the finding that real exchange rate appreciation is expansionary (except in Bulgaria) strengthens further the argument in favour of the use of the exchange rate as the prime anti-inflationary instrument. This conclusion is the outcome of two conflicting effects related to real exchange changes. That is, it reflects the fact that in the transition economies the demand-side effect of exchange rate depreciation on output does not appear as strong as the corresponding supply-side effect. There are in fact two basic reasons for the weak demand-side effect. The first has to do with the low-quality of the products which makes them poor substitutes for the products of the developed market economies. The second, which is related to the first, refers to the high pass-through of exchange rate changes, primarily due to the lack of domestic competition, which limits the change in the real exchange rate and thus the impact on relative prices. On the other hand, the supply-sides of the transition economies dominate in transmitting the effect of exchange rate changes onto output. This is primarily due to the fact that real appreciation will lead to lower import costs, and hence production costs, that will tend to encourage profits and expand supply leading to positive output growth. Thus an important implication for policy-makers, which is indicative of the state of development of these economies, is that exchange rate policies that are aimed at affecting output through the demand-side are of limited short-run effectiveness with no long-lasting effects. The fact that the supply-side channel is more important means that lower domestic inflation is vitally important if domestic industrial output is to grow. This constitutes an additional argument that calls for an effective disinflation in the transition economies. Furthermore, the fact that real exchange rate changes do not foster output growth through the altering of relative prices means that policy-makers must give emphasis to the supply-side of the economy through improvements in product quality, productivity and the use of more advanced technology. That is, they can make the transition economies more competitive through policies that will encourage exporters to invest in new technologies and introduce new products.

Another issue with important policy recommendations refers to the concept of an equilibrium exchange rate. The fact that positive output growth is accompanied with real exchange rate appreciation may also reflect movements in the equilibrium real exchange rate. That is, to the extent that there is a gradual transformation in the production base of these countries towards better quality products it could be reflected in an appreciating exchange rate which by no means constitutes an

obstacle to growth. This, in turn, has important implications with respect to the correct assessment of the equilibrium exchange rate for these economies. More specifically, policy-makers must take into consideration changes in quality, market structure, productivity and the terms of trade when evaluating the equilibrium exchange rate and assessing the impact of a real appreciation on competitiveness.

A final point is related to the fact that successful stabilization constitutes a vital precondition to growth and therefore an exchange rate policy that serves the stabilization objective is indirectly leading to higher growth. An implication that comes out of this point concerns the choice of the most appropriate exchange rate regime during transition. In particular, to the extent that exchange rate stability or, more specifically, the use of the exchange rate as a nominal anchor, brings in greater discipline by the authorities contributing more to the disinflation process, means that a fixed exchange rate regime may seem more appropriate. This is further strengthened by the fact that the resulting real appreciation does not lead to a fall in output. This point is particularly important for countries like Bulgaria, in our sample of countries, which is lagging behind the other transition economies in its progress made towards stabilization and growth. It suggests that the monetary authorities of the particular country must persist with the currency-board arrangement until the economy's inflation rate is stable and low. That is, to the extent that the specific policy is successful in stabilizing the economy, it will also have a favourable impact on economic growth.

Part I
The Theoretical Framework

2 Output Dynamics in Transition Economies under Alternative Exchange Rate Regimes

Christos Papazoglou and Eric J. Pentecost

INTRODUCTION

It has become a stylized fact that transition economies suffer falls in output in the early years of liberalization, and several reasons have been postulated for this fall in real GDP. Borensztein, Demekas and Ostry (1993) argue, for example, that for Bulgaria and the Czech Republic supply shocks were the most important explanation with national factors capable of explaining nearly all the variation in output with sector-specific factors playing only a minor role. An alternative hypothesis due to Calvo and Coricelli (1992) is the credit-crunch hypothesis, whereby high real interest rates were imposed on enterprises, which responded by reducing their demand for credit and output levels. A third hypothesis is that at least part of the fall in output is a statistical exaggeration due to underreporting of private sector activity (Berg and Sachs, 1992; and Berg and Blanchard, 1994).

This chapter attempts to provide a theoretical rationale for the stylized fact of falling real output, by setting out an aggregate model of a typical transitional economy. Such a model is characterized by the absence of a fully developed system of property rights, hoarding of labour and the lack of flexibility of labour markets. The model therefore emphasizes the real sector – particularly the goods market – although there is assumed to be a domestic money market and a rudimentary market for government debt, the degree of international capital mobility is not necessarily assumed to be high. Indeed a large risk premium is likely to be needed by foreign residents if they are to hold domestic assets, although this is left implicit in the model developed here.

Our model, however, differs from previous models in other ways. First, because we are interested primarily in output dynamics, especially as a result of liberalization shocks, aggregate output is endogenous and not fixed at the full employment level. In particular, we assume that output will adjust gradually to the level of demand and respond directly to changes in the structure of production as a result

11

of the gradual liberalization of the production process. Prices are endogenous to the model determined by a labour demand function combined with a fixed money wage. Second, the model can be applied to countries with either fixed or floating exchange rate policies. This is important because the transition economies of Central and Eastern Europe exhibit both kinds of exchange rate policy, and indeed exchange rate policy may change during the transition process.[1] Third, the transition process is characterized by three parameters in the relations for the demand for financial assets, the demand for goods and the supply of goods. By considering the impact of changes in these parameters the effect of the transition process on the development through time of output, the money stock and the exchange rate can be examined. This model is able to distinguish between financial liberalization, characterized by a rise in domestic nominal interest rates (see McKinnon, 1973), and the liberalization of production characterized by a rise in productivity (or, what is analytically equivalent, a fall in the money-wage rate) and a permanent fall in core inflation.

The chapter is set out as follows. The next section sets out the model, and we then examine the output dynamics under a fixed exchange rate policy following liberalization shocks to money demand and goods supply. This is followed by an examination of the evolution of output and the nominal exchange rate under a floating exchange rate policy. Finally, we conclude with some general policy implications of the model for transition economies.

THE MODEL

The basic model consists of six equations: the demand for goods, the supply of goods, domestic money-market equilibrium, expected inflation, the growth of output and the balance of payments. Note that all variables are in logs and Greek letters denote constant parameters.

The demand for domestic output depends inversely upon the real rate of interest and directly on the real exchange rate as shown in equation (2.1). The level of domestic absorption is given as a, which depends inversely on the real rate of interest, defined as the nominal interest rate, i less π, the expected rate of inflation, and directly on the real exchange rate defined as the domestic price of a unit of foreign currency, e less p, the domestic price level:

$$a = -\alpha(i - \pi) + \beta(e - p) \qquad (2.1)$$

The money market is given by a conventional LM relation, with the exception that the income elasticity of money demand is assumed to be unity and

v denotes a demand for money shock, such as an interest-rate liberalization. Hence

$$m = p + y - \gamma(i + v) \qquad (2.2)$$

where m is the nominal money supply and y is the level of output.

The third static equation represents the supply-side of the model. It is assumed that money wages are set exogenously, but that on the demand-side labour is employed until the marginal revenue product is equal to the money-wage rate, w. Thus if the marginal product of labour exceeds the real wage rate output will rise. Inverting this relation gives the standard upward-sloping aggregate supply curve of the form:

$$p = w + \eta y \qquad (2.3)$$

where the real wage rate is inversely related to the level of output.

The dynamic part of the model also consists of three equations – for inflation, output growth and the balance of payments. Expected inflation, π, is assumed to be the same as actual inflation by perfect foresight expectations, and simply assumed to be directly related to excess demand in the goods market plus some exogenous rate of core inflation, $\bar{\pi}$, hence

$$\pi = \dot{p} = \lambda(a - y) + \bar{\pi} \qquad (2.4)$$

where $\lambda \geq 0$ denotes the speed of adjustment of inflation expectations to excess demand in the goods market. This equation is used to eliminate expected inflation from the demand for goods equation, since we are really concerned to model output effects.

The growth of output is also assumed to repsond to the excess demand for output, such that

$$\dot{y} = \phi(a - y) \qquad (2.5)$$

where $\phi \geq 0$ denoting the responsiveness of output to excess demand for goods. As full employment is approached, then $\phi \to \infty$, but in general it is expected that $0 < \phi < \infty$.

The final dynamic equation represents the balance of payments and foreign exchange market adjustment. The equation is

$$\dot{f} = \tau(e - p) + \theta(i - E\dot{e}) \qquad (2.6)$$

where f is the stock of foreign exchange reserves, τ is the Marshall–Lerner condition for a successful devalution and θ is the degree of capital mobility. Assuming

agents have perfect foresight the expected change in the exchange rate, $E\dot{e}$, is set equal to the actual change in the analysis that follows. The relationship between m and f is

$$m = \mu f + (1 - \mu)d \tag{2.7}$$

where d is the domestic money base, and μ the proportion of reserves backing base money.[2] It is generally assumed that reserve changes are not sterilized by the authorities, although this can in principle be handled by the model by specifying a relationship between domestic money base changes and reserve changes.

This model can be solved for ouput under conditions of fixed and flexible exchange rates, thus enabling us to show in the context of a standard macroeconomic model the likely effects of liberalization in the context of transition economies. The first stage is to solve the static equations for absorption, the rate of interest and the price level, using equation (2.4) to also eliminate any inflation dynamics thereby enabling us to focus on output developments. Substituting (2.3) and (2.4) into (2.1) and (2.2) gives

$$\begin{bmatrix} 1 - \alpha\lambda & \alpha \\ 0 & \gamma \end{bmatrix}\begin{bmatrix} a \\ i \end{bmatrix} = \begin{bmatrix} \beta e + \alpha\bar{\pi} - \beta w - (\alpha\lambda + \beta\eta)y \\ -m - \gamma v + w + (1 + \eta)y \end{bmatrix} \tag{2.8}$$

Solving (2.8) for a and i gives

$$a = [\gamma(1 - \alpha\lambda)]^{-1}[\beta\gamma e + \alpha m + \alpha\bar{\pi} + \alpha\gamma v$$
$$- (\alpha + \beta\gamma)w - (\alpha(1 + \eta + \gamma\lambda) + \beta\gamma\eta)y] \tag{2.9}$$

$$i = -\left(\frac{1}{\gamma}\right)m - v + \left(\frac{1}{\gamma}\right)w + \left[\frac{1 + \eta}{\gamma}\right]y \tag{2.10}$$

FIXED EXCHANGE RATES

A fixed exchange rate regime is characterized by setting $E\dot{e} = \dot{e} = 0$ and normalizing the spot exchange rate to unity so that the log of the spot rate is also zero. In this case (2.6) becomes

$$\dot{f} = -\tau p + \theta i \tag{2.11}$$

Substituting for a, i and p in (2.11) and (2.5) gives the second-order dynamic system as follows:

$$
\begin{bmatrix} \dot{f} \\ \dot{y} \end{bmatrix} = \begin{bmatrix} -F_f & F_y \\ -Y_f & -Y_y \end{bmatrix} \begin{bmatrix} f \\ y \end{bmatrix}
$$
$$
+ \begin{bmatrix} -(\theta(1-\mu)/\gamma)d - \theta v - (\tau - \theta/\gamma)w \\ \Delta^{-1}\phi\alpha(1-\mu)d + \Delta^{-1}\phi\alpha\gamma(\bar{\pi}+v) - \Delta^{-1}\phi(\alpha+\beta\gamma)w \end{bmatrix}
$$
(2.12)

where the elements of the 2×2 matrix, A, are defined as

$$F_f = \theta\mu/\gamma$$
$$F_y = \frac{\theta(1+\eta) - \gamma\eta\tau}{\gamma}$$
$$Y_f = \phi\Delta^{-1}\alpha\mu$$
$$Y_y = \phi\Delta^{-1}(\gamma(\alpha\lambda + \beta\eta) + \alpha(1+\eta) + 1)$$
$$\Delta = \gamma(1 - \alpha\lambda) > 0$$

Since $Det(A) = F_f Y_y + Y_f F_y > 0$ and $Tr(A) = -(F_f + Y_y) < 0$ the model is dynamically stable. This is shown in Figure 2.1 where the slopes of the $\dot{f} = 0$

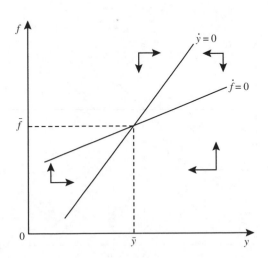

Figure 2.1 Model stability

and $\dot{y} = 0$ schedules are as follows:

$$\left.\frac{\partial f}{\partial y}\right|_{\dot{f}=0} = \frac{\theta(1+\eta) - \gamma\eta\tau}{\mu\theta} > 0 \quad \text{and}$$

$$\left.\frac{\partial f}{\partial y}\right|_{\dot{y}=0} = \frac{\gamma(\alpha\lambda + \beta\eta) + \alpha(1+\eta) + 1}{\alpha\mu} > 0$$

so that if $\tau\alpha\eta + \alpha\theta[\gamma(\lambda+\eta) - 1] + \theta\gamma(1+\beta\eta) > 0$, as seems likely, the goods-market line is steeper than the balance of payments locus. Note that this is true regardless of the degree of capital mobility in this case.

There are three shocks that we can consider using this model: a reduction in core inflation, $\bar{\pi}$, a financial innovation shock, v, and a supply-side shock through w, by which a rise in productivity is regarded as a fall in w. To assess the final effects of these shocks on the money supply and output the model equilibrium needs to be computed.[3]

The simplest shock to consider is a fall in core inflation. This causes the goods-market equilibrium line to shift to the left, in Figure 2.2, which leads to a fall in output and reserves. The reduction in core inflation has been a common objective of the transition economies and so has output reduction – at least in the early years of transition – and so this model is consistent with the stylized facts noted in the introduction. The mechanism by which this operates in this model is through an increase in the real rate of interest, which reduces investment demand and output.

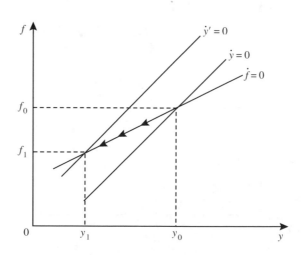

Figure 2.2   A fall in core inflation

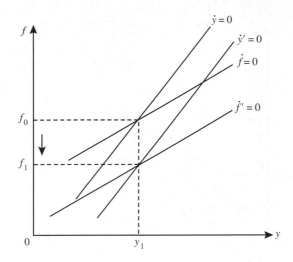

Figure 2.3   A rise in v: financial liberalization shock

A rise in v represents a rise in the interest rate, as a result of financial liberalization, and hence a fall in the demand for money which curtails currency substitution and capital flight. In this case, as Figure 2.3 shows, the effect of financial innovation has no effect on the level of output. Both the goods market and balance of payments equilibrium locii shift to the right, as the lower demand for money is met by a decrease in the supply of foreign money base, leaving output unchanged.

Perhaps the most interesting shock to consider in this model is a supply-side shock to w. An increase in productivity can be represented by a fall in w, which has an unambiguous effect on output leading the goods-market schedule to shift to the right. The effect on the balance of payments is ambiguous, depending on the assumed degree of capital mobility. If capital mobility is relatively high then foreign reserves will increase, whereas if there is low, say zero capital mobility, then reserves will fall. In Figure 2.4 it is assumed that capital mobility is relatively high so that both output and reserves increase. The mechanism is through a fall in the domestic price level, which stimulates the domestic demand for output thus inducing a higher supply of output. The fall in domestic prices increases competitiveness that leads to a trade balance surplus and an increase in reserves. On the other hand, lower prices imply a lower demand for domestic money and a fall in the rate of interest, which results in a capital outflow and a lower level of reserves, until output rises to restore the demand for money and the initial level of interest rates.

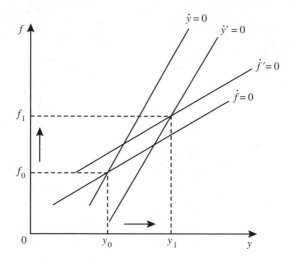

Figure 2.4   A fall in the money wage (rise in productivity)

THE MODEL WITH A FLOATING EXCHANGE RATE REGIME

In the case of a floating exchange rate regime, $\dot{f} = 0$, equations (2.5) and (2.6) are solved for $\dot{e}$ and $\dot{y}$ assuming perfect foresight expectations. Under floating rates (2.6) becomes

$$\dot{e} = i + (\tau/\theta)(e - p) \tag{2.13}$$

so that as capital mobility increases this equation reduces to uncovered interest-rate parity. Substituting (2.3), (2.8) and (2.10) into (2.13) and (2.5) gives the second-order dynamic system:

$$\begin{bmatrix} \dot{e} \\ \dot{y} \end{bmatrix} = \begin{bmatrix} (\tau/\theta) & E_y \\ Y_e & -Y_y \end{bmatrix} \begin{bmatrix} e \\ y \end{bmatrix}$$
$$+ \begin{bmatrix} -\gamma m - \gamma v + (\gamma - \tau/\theta)w \\ \Delta^{-1}\phi\alpha(1-\mu)d + \Delta^{-1}\phi\alpha\gamma(\bar{\pi}+v) - \Delta^{-1}\phi(\alpha+\beta\gamma)w \end{bmatrix} \tag{2.14}$$

where $Det(B) = -Y_y(\tau/\theta) - Y_e E_y < 0$, if $E_y > 0$. The condition for $E_y > 0$ is simply that the degree of capital mobility is greater than the trade balance response to real exchange rate changes, that is $\theta > \tau$.[4] This seems likely since the degree of price responsiveness is likely to be low in transition economies. The negatively

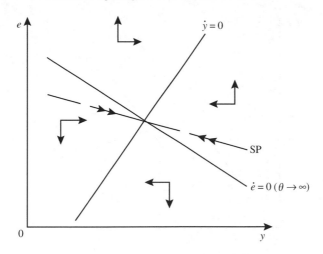

Figure 2.5 Stability with floating rates

signed determinant suggests that the model is unstable unless there is a free variable in the system that can jump discreetly to place the model on the stable manifold. If there is a sufficiently high degree of capital mobility then the exchange rate could be this jump variable. The equilibrium schedules for $\dot{e} = 0$ and $\dot{y} = 0$ have the following slopes:

$$\left.\frac{\partial e}{\partial y}\right|_{\dot{e}=0} = \frac{-\gamma\theta(1 + \eta) + \tau\eta}{\tau} < 0, \qquad \left.\frac{\partial e}{\partial y}\right|_{\dot{y}=0} = \frac{Y_y}{Y_e} > 0$$

The two schedules appear in Figure 2.5. The $\dot{e} = 0$ schedule shows combinations of the exchange rate and output that are consistent with foreign exchange market equilibrium. It is negatively sloped since a decrease in output lowers the demand for domestic money, through the fall in output demand, leading to a capital outflow from the home economy that serves to depreciate the exchange rate. Note, however, that the slope is positive in the case where there is no capital mobility. The $\dot{y} = 0$ locus is upward-sloping as before, since a rise in the exchange rate increases domestic competitiveness that leads to a higher demand for output. As is evident from Figure 2.5, there exists a unique stable path (SP schedule) that yields a dynamic movement with e and y converging to the steady state of the system. Given the parameters of the model, any combination of e and y other than those along the SP locus will set in motion dynamic forces that move the economy away from the steady state.

Under a floating exchange rate a fall in core inflation gives rise to a fall in output and a depreciation of the currency. The mechanism is that a fall in core

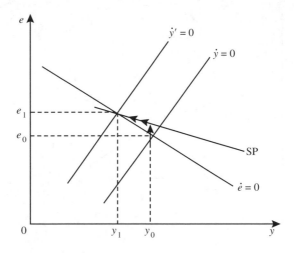

Figure 2.6   A fall in core inflation

inflation directly lowers the demand for output and domestic output prices. The resulting excess supply of money leads to a fall in the rate of interest and a capital outflow, which depreciates the exchange rate. Figure 2.6 shows that the exchange rate initially jumps but still undershoots its final equilibrium. Thus exchange rate depreciation is linked with a fall in output.[5]

A rise in v, due to financial liberalization, leads to a rise in both e and y, but the exchange rate initially overshoots in the short run as indicated by Figure 2.7. The rise in v leads to a fall in the demand money and an excess supply of money. With prices and output sticky in the short run, the interest rate must fall to clear the money market, which leads to a capital outflow and an immediate depreciation of the exchange rate. The exchange rate depreciation leads to an increase in competitiveness, which together with the fall in the interest rate leads to rise in the demand for domestic output, causing output and the price level to rise. As nominal income rises the demand for money increases enabling the interest rate to rise and the exchange to appreciate along the saddle path. The interesting feature of the adjustment process is that because output is slow to rise, the rise in output occurs at the same time as the exchange rate appreciation. This positive association between appreciation and output growth is a stylized fact for many transition economies.

A fall in the money-wage rate (a rise in productivity) causes both equilibrium schedules to shift out to the right generating rises in both e and y, but again only after some short-run exchange rate overshooting as in Figure 2.7. A fall in wages reduces prices, which leads to greater domestic competitiveness that raises the demand for domestic output. In the short run before output can be expanded, the

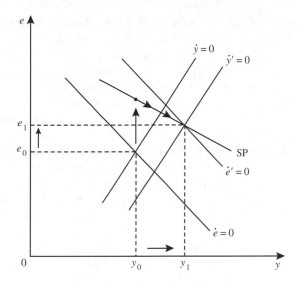

Figure 2.7 A rise in v: financial liberalization shock

excess supply of money caused by the decline in the price level means a fall in the interest rate and a capital outflow, which immediately causes the exchange rate to depreciate. As output starts to rise and with it the demand for money, interest rates can rise again and the exchange rate appreciates gradually back to its long-run equilibrium. Thus exchange rate appreciation is again associated with rising output, which is consistent with the observed performance of the transition economies.

CONCLUSIONS

This chapter has examined output adjustment in transition economies as a result of liberalization shocks in the context of a Keynesian-style open-economy macroeconomic model, whereby prices are slow to respond to excess demand and the supply of labour is considered as infinite at the given money-wage rate. In particular, we have developed a theoretical macroeconomic model that captures some of the basic characteristics of transition economies under both fixed and floating exchange rate regimes. The model is broadly consistent with the stylized facts appertaining to transition economies, in that it shows that the process of transition from command to a market-based economy may be characterized by a fluctuating level of output and by real exchange rate appreciation.

There are, however, differences between the fixed and floating-rate cases, both with regards to the likely stability of the model and the adjustment dynamics. For example, with floating rates instability seems more likely, especially if capital mobility is low, whereas under fixed rates instability seems unlikely for reasonable values of the parameters. This adds weight to Williamson's argument (Williamson, 1994) that some kind of pegged exchange rate is preferable for transition economies, in that such regimes are more robust against financial shocks. On the other hand, financial liberalization seems to have a larger effect on output growth under floating than under fixed exchange rates, at least if capital mobility is reasonably high, since the exchange rate is assumed to respond to interest-rate changes, thus generating a strong link to the real side and the demand for output. A productivity shock seems to raise output under both exchange rate scenarios, although nominal exchange rate overshooting is a feature of the adjustment path under floating rates.

This chapter also serves to illustrate the fact that a large number of alternative responses are plausible, even in the context of a relatively standard model. Thus the issue of the output response to real exchange rate changes cannot be resolved by theoretical analysis alone, being essentially an empirical issue. It follows, therefore, that most of the remaining chapters focus on the empirical relationships between output, the price level and the exchange rate.

APPENDIX

In the long-run equilibrium the dynamic equations, with fixed exchange rates, become

$$\dot{f} = \dot{p} = \dot{y} = 0$$

Thus we get from the goods and balance of payments equations:

$$y = a \tag{A2.1}$$

$$i = (\tau/\theta)p \tag{A2.2}$$

Substituting these relations into equations (2.1), (2.2), (2.3) and (2.7) gives the equilibrium values for f and y as

$$y = -B^{-1}(\beta + \alpha\tau/\theta)w + \beta^{-1}\alpha\bar{\pi}$$

$$f = \mu^{-1}[(1 - \gamma\tau/\theta) - (1 + \eta)B^{-1}(1 - \gamma\tau/\theta)(\beta + \alpha\tau/\theta)]w$$

$$\quad - \mu^{-1}(1 - \mu)d - \mu^{-1}\gamma v$$

where $B = 1 + \eta(\beta + \alpha\tau/\theta) > 0$

Under floating exchange rates the position is more complex with (A2.2) becoming

$$i = -(\tau/\theta)(e - p) \tag{A2.3}$$

Substituting (A2.1) and (A2.3) into equations (2.1), (2.2) and (2.3) gives an indeterminant solution under low (zero) capital mobility. Under perfect capital mobility we get:

$$e = C^{-1}[-\alpha(1 + \eta)\bar{\pi} + (1 + \beta\eta)m + \gamma(1 + \beta\eta)v - (1 - \beta)w]$$

$$y = C^{-1}[\beta m - \beta w + \beta\gamma v]$$

$$C = \beta(1 + \eta) > 0.$$

Notes

1. Indeed this has been the case for both Bulgaria and the Czech Republic. Bulgaria switched from a flexible exchange rate policy to a currency-board arrangement in July 1997. The Czech Republic, on the other hand, switched from a fixed exchange rate policy to a more flexible arrangement following a speculative attack in May 1997.
2. This specification assumes that $M = F^{\mu}D^{1-\mu}$ given the log-linear nature of the model. This is not crucial in this context and has a precedent in Driskill and McCafferty (1985), who use a log-linear specification for wealth.
3. This is undertaken in the Appendix.
4. $E_y = \gamma(1 + \eta) - \eta\tau/\theta$ which is most likely positive unless the degree of capital mobility is very low.
5. This result relies on high, but imperfect capital mobility. As the appendix shows with perfect capital mobility output remains at its initial level of y_0, since the $\dot{e} = 0$ schedule becomes vertical.

3 Currency Options and Trade Smoothing under an Exchange Rate Regime Shift

Alexis Derviz

INTRODUCTION

This chapter describes a dynamic stochastic model of investment, production and consumption in an open economy. Equilibrium supplies and demands for goods and securities are obtained under the assumption of optimally behaving producers, exporters, importers, households and foreign investors. These supplies and demands are derived in terms of their shadow prices, which are adjoint processes of the optimization problems of the agents. The shadow prices prove to be diffusion processes with parameters expressed in terms of utilities, production functions, and asset returns and growth/goods attrition rates. Therefore, the equilibrium trade volumes and prices may have non-stationary characteristics. Accordingly, problems may arise if one attempts to estimate time series for prices directly. It is more natural to estimate the dynamics of the shadow prices and derive from them the predictions of price behaviour, including the effects of real exchange rate and other exogenous shocks.

The same shadow-price method yields the impact of asset-price behaviour on the goods markets, export and import equilibrium prices, a thing seldom made transparent in international trade models.

The proposed model can be applied, among other things, to a transition economy with an ongoing privatization process, when new equity is continuously enlarging the supply. The traditional assumption of finance theory (Merton, 1971; Cox *et al.*, 1985, and many others since then), positing zero net supply of bonds and constant amount of equity, must be abandoned. Instead, the inflow of new securities must be regarded as one of the basic uncertainty factors of the economy, with consequences for the optimal portfolio choice, especially for the demand for money (see Derviz, 1997a,b, for details).

The model is used in conjunction with the currency options approach to the exchange rate regime analysis. The first case is the freely-floating exchange rate, when the equilibrium in the goods and asset markets is shown to be independent

24

of the drift parameter of the (exogenous) exchange rate process. The exchange rate then affects equilibrium prices only through its diffusion parameter – a result analogous to the well-known 'risk-neutral' asset valuation in the standard portfolio theory (Merton, 1971). The next step is to introduce the exchange rate regime based on an officially fixed nominal fluctuation band (target zone) and to study the possibility of its breakdown for the reason of imperfect credibility. This spontaneous regime change (transition to the free float) must have an impact on the real economy: exports, imports and the trade balance. Here, important empirical phenomena have been observed, to which the proposed model offers a rational explanation.

The experience of the Czech economy with exchange rate regime changes since the start of the reform (1990) is associated with two episodes. First, hand in hand with the price liberalization (January 1991), three consecutive devaluations of the Czech koruna (CZK) put its fixed value *vis-à-vis* a basket of five foreign currencies (USD, DEM, ATS, GBP, SFR) on a truly competitive level. Only a narrow, that is purely formal fluctuation band (0.5 per cent in each direction from the central parity) had been allowed till February 1996. Although the basket composition was changed twice during that period: GBP was replaced by the French franc and, later, all the currencies except for DEM at 65 per cent and USD at 35 per cent were removed, the nominal exchange rate level can be considered fixed for macroeconomic purposes. No significant changes could be observed even after the formal introduction of a wide target zone in February 1996 (7.5 per cent each way); the exchange rate did not deviate too far from the central parity for at least another year. Accordingly, the behaviour of most importers, exporters and financial intermediaries was based on the assumption of an almost immobile medium-term level of the nominal exchange rate.

It is rather difficult to analyse the impact of the foreign exchange liberalization and devaluation of 1991 on the exporter and importer behaviour reliably. That very period was characterized by several other important shocks: the breakdown of the former COMECON markets, foreign trade liberalization and the start of the privatization process.

The second substantial exchange rate shock was registered in the second half of May 1997. Then, after two weeks of turbulence in the koruna market, the Czech National Bank agreed with the government on the necessity to give up the protection of the target zone. Koruna then entered the freely-floating regime with a sharp depreciation on 28 May. After that, it continued to fluctuate around a mean value lying somewhat above the upper bound of the former target zone (see Figure 3.1).

Had one wanted to identify the date of the above described exchange rate regime shift on the basis of foreign trade data alone, the correct result would have been highly improbable. Indeed, on the export side, the accelerated growth registered at

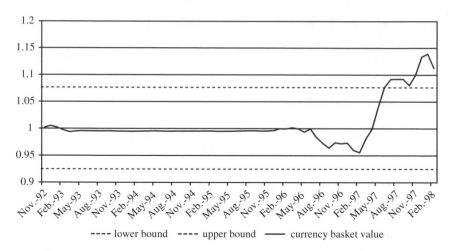

Figure 3.1   The Czech koruna exchange rate with respect to the currency basket

the beginning of 1997 can barely be explained by the export-promoting exchange rate movement (the koruna values had stably remained in the appreciation half of the target zone till shortly before the crisis in May). The turning point in exports (February–March 1997) could instead be attributed to (a) the first effects of post-privatization restructuring in the export-oriented companies, (b) the advent of the long-awaited export-friendly government policies, and (c) growth in Western Europe.

The import picture is no less surprising. There was no growth slow-down for the whole Summer and early Autumn 1997. Although more recent import figures do show an import setback, the reason, however, is not the koruna fall itself, but rather the austerity policy of the government aimed at restricting private demand. In any case, it remains to explain an astounding insensitivity of imports to the forex market turbulences for several consecutive months.

There exists some preliminary evidence pointing at a heavy use of derivatives in the Czech forex market during the whole year 1997. Most importantly, the derivative products (futures and options) were popular instruments in the hands of importers and not just a security in the portfolios of currency speculators.

The preceding discussion provides a good background to my attempt to rationalize the participation of non-financial agents in the currency option market. Specifically, I want to visualize the consequences of this phenomenon for the country's foreign trade.

The chapter proposes an application of the maximum principle and shadow-price techniques to modelling a loss of credibility of a target zone and its collapse followed by the transition to a freely-floating exchange rate. I assume that at or

prior to a predetermined time moment T there is a possibility that the monetary authority stops protecting the official upper bound $\bar{S}$ of the target zone for the nominal exchange rate S (number of domestic currency units to be paid for one unit of an aggregate foreign currency, that is a basket of those that are used in the country's foreign trade). Put differently, the target zone is but partially credible as soon as the agents start attributing a non-zero probability to the transition to free float some time arount $t = T$.

The loss of credibility will be modelled in terms of an implicit market for American call options on the foreign currency, with the common expiration date T and exercise price $\bar{S}$. As long as the bound $\bar{S}$ is fully credible, such options are expected to be out of the money forever. Therefore, the demand for them is zero and they do not even have to exist physically. On the contrary, the very fact of incomplete credibility of bound $\bar{S}$ can be equivalently characterized as a situation when the probability of being in the money for such an option is positive for certain future time moments. Thus, one would observe a non-trivial price and transaction volume of them in the option market.

The question to be answered is whether the agents would benefit from the real existence of the outlined American call market at the times surrounding a collapse of the target zone. Namely, can writing, purchasing and exercising these options prior to date T be optimal for anyone in the economy?

I am going to show that, under certain conditions, consumers prefer to buy and subsequently exercise currency calls for at least some small interval of times preceding T. The exercise proceeds, that is the foreign currency so acquired, serve to finance imports. Moreover, during the said time interval it is optimal for households to ignore the spot forex market completely. On the other side of the option market, exporters prefer to write and sell currency calls in expectation of future export revenues in the foreign currency, a part of which can be used to honour exercised calls. This can lead to a non-trivial transaction volume in the option market, provided that the exogenous export price is high enough.

As a consequence, one does not observe a complete pass-through of the abrupt shift in the exchange rate behaviour into the export and import flows. Prior to the abolition of the target zone upper edge, the *effective* supply of exports and demand for imports evolve towards the schedules to become prevalent under free float. Thus, currency options contribute to a smooth transition to a new exchange rate regime in the country's international trade.

The technical explanation of this phenomenon has to do with restrictions posed in the model on the use of option sale or exercise proceeds. Neither the households nor the exporters are financial wealth-maximizing traders in the financial markets. The households only use the currency received for exercised options to pay for imported goods. The exporters honour exercise calls by depleting their currency reserves constituted by export revenues. This means that neither of these

two agent categories combine spot and derivative forex market operations, as traditional investors (the international ones in the present model) would do. Neither the households nor the exporters guide themselves by arbitrage considerations in the classical sense (of course, there is the arbitrage of marginal utilities, implicitly present in any utility-optimizing behaviour), and options are not redundant securities in this setting. A decision to exercise by a household is analogous to the decision to purchase imported goods: both demands are generated by strictly increasing concave preferences for foreign consumption. In its turn, option supply by an exporter is non-zero while it is a source of a positive cash flow, not too costly in terms of the shadow price of a short-option position.

The next section describes the variables, uncertainty factors, information structure, and the preferences of agents. I then give the formulation of the optimization problems of households, representative firms in the three productive sectors, and the international investors. The demand and supply functions for the consumption good, bond and equity markets, and the import and export goods are then obtained after which we study the time period from the introduction to the expiration date of American calls on the foreign currency. Decision problems of households and exporting firms are reformulated to account for option positions. Supply and demand for a currency call is derived and shown to be non-zero at least during a short period prior to the expiration date. I conclude by discussing the real economy consequences of the exchange rate and other financial market shocks, as well as of the possibility of estimating and/or simulating them with the help of the proposed model.

THE MODEL

The prime objective of the model is to analyse transitional economies. Thus, to capture the possible effects of privatization and an unstable money supply it was necessary to separate equity and outstanding debt on the liability side of the firms' balance sheets and model two different security markets: for shares and bonds. The results about the currency option market will be derived later by analysing households and exporters in more detail.

Actors, Goods and Uncertainty Factors

The agents in the economy are households, international investors and firms in the real business sector producing domestic consumption goods, imported goods and exported goods, for which the shorthands H, INV, FC, FI, FX are used throughout. A representative agent in each category is assumed.

The economy offers three investment possibilities: cash and other domestic liquid assets $\mathcal{M}$, domestic bonds $\mathcal{B}$ with infinite maturity (an aggregate consisting

of individual bonds with different finite maturities; the change of this aggregate in time associated with expiration of older titles at maturity is expressed by a random expiration rate, see below); domestic equity $\mathcal{E}$. The two latter categories are further split into three compartments according to which productive sector issues them. These investment opportunities are open to both H and INV.

The agents trade in the markets for: $\mathcal{C}$, domestic consumption goods; $\mathcal{C}^*$, imported goods; $\mathcal{I}$, foreign currency (spot trade); $\mathcal{B}$, domestic bonds; and $\mathcal{E}$, domestic equity. $\mathcal{M}$ can be traded against everything else, while durables and securities, that is $\mathcal{C} \oplus \mathcal{C}^*$, $\mathcal{B}$, $\mathcal{E}$ and $\mathcal{I}$ must be first exchanged for $\mathcal{M}$ before they can be transmitted to another investment, consumption or production use.

There is a stochastic instantaneous rate of return $d\pi^m$ on $\mathcal{M}$, dj on $\mathcal{I}$ and dh on $\mathcal{B}$. Deterioration rates of $\mathcal{E}$ and $\mathcal{C} \oplus \mathcal{C}^*$ are denoted by $d\pi^e$ and $d\pi^c$. The maturity/default rate of $\mathcal{B}$ is $d\pi^b$. Cumulative growth or deterioration variables π^m, π^e, π^c, h, π^b and j are Itô processes, as well as the nominal exchange rate S of the national currency (the number of national units for one foreign unit).

Other risky variables appearing in the model are γ^c, γ^i and γ^x – cumulative cash dividends on the three categories of productive assets, so that $d\gamma^c$ is the dividend rate in $\mathcal{M}$-units on one share of FC, etc.

The price indices in markets for $\mathcal{C}$, $\mathcal{C}^*$, $\mathcal{X}$ (exported goods), $\mathcal{B}$ and $\mathcal{E}$ are p, p^i, p^x, P^b (three components) and P^e (three components). If p^* is the foreign currency price of $\mathcal{C}^*$, then $Q = p^i/p = Sp^*/p$ is the real exchange rate for importers and p^i/p^x corresponds to the terms of trade. For notational simplicity, I will unify attrition rates, returns and equity prices in the three productive sectors by 3-dimensional vectors π^e, γ and P^e.

The global risk factors represented by the Itô processes named above, have the diffusion parts spanned by a d-dimensional vector Z of standard mutually independent Brownian motions, generating the filtration $\mathcal{F} = (\mathcal{F}_t)_{t \in \mathbf{R}^+}$ satisfying 'the usual conditions' (Elliott, 1982), whose tth element represents the time-t information available to all agents. All the processes appearing in the sequel are Markov diffusions with respect to basis Z. In particular, the law of motion of the nominal exchange rate will be

$$dS = S(n^0 \, dt + n^1 \, dZ) \tag{3.1}$$

The action of random shocks comprising Z is described by (3.1), plus the following list of Itô evolution equations:

$$d\pi^k = \mu^k \, dt + \sigma^k \, dZ, \quad k = m, c, i, b, e$$

$$dj = j^0 \, dt + j^1 \, dZ$$

$$d\gamma^\iota = g^\iota \, dt + v^\iota \, dZ, \quad \iota = c, i, x$$

plus the three production process shocks to be introduced in the next subsection.

State-Transition Equations, Production and Preferences

From here up to p. 43, we consider the economy without the possibility of using currency options, and with a freely-floating exchange rate.

Households

Households are allowed to consume $\mathcal{C}$ and spend their remaining income in $\mathcal{M}$-units, on investment in $\mathcal{B}$ and $\mathcal{E}$. The representative household is assumed to be a price- (p, P^b and P^e) and asset return- (j, γ^c, γ^i and γ^x) taker. Households also receive a stochastic labour income from the three sectors of production: $dw = dw^c + dw^i + dw^x$, which they take as exogenous.

For notational simplicity, let us unify attrition rates, returns, prices, positions and position adjustment rates of a representative household in the three existing productive sectors by 3-dimensional vectors π^e, γ, P^e, y^e and ψ^e.

With this in mind, the state variables of the representative household will be: y^m, the amount of held $\mathcal{M}$-units; y^b, the amount of held bonds; y^e, the amount of held shares of real assets; y^c, the current stock of $\mathcal{C}$. Its control variables are: c, newly-acquired consumption good per period; ψ^b, net bond purchase/sale rate; ψ^e, net equity purchase/sale rate.

The law of motion of the household's state variables is given by the stochastic differential equation system:

$$dy^m = y^m\,d\pi^m + y^b(dj + P^b\,d\pi^b) + y^e \cdot d\gamma$$
$$\qquad - P^b \cdot \psi^b\,dt - P^e \cdot \psi^e\,dt - pc\,dt + dw \tag{3.2a}$$
$$dy^b = -y^b\,d\pi^b + \psi^b\,dt \tag{3.2b}$$
$$dy^e = -y^e\,d\pi^e + \psi^e\,dt \tag{3.2c}$$
$$dy^c = -y^c\,d\pi^c + c\,dt \tag{3.2d}$$

Defining the following two matrix-valued stochastic processes by

$$dA^H = \begin{bmatrix} d\pi^m & dj + P^b\,d\pi^b & d\gamma & 0 \\ 0 & -d\pi^b & 0 & 0 \\ 0 & 0 & -d\pi^e & 0 \\ 0 & 0 & 0 & -d\pi^c \end{bmatrix}, \text{ and}$$

$$B^H = \begin{bmatrix} -P^b & -P^e & -p \\ 1 & 0 & 0 \\ 0 & 1 & 0 \\ 0 & 0 & 1 \end{bmatrix}$$

This can be rewritten as a single vector-valued transition equation:

$$dy = dA^H \cdot y + B^H \cdot \begin{bmatrix} \psi^e \\ \psi^b \\ c \end{bmatrix} dt \qquad (3.3)$$

The household utility is a function:

$$(y^m, y^c; c, \psi) \mapsto u(y^m, y^c; c, \psi) = u^w(y^m, y^c) + u^c(c) - u^a(\psi) \qquad (3.4)$$

Here, the component u^w (wealth utility) reflects the preference for solvency (cash holdings y^m may not fall too low, since otherwise, the utility goes to $-\infty$) and sufficient consumption goods supplies (it is increasing in z but strictly concave in it). The term u^c reflects the felicity of current addition to the stock of C, but with disutility resulting from too big purchases, that is, u^c starts to decrease after some critical level of c has been exceeded. For example, one can think of the quadratic function $\alpha_0 c - (\alpha_1/2)c^2$. Finally, the third component is the disutility of portfolio adjustment. Again, one can think of the quadratic function like

$$u^a(\psi) = \frac{\alpha_b}{2}(\psi^b)^2 + \frac{\alpha_e}{2}(\psi^e)^2$$

In the above formula, α_1, α_b and α_e are constant adjustment disutility coefficients. They are introduced to ensure finite adjustment speeds in any dynamic equilibrium. Observe that the existing literature on portfolio selection usually deals with zero adjustment cost cases. This leads to simplified formulae but, at the same time, prevents explicit analysis of agents' behaviour outside the steady state.

The modelling principle applied to representative firms in the three production subsectors consists in direct utilizing of the cost function instead of a more traditional production function. Also, the principle of valuation of a productive firm will be different from the traditional adding up expected discounted cash flows (cf. Cox *et al.*, 1985; Duffie, 1992; Grinols and Turnovsky, 1993). The idea is borrowed from the literature on recursive utility (Duffie and Epstein, 1992a,b). The expected future value of the firm's assets and dividends is evaluated by a certain *aggregator* function, which includes the measure of uncertainty of the firm's performance. Differently from the recursive utility theory, however, I do not include the value function itself into the list of the arguments of the aggregator, preferring to deal with several state variables instead – a technical possibility equivalent to the original recursive one.

The exact formulation of the representative firm variables, production possibilities and state-transition equations follows for the three defined sectors, FC, FI and FX. Their optimization problems are then discussed later.

Consumption Good Producers

The representative firm is characterized by four state variables: x^m, liquidity, that is number of cash ($\mathcal{M}$-) units on the current account; x^i, amount of the intermediate input units ($\mathcal{I}$); x^b, amount of currently outstanding bonds issued by the company; x^e, amount of currently outstanding shares issued by the company.

The amount of output ($\mathcal{C}$) produced per period has a variable (labour) cost of $L(x^m, x^i; c)$. The dependence on x^m means that the firm needs free liquidity to run the production, with decreasing marginal benefits, that is L goes to $-\infty$ when x^m falls to zero, while the partial derivative L_{x^m}, which will be abbreviated to L_m, decreases to zero as x^m increases. Dependence on x^i means simply that the production requires inputs of the intermediate good (with the intuitive properties of a positive derivative L_i and decreasing marginal effect). The dependence on c is assumed to possess the usual properties, so that it generates a smoothly increasing marginal cost function $c \mapsto L_c(x^m, x^i; c)$, which gives rise to the traditional component of the $\mathcal{C}$-market inverse supply function coming from FC. I shall later derive another component of this supply function resulting from intertemporal optimal behaviour considerations.

The labour costs will have one more stochastic, component, $\zeta(c)\, dZ$, with ζ an increasing function of output c (in the vector norm). Then the total labour expenditure per period, that is variable production costs, of the firm are

$$dw^c = L\, dt + \zeta\, dZ$$

The control variables in the company's decision-making process are, beside c, the rate of adding to the stock of $\mathcal{I}$, denoted by χ^i, and the rates of issue of new bonds, χ^b, and new equity, χ^e.

The dividends that the company pays out in cash are assumed proportional to the available cash at the end of each period, with a stochastic rate dr, that is $x^m\, dr$ is paid out per period in total, with $d\gamma^c = x^m\, dr/x^e$ $\mathcal{M}$-units received by the holder of one share.

From the given definitions it is clear that the state-transition equation for the state process $x = [x^m, x^i, x^b, x^e]^\mathsf{T}$ must be

$$dx^m = x^m(d\pi^m - dr) - x^b(dj + P^b\, d\pi^b) + \{pc - L(x^m, x^i; c)\}\, dt$$

$$\qquad - \zeta(c)\, dZ - p^i \chi^i\, dt + P^b \chi^b\, dt + P^e \chi^e\, dt \qquad (3.5\text{a})$$

$$dx^i = -x^i\, d\pi^i + \chi^i\, dt \qquad (3.5\text{b})$$

$$dx^b = -x^b\, d\pi^b + \chi^b\, dt \qquad (3.5\text{c})$$

$$dx^e = -x^e\, d\pi^e + \chi^e\, dt \qquad (3.5\text{d})$$

Defining the two matrix-valued stochastic processes by

$$
dA^c = \begin{bmatrix} d\pi^m - dr & 0 & -dj - P^b\,d\pi^b & 0 \\ 0 & -d\pi^i & 0 & 0 \\ 0 & 0 & -d\pi^b & 0 \\ 0 & 0 & 0 & -d\pi^e \end{bmatrix},
$$

$$
B^c = \begin{bmatrix} p & -p^i & P^b & P^e \\ 0 & 1 & 0 & 0 \\ 0 & 0 & 1 & 0 \\ 0 & 0 & 0 & 1 \end{bmatrix}
$$

and vector processes $\mathcal{L}(x; c) = [L(x^m, x^i; c), 0, 0, 0]^\mathsf{T}$, $d\mathcal{Z}(c) = [\zeta(c)\,dZ, 0, 0, 0]^\mathsf{T}$, I can rewrite this as a single vector-valued transition equation:

$$
dx = dA^c \cdot x - \mathcal{L}(x; c)\,dt + B^c \cdot \begin{bmatrix} c \\ \chi \end{bmatrix} dt - d\mathcal{Z}(c)
$$

$$
= \mu(x)\,dt + \sigma(x)\,dZ
$$

For future use, the drift and diffusion parts of matrix process A^c are called A^{c0} and A^{c1}: $dA^c = A^{c0}\,dt + A^{c1}\,dZ$.

Next, I define the aggregator function for instantaneous valuation of the firm's assets and operations in a given moment of time. It is assumed to have the form:

$$
F(x; c, \chi) = f(x^m, x^e) - f^a(\chi) - \frac{\beta_c}{2}\,|\,\zeta(c)\,|^2 \tag{3.6}
$$

Individual terms have the follwing meaning. Function f measures the firm's ability to pay dividends and finance operations out of the current cash holdings x^m, relative to the ownership structure, that is the number of outstanding shares, x^e. Function f^a expresses the costliness of new bond and equity issues. It is easiest to think of the quadratic cost function:

$$
f^a(\chi) = \frac{\beta_b}{2}(\chi^b)^2 + \frac{\beta_e}{2}(\chi^e)^2
$$

The last term in (3.6) expresses the negative valuation in the production process risk given by ζ.

In view of widely differing, not to say controversial opinions found in the literature concerning the methods with which productive firm valuation should be modelled, I prefer at the present stage to abstain from any further concretization of the functional form of F.

Importers

Regarding the firms which import the inputs for the consumption-goods sector, I assume that they utilize an 'internationalized' valuation of their current cash holdings. The reason is that their inputs must be paid in foreign currencies, so that the operations must be financed from the account where domestic revenue is being transferred at the current exchange rate.

To wit, define by k^0 the value of foreign cash of a representative member of FI. It is related to the cash holdings expressed in domestic (that is $\mathcal{M}$-) units k^m by the formula $k^m = Sk^0$.

Labour costs will be assumed to emerge primarily abroad, therefore their functional form is $L^i(k^0; \chi)$ where χ is the output in $\mathcal{I}$-units purchased by FC. Otherwise, the properties of L^i are analogous to those of labour costs L in FC. Taking into account the risky part $\zeta^i(\chi)\,dZ$ of the variable costs, the wage payments in FI are

$$dw^i = SL^i\,dt + S\zeta^i \cdot dZ$$

As in the case of FC, let us introduce the state variables k^b (outstanding bonds) and k^e (outstanding shares), as well as the control variables for the augmentation rates of the firm's assets: ρ^b for the newly-issued bonds and ρ^e for the newly-issued shares per period. Altogether, the evolution of domestic cash k^m looks like

$$dk^m = k^m(d\pi^m - dr^i) - k^b(dj + P^b\,d\pi^b) + \{p^i\chi - SL^i(k^0; \chi)\}\,dt$$

$$- S\zeta^i(\chi)\,dZ + P^b\rho^b\,dt + P^e\rho^e\,dt \tag{3.7}$$

where dr^i is the dividend rate paid out of the available liquidity, so that an investor receives $\gamma^i = k^m\,dr^i/k^e$ per share.

Recalling (3.1) and using Itô's lemma, the following state-transition equation system is obtained for the state vector process $k = [k^0, k^b, k^e]^\mathsf{T}$ of the importing firm:

$$dk^0 = k^0(d\pi^m - d\pi^S - \sigma^m \cdot (n^1)^\mathsf{T}dt + |n^1|^2\,dt - dr^i)$$

$$- k^b\frac{dj + P^b\,d\pi^b - (j^1 + P^b\sigma^b) \cdot (n^1)^\mathsf{T}\,dt}{S}$$

$$+ \left\{\frac{p^i}{S}\chi - L^i(k^0; \chi)\right\}dt - \zeta^i(\chi)\,dZ + \zeta^i(\chi) \cdot (n^1)^\mathsf{T}\,dt$$

$$+ \frac{P^b\rho^b}{S}\,dt + \frac{P^e\rho^e}{S}\,dt \tag{3.8a}$$

$$dk^b = -k^b\,d\pi^b + \rho^b\,dt \tag{3.8b}$$

$$dk^e = -k^e\,d\pi^e + \rho^e\,dt \tag{3.8c}$$

Put $d\pi^0 = d\pi^m - d\pi^S - \sigma^m \cdot (n^1)^T dt + |n^1|^2 dt - dr^i$ and define the matrix-valued stochastic processes A^i and B^i by

$$
dA^i = \begin{bmatrix} d\pi^0 & -dj + P^b\,d\pi^b - (j^1 + P^b\sigma^b) \cdot (n^1)^T dt/S & 0 \\ 0 & -d\pi^b & 0 \\ 0 & 0 & -d\pi^e \end{bmatrix},
$$

$$
B^c = \begin{bmatrix} p^i/S & P^b/S & P^e/S \\ 0 & 1 & 0 \\ 0 & 0 & 1 \end{bmatrix}
$$

and vector processes

$$
\mathcal{L}^i(k; \chi) = [L^i(k^0; \chi) - \zeta^i(\chi) \cdot (n^1)^T, 0, 0]^T
$$

$d\mathcal{Z}^i(\chi) = [\zeta^i(\chi)\,dZ, 0, 0]^T$, rewrite this as a single vector-valued transition equation:

$$
dk = dA^i \cdot k - \mathcal{L}^i(k; \chi)\,dt + B^i \cdot \begin{bmatrix} \chi \\ \rho \end{bmatrix} dt - d\mathcal{Z}^i(\chi)
$$

$$
= \mu(k)\,dt + \sigma(k)\,dZ
$$

The drift and diffusion parts of matrix process A^i receive the names A^{i0} and A^{i1}: $dA^i = A^{i0}\,dt + A^{i1}\,dZ$.

The aggregator function G for instantaneous valuation of the firm's assets and operations in a given moment of time is assumed to have the form:

$$
G(k; \chi, \rho) = g(k^0, k^e) - g^a(\rho) - \frac{\delta_i}{2}|\zeta^i(\chi)|^2 \tag{3.9}
$$

In the same way as in the case of FC, individual terms have the following meaning. Function g measures the firm's ability to pay dividends and finance operations out of the current cash holdings k^0, relative to the ownership structure, that is, number of outstanding shares, k^e. Function g^a expresses the costliness of new bond and equity issues. I will use the quadratic cost function:

$$
g^a(\chi) = \frac{\delta_b}{2}(\rho^b)^2 + \frac{\delta_e}{2}(\rho^e)^2
$$

The last term in (3.9) expresses the negative valuation in the production process risk given by ζ^i.

Exporters

The exporter's model will be formally very similar to that of the FC-firm, with the obvious adjustments due to the external source of its revenue.

The four state variables of the FX-representative firm are: q^m, the liquidity on the current account; q^c, the amount of the C-input units entering the production process; q^b, the amount of currently outstanding bonds issued by the company; q^e, the amount of currently outstanding shares issued by the company.

The amount ε of output ($\mathcal{X}$) produced per period has a variable (labour) cost of $L^x(q^m, q^c; \varepsilon)$. The dependence on q^m means that the firm needs free liquidity to run the operations, with decreasing marginal benefits, that is L^x goes to $-\infty$ when q^m falls to zero, while the partial derivative $L^x_{q^m}$, abbreviated to L^x_m in the sequel, decreases to zero as q^m increases. Dependence on q^c means that the production requires inputs of the FC-output, with the intuitive properties of a positive derivative L^x_c and decreasing marginal effect. The dependence on ε is assumed to possess the usual properties, so that it generates a smooth increasing marginal cost function $\varepsilon \mapsto L^x_\varepsilon(q^m, q^c; \varepsilon)$, which gives rise to the principal component of the $\mathcal{X}$-market inverse supply function coming from FX. FX-firms are assumed to be price-takers in international markets, that is take their output price p^x as exogenous.

The labour costs have the stochastic component, $\zeta^x(\varepsilon) \, dZ$, with ζ^x an increasing function of output ε (in the vector norm). Then the total labour expenditure per period, that is variable production costs of the firm, are

$$dw^x = L^x \, dt + \zeta^x \, dZ$$

The control variables in the company's decision-making process are, beside ε, the rate of adding to the stock of C, denoted by v^c, and the rates of issue of new bonds, v^b, and new equity, v^e.

The dividends that the company pays out in cash are proportional to the available cash at the end of each period, with a stochastic rate dr^x, that is $q^m \, dr^x$ is paid out per period in total, with $d\gamma^x = q^m \, dr^x / q^e$ $\mathcal{M}$-units received by the holder of one share.

The state-transition equation for the state process $q = [q^m, q^c, q^b, q^e]^{\mathsf{T}}$ is easily seen to be

$$dq^m = q^m(d\pi^m - dr^x) - q^b(dj + P^b \, d\pi^b) + \{Sp^x\varepsilon - L^x(q^m, q^c; \varepsilon)\} \, dt$$

$$\qquad - \zeta^x(\varepsilon) \, dZ - pv^c dt + P^b v^b \, dt + P^e v^e \, dt \tag{3.10a}$$

$$dq^c = -q^c \, d\pi^c + v^c \, dt \tag{3.10b}$$

$$dq^b = -q^b \, d\pi^b + v^b \, dt \tag{3.10c}$$

$$dq^e = -q^e \, d\pi^e + v^e \, dt \tag{3.10d}$$

Defining the two matrix-valued stochastic processes by

$$
dA^x = \begin{bmatrix} d\pi^m - dr^x & 0 & -dj - P^b \, d\pi^b & 0 \\ 0 & -d\pi^c & 0 & 0 \\ 0 & 0 & -d\pi^b & 0 \\ 0 & 0 & 0 & -d\pi^e \end{bmatrix},
$$

$$
B^x = \begin{bmatrix} Sp^x & -p & P^b & P^e \\ 0 & 1 & 0 & 0 \\ 0 & 0 & 1 & 0 \\ 0 & 0 & 0 & 1 \end{bmatrix}
$$

and vector processes

$$
\mathcal{L}^x(q; \varepsilon) = [L^x(q^m, q^c; \varepsilon), 0, 0, 0]^\mathsf{T},
$$

$d\mathcal{Z}^x(\varepsilon) = [\zeta^x(\varepsilon) \, dZ, 0, 0, 0]^\mathsf{T}$; and rewriting this as a single vector-valued transition equation:

$$
dq = dA^x \cdot q - \mathcal{L}^x(q; \varepsilon) \, dt + B^x \cdot \begin{bmatrix} \varepsilon \\ \upsilon \end{bmatrix} dt - d\mathcal{Z}^x(\varepsilon)
$$

$$
= \mu(q) \, dt + \sigma(q) \, dZ
$$

For future use, the drift and diffusion parts of matrix process A^x receive the names A^{x0} and A^{x1}: $dA^x = A^{x0} \, dt + A^{x1} \, dZ$.

The aggregator function for instantaneous valuation of the firm's assets and operations in a given moment of time is assumed to have the form:

$$
H(q; \varepsilon, \upsilon) = h(q^m, q^e) - h^a(\upsilon) - \frac{\kappa_x}{2} |\zeta^x(\varepsilon)|^2 \tag{3.11}
$$

Here, the meaning of individual terms is that function h measures the firm's ability to pay dividends and finance operations out of the current cash holdings q^m, relative to the ownership structure, that is the number of outstanding shares, q^e. Function h^a expresses the costliness of new bond and equity issues. I will use the quadratic cost function:

$$
h^a(\upsilon) = \frac{\kappa_b}{2} (\upsilon^b)^2 + \frac{\kappa_e}{2} (\upsilon^e)^2
$$

The last term in (3.11) expresses the negative valuation in the production process risk given by ζ^x.

International Investors

The model of a representative international investor will resemble that of the representative household, except for lacking a consumption rate.

The international investor spends his disposable income, when expressed in $\mathcal{M}$-units, on investment in $\mathcal{B}$ and $\mathcal{E}$. He is a price- (P^b and P^e) and asset return- (j and γ) taker.

The international investor measures his cash in international units of account, so that if v^m are his $\mathcal{M}$-holdings, the relevant liquidity must be measured as $v^0 = v^m/S$ (cf. the model for FI above). Other two-state variables will be v^b, the amount of held bonds; and v^e, the amount of held shares of real assets. The control variables are ϕ^b, the net bond purchase/sale rate; ϕ^e, the net equity purchase/sale rate. The investor pays the dividend rate dr^i (the same as FI) out of his v^0-holdings.

Remembering that the attrition rates, returns, prices, positions and position adjustment rates of any investor in the three existing productive sectors must be 3-dimensional vectors, and using Itô's lemma in the same way as in the FI-model (cf. 3.8), one gets the following state-transition equation system for the state vector process $v = [v^0, v^b, v^e]^\mathsf{T}$:

$$dv^0 = v^0(d\pi^m - d\pi^S - \sigma^m \cdot (n^1)^\mathsf{T} dt + |n^1|^2 dt - dr^i)$$

$$+ v^b \frac{dj + P^b \, d\pi^b - (j^1 + P^b\sigma^b) \cdot (n^1)^\mathsf{T} dt}{S}$$

$$+ v^e \frac{d\gamma - \gamma^1 \cdot (n^1)^\mathsf{T} dt}{S} - \frac{P^b\phi^b}{S} dt - \frac{P^e\phi^e}{S} dt \qquad (3.12a)$$

$$dv^b = -v^b \, d\pi^b + \phi^b \, dt \qquad (3.12b)$$

$$dv^e = -v^e \, d\pi^e + \phi^e \, dt \qquad (3.12c)$$

Defining the following two matrix-valued stochastic processes by

$$dA^* = \begin{bmatrix} d\pi^0 & \frac{(dj + P^b \, d\pi^b - (j^1 + P^b \cdot \sigma^b) \cdot (n^1)^\mathsf{T} dt)}{S} & (d\gamma - \gamma^1 \cdot (n^1)^\mathsf{T} dt)/S \\ 0 & -d\pi^b & 0 \\ 0 & 0 & -d\pi^e \end{bmatrix},$$

$$B^* = \begin{bmatrix} -P^b/S & P^e/S \\ 1 & 0 \\ 0 & 1 \end{bmatrix}$$

one can rewrite this as a single vector-valued transition equation:

$$dv = dA^* \cdot v + B^* \cdot \phi \, dt$$

The international investor utility is a function:

$$(v^0; \phi) \mapsto u^*(v^0; \phi) = u^{*w}(v^0) - u^{*a}(\phi)$$

Here, the component u^{*w} (wealth utility) reflects the preference for solvency (cash holdings v^0 may not fall too low, since otherwise, the utility goes to $-\infty$). The second component is the disutility of portfolio adjustment. One can think of the quadratic function like

$$u^{*a}(\phi) = \frac{\iota_b}{2}(\phi^b)^2 + \frac{\iota_e}{2}(\phi^e)^2$$

where ι_b and ι_e are constant adjustment disutility coefficients.

OPTIMAL PRODUCTION, CONSUMPTION, SECURITY ISSUE AND INVESTMENT DECISIONS

Equilibrium behaviour of agents in the goods and asset markets (topic of the next section) will follow from the solutions of the agents' optimization problems. Technically, the methods used are closest to those used in Stulz (1984), Claessens (1991) and Zapatero (1995).

I shall need a suitable formulation of the stochastic maximum principle (Hausmann, 1981; Peng, 1990). My way of applying stochastic control differs from most standard finance theory textbooks (see, for example, Merton, 1991; or Duffie, 1992). The techniques I invoke are based on the adjoint Itô equation. Examples of its utilization in finance can be found in Cadenillas and Karatzas (1995). The present version is based upon Derviz (1997b).

For simplicity, I assume that the agents in all considered sectors, that is H, FC, FI, FX and INV, discount future utilities by means of the same rate:

$$\Theta_t^s = [\theta]_t^s = \int_t^s \theta(\tau) \, d\tau$$

a locally riskless discount rate between times t and $s > t$. Then the general form of the optimization problem studied here is

$$\max_l \mathbf{E}\left[\int_0^T e^{-[\theta]_0^t} \mathbf{U}(X_t; l_t) \, dt + e^{-[\theta]_0^T} B(T, X_T) \right] \tag{3.13}$$

w.r.t. controls l, subject to the state-transition equation:

$$dX = \mu(X, l)\, dt + \sigma(X, l)\, dZ \tag{3.14}$$

the holdings of assets and goods X_0 at time $t = 0$ given. B is the so-called final-bequest function. It is equal to zero by definition if the time horizon of the optimization problem is infinite ($T = \infty$).

When $T < \infty$, a special case of the final-bequest function will be used later. Define by V_t the time t-value function of the problem (3.13) with infinite horizon:

$$V_t(x) = \max_l \mathbf{E}\left[\int_t^T e^{-[\theta]_t^s} \mathbf{U}(X_s; l_s)\, ds \mid \mathcal{F}_t \right] \tag{3.15}$$

where $X_t = x$ is an $\mathcal{F}_t$-measurable initial condition for the transition equation (3.14), and assume that it exists and depends smoothly on all variables. In a later section I shall take $B(T, X_T) = V_T(X_T)$. In this way, the optimization problem will be split into two periods. Period $0 \leq t < T$ will be characterized by the presence of an additional state variable X^* whose value at $t = T$ is included into X_T (which enters $B = V$ in (3.13)) in a predefined way.

To obtain the optimization problem of the specific sector representative, one should replace $\mathbf{U}$ by u, F, G, H or u^*, the state variable X by y, x, k, q or v, and the equation (3.14) by (3.2), (3.5), (3.8), (3.10) or (3.12). For instance, the representative household solves

$$\max_{c, \psi} \mathbf{E}\left[\int_0^T e^{-[\theta]_0^t} u\left(y_t^m, y_t^c; c_t, \psi_t\right) dt \right.$$

$$\left. + e^{-[\theta]_0^T} V^H\left(y_T^m + g_T^m y_T^*, y_T^c + g_T^c y_T^*, y_T^e, y_T^b\right) \right] \tag{3.16}$$

(where parameters g^m and g^c will be defined in due course), subject to either (3.2) or (3.3), the holdings of assets and goods y_0 at time $t = 0$ given.

The solution to the above problem can be characterized in terms of the value function by dynamic programming methods (Fleming and Rishel, 1975; Karatzas *et al.*, 1986; or Fleming and Soner, 1993). I prefer to apply the stochastic maximum principle (Elliott, 1982) adapted for the utility with state-dependence and non-zero portfolio adjustment costs (Derviz, 1997b) and invoking the adjoint process.

To be specific, the problem (3.13), (3.14) can be solved by forming the current-value Hamiltonian

$$\mathcal{H}(t, X, l, \xi, \Xi) = \mathbf{U}(X, l) + \xi \cdot \mu(X, l) - tr(\Xi \cdot \sigma(X, l))$$

where ξ and Ξ are the so-called first- and second-order adjoint processes (ξ is of the same dimension n as X, and Ξ is a $n \times d$-matrix), with $\Xi = \xi \cdot D_X \sigma$. The Hamiltonian must be maximized with respect to l_t.

Let us define by $[f, g]$ the predictable covariation of diffusion processes f and g, and put $d[f, g] = \langle f, g \rangle \, dt$ ($\langle f, f \rangle$ will be standardly shortened to $\langle f \rangle$). Then the (first-order) adjoint process ξ satisfies the stochastic differential equation:

$$d\xi = \xi \cdot (\vartheta \mathbf{1} \, dt - dA + \langle A \rangle \, dt) - D_X \mathbf{U} \, dt \qquad (3.17)$$

with the $n \times n$-matrix valued process A defined by

$$dA = D_X \mu \, dt + D_X \sigma \, dZ$$

The co-state process ξ, which appears in the above formulae, can also be described as the X-gradient of the value function of the problem (3.13), (3.14), provided it exists.

In the problems of this paper, state X represents asset and other durable-goods holdings. Therefore, the adjoint, or co-state variable ξ can be called the *shadow price* vector of the corresponding group of investment goods, specific for each sector and optimization problem.

The next step is to apply the Hamiltonian optimization result to the individual sectors and obtain the description of the supply and demand schedules. The latter will be functions of prevailing market prices which the agents treat as exogenous, and the agents' shadow prices.

SUPPLIES, DEMANDS AND EQUILIBRIUM PRICES

The following symbols will be reserved for the shadow price vectors in H, FC, FI, FX and INV: ξ, λ, μ, ν and η. Subscripts refer to the component corresponding to a specific investment good. For example, μ_0 is the importer's shadow price of international liquidity, and so forth.

Households

Optimal spending is given by the first order conditions:

$$\frac{du^c}{dc}(c) = \xi_m p - \xi_c \qquad (3.18a)$$

$$u^a_{\psi^b} = \xi_b - \xi_m P^b \qquad (3.18b)$$

$$u^a_{\psi^e} = \xi_e - \xi_m P^e \qquad (3.18c)$$

These conditions can be rewritten as inverse demand functions, using the specific utility function defined in the previous section:

$$c = \frac{\alpha_0 + \xi_c}{\alpha_1} - \frac{\xi_m}{\alpha_1} p \tag{3.19a}$$

$$\psi^b = \frac{\xi_b}{\alpha_b} - \frac{\xi_m}{\alpha_b} p^b \tag{3.19b}$$

$$\psi^e = \frac{\xi_e}{\alpha_e} - \frac{\xi_m}{\alpha_e} p^e \tag{3.19c}$$

Consumption Goods Producers

Skipping the first order condition equations of the type (3.18), I write out the results in terms of the relevant inverse supply and demand functions:

supply of $\mathcal{C}$:
$$p = L_c(x^m, x^i; c) + \left[\frac{\beta_c}{\lambda_m} \zeta(c) - \sigma^m + r^1 \right] \cdot [\zeta'(c)]^{\mathsf{T}} \tag{3.20}$$

demand for $\mathcal{I}$:
$$p^i = \frac{\lambda_i}{\lambda_m} - \frac{\beta_i}{\lambda_m} \chi^i \tag{3.21}$$

supply of $\mathcal{B}$:
$$P^b = -\frac{\lambda_b}{\lambda_m} + \frac{\beta_b}{\lambda_m} \chi^b \tag{3.22}$$

supply of $\mathcal{E}$:
$$P^e = -\frac{\lambda_e}{\lambda_m} + \frac{\beta_e}{\lambda_m} \chi^e \tag{3.23}$$

Importers

The relevant inverse supply functions of FI-firms are explicitly dependent on the current nominal exchange rate:

supply of $\mathcal{I}$:
$$p^i = S \left\{ L_\chi^i(k^0; \chi) + \left[\frac{\delta_i}{\mu_0} \zeta^i(\chi) - \sigma^m + r^{i1} \right] \cdot \left[\frac{d\zeta^i(\chi)}{d\chi} \right]^{\mathsf{T}} \right\} \tag{3.24}$$

supply of $\mathcal{B}$:
$$P^b = S \left(\frac{\delta_b}{\mu_0} \rho^b - \frac{\mu_b}{\mu_0} \right) \tag{3.25}$$

supply of $\mathcal{E}$:
$$P^e = S \left(\frac{\delta_e}{\mu_0} \rho^e - \frac{\mu_e}{\mu_0} \right) \tag{3.26}$$

Exporters

Here, one specific feature to point out is the inverse supply function of exported good $\mathcal{X}$ is given in terms of the foreign unit of account. Other supplies and demands are as usual:

supply of $\mathcal{X}$:
$$p^x = \frac{1}{S} \left\{ L^x_\varepsilon (q^m, q^c; \varepsilon) + \left[\frac{\kappa_x}{v_m} \zeta^x(\varepsilon) - \sigma^m + r^{x1} \right] \right.$$

$$\left. \cdot \left[\frac{d\zeta^x(\varepsilon)}{d\varepsilon} \right]^{\mathsf{T}} \right\} \tag{3.27}$$

demand for $\mathcal{C}$:
$$p = \frac{v_c}{v_m} - \frac{\kappa_c}{v_m} v^c \tag{3.28}$$

supply of $\mathcal{B}$:
$$P^b = \frac{\kappa_b}{v_m} v^b - \frac{v_b}{v_m} \tag{3.29}$$

supply of $\mathcal{E}$:
$$P^e = \frac{\kappa_e}{v_m} v^e - \frac{v_e}{v_m} \tag{3.30}$$

International Investors

Their demands for assets are formally very similar to those of the households, except for the utilized units of account:

demand for $\mathcal{B}$:
$$P^b = S \left(\frac{\eta_b}{\eta_0} - \frac{\iota_b}{\eta_0} \phi^b \right) \tag{3.31}$$

demand for $\mathcal{E}$:
$$P^e = S \left(\frac{\eta_e}{\eta_0} - \frac{\iota_e}{\eta_0} \phi^e \right) \tag{3.32}$$

One can check that both sides of every market in the model have been described by the above supply and demand schedules. The shadow prices ξ, λ, μ, ν and η appearing in the above formulae are characterized by the adjoint equations which one obtains by specializing the general adjoint stochastic differential equation (3.17) to the particular sector's problem.

EARLY EXERCISE OF AMERICAN CALLS ON FOREIGN CURRENCY AND TRADE SMOOTHING

Households' Consumption and Demand for Options

To account for a representative household's positions in American options on the foreign currency with expiration date T and strike price $\bar{S}$, let us define an

additional state variable y_t^* for $0 \leq t \leq T$. It will denote the number of currently held option contracts (with $y^* < 0$ indicating a short position). In addition, H will receive two more decision variables: $0 \leq \delta^*$ – purchase rate of new options, and δ^S – options exercise rate.

The modified household's optimization problem will accomodate the possibility of early currency option exercise with the subsequent spending of the acquired currency on purchases of the foreign consumption good C^*. Therefore, one must modify the period utility function (3.4), which becomes

$$u(y; c, c^*, \psi, \delta) = u^w(y^m, y^c) + u^c\left(c, c^* + \frac{\vartheta(y^*)\delta^S}{p^*}\right) - u^a(\psi, \delta) \quad (3.33)$$

where c^* is the amount of C^* obtained by means of the spot forex market. The rest of C^* is exchanged for the amount $\vartheta(y^*)\delta^S$ of the foreign currency available after the excercise of currency calls. Here, $z \mapsto \vartheta(z)$ is a smooth function identically equal to zero when $z \leq 0$, identically equal to 1 when $z \geq \bar{z}$ for $\bar{z}$ a small positive number, and increasing from 0 to 1 for $0 < z < \bar{z}$. Multiplier $\vartheta(y^*)$ reflects the fact that only options that are owned ($y^* > 0$) can be exercised.

Let us fix a household $h \in H$. Provided $y^* > 0$ for h, the total number of currency options exercised by this household during time interval dt will be assumed to equal $\delta^S dt + d\rho^h$, where ρ^h is an idiosyncratic (that is h-specific) noise. It can be understood as a 'trembling hand' effect in the decisions of h, causing purely random deviations from the desired exercise volume $\delta^{Sh} dt$. Accordingly

$$t \mapsto R_t^S = \sum_{h \in H} \left\{ \int_0^t \delta_s^{Sh} \, ds + \rho_t^h \right\}$$

is the aggregate cumulative process of option exercise. I assume that R^S has a diffusion form. Since individual households are small, only dR^S and not the individual $d\rho^h$'s is observed by the markets. As the processes ρ^h do not affect the household decisions in any way significant for the discussed problem, I am not specifying their nature in further detail. Also, index h will be omitted wherever possible.

For $0 \leq t < T$, let X_t^* be the current option price. The state-transition equation system (3.2) of household h, must be modified as regards the laws of motion of y^m and y^c. Another transition equation (law of motion of y^*) must be added to the system (3.2) for times periods between 0 and T. Consequently, in the presence of currency calls, one obtains the following state-transition equations for

y^m, y^c and y^*:

$$dy^m = y^m \, d\pi^m + y^b (dj + P^b \, d\pi^b) + y^e \cdot d\gamma$$
$$+ \, dw - P^e \cdot \psi^e \, dt - P^b \cdot \psi^b \, dt - pc \, dt$$
$$- \, Sp^* c^* \, dt - \bar{S}\vartheta(y^*)(\delta^S \, dt + d\rho^h) - X^*\delta^* \, dt \tag{3.34a}$$

$$dy^c = -y^c \, d\pi^c + \left\{ c + Qc^* + Q\frac{\vartheta(y^*)\delta^S}{p^*} \right\} dt \tag{3.34b}$$

$$dy^* = -\vartheta(y^*)(\delta^S \, dt + d\rho^h) + \delta^* \, dt \tag{3.34c}$$

while their counterparts for y^e and y^b remain unchanged. Note that $Q \, d\rho^h / p^*$ does not appear in (3.34b): the corresponding amount of foreign currency is not converted into C^*. It remains on the household's account as an odd residual.

The household's optimization problem is now

$$\max_{c,\psi,\delta} \mathbf{E} \left[\int_0^T e^{-[\theta]_0^t} u(y_t^m, y_t^c; c_t, c_t^*, \psi_t, \delta_t) \, dt + e^{-[\theta]_0^T} \right.$$
$$\left. \times V^H \left(y_T^m - \bar{S}\vartheta(S_T - \bar{S})y_T^*, y_T^c + \vartheta(S_T - \bar{S})\frac{Q_T}{p_T^*} y_T^*, y_T^e, y_T^b \right) \right] \tag{3.35}$$

subject to (3.34) and the initial values of asset holdings y_0 (where $y_0^* = 0$).

Formulation (3.35) of the household's decision problem involves the time T-bequest function equal to V^H – the value function of the household's original infinite-horizon problem in the absence of currency options.[1] The household's life is split into two periods, $[0, T)$ and $[T, +\infty)$. Only the first period needs to be studied explicitly in this section, since after time T (the currency option expiration time) the economy returns to the situation discussed above. If, shortly before expiration, that is at $t = T - 0$, there still exists a stock y_T^* of outstanding options, they are exercised as European ones if in the money. Amount $\bar{S}y_T^*$ of $\mathcal{M}$ is paid as the strike price, and the received currency is immediately exchanged for the corresponding amount of C^*, which is added to the existing stock y_T^c. Factor $\vartheta(S_T - \bar{S})$ is present in (3.35) to guarantee that out of the money options are not exercised.

The solution to the finite horizon optimization problem (3.35) is characterized by the stochastic maximum principle discussed above, pp. 39–41. In particular, time T-values of the co-state variables are given by the partial derivatives of the final-bequest function. Specifically, for the co-state variable ξ_*, that is the shadow

price of American currency options $\mathcal{O}^*$, the expression

$$\xi_*(T-0) = \frac{\partial V^H}{\partial y^*}(T-0)$$

$$= -\frac{\partial V^H}{\partial y^m}(T)\vartheta(S_T - \bar{S})\bar{S} + \frac{\partial V^H}{\partial y^c}(T)\vartheta(S_T - \bar{S})\frac{Q_T}{p_T^*}$$

$$= \left[\xi_c(T)\frac{Q_T}{p_T^*} - \xi_m(T)\bar{S}\right]\vartheta(S_T - \bar{S}) \tag{3.36}$$

is valid. I shall also need the partial derivatives of the current value Hamiltonian of problem (3.35) w.r.t. c^*, δ^* and δ^S:

$$\frac{\partial \mathcal{H}^H}{\partial c^*} = u_*^c - \xi_m S p^* + \xi_c Q$$

$$\frac{\partial \mathcal{H}^H}{\partial \delta^*} = -\alpha_* \delta^* - \xi_m X^* + \xi_* \tag{3.37}$$

$$\frac{\partial \mathcal{H}^H}{\partial \delta^S} = \vartheta(y^*)\left\{\frac{u_*^c}{p^*} - \xi_m \bar{S} + \xi_c \frac{Q}{p^*} - \xi_*\right\}$$

Now, I ask two questions regarding the properties of solutions of the household's problem in the presence of currency options. First, is there a period of time prior to expiration when options are no longer purchased? Second, is there a period when C^* is not being acquired with the currency obtained in the spot forex market?

The answer to the first question would be positive if I could demonstrate the possibility of inequality $X^* > \xi_*/\xi_m$ which would imply $\partial \mathcal{H}^H/\partial \delta^* < 0$. In that case, the natural constraint $\delta^* \geq 0$ on the option purchase variable would imply that no-purchase ($\delta^* = 0$) is optimal.

Analogously, the second question is answered positively for the time moments when $\partial \mathcal{H}^H/\partial c^* < 0$, that is when taking $c^* = 0$ is optimal for the household.

To establish the conditions under which $X^* > \xi_*/\xi_m$, take the case of a single representative household and observe that its (linear) inverse demand for $\mathcal{O}^*$ is given by

$$X^* = \frac{\xi_*}{\xi_m} - \frac{\alpha_*}{\xi_m}\delta^*$$

(see Figure 3.2, where this demand schedule is denoted by line H). The household is not the only potential buyer of currency calls. Another one is the community of international investors, INV. Their preferences can generate either a demand for $\mathcal{O}^*$ or a supply of them, depending on the current shadow prices. Nevertheless, a period

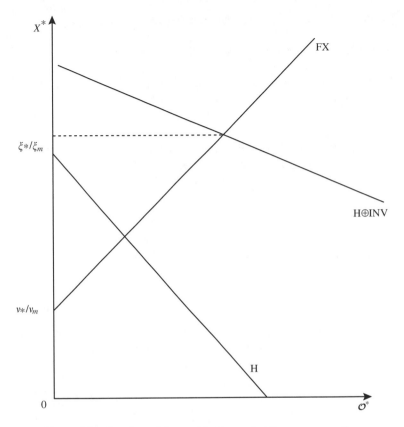

Figure 3.2 Supply and demand in the market for currency calls

can be identified when the net effect is that of a non-zero demand. This happens at times preceding the exchange rate target zone collapse, when the shadow price of foreign currency (and also of $\mathcal{O}^*$ which can be converted into it by option exercise) is high enough. The joint $\mathcal{O}^*$-demand of H and INV at such times is shown by the line $H \oplus INV$ in Figure 3.2.

The instantaneous equilibrium in the $\mathcal{O}^*$-market is achieved by the demand $H \oplus INV$ meeting the supply of newly written $\mathcal{O}^*$ coming from exporters (it will be shown to be positive in the next subsection), represented by line *FX* in Figure 3.2. Altogether, the intersection point may lie so high that the equilibrium price X^* is too big for H to take part in the transactions. Then, only INV-demand is non-zero. This is exactly the case when H no longer purchases $\mathcal{O}^*$ (although exercises earlier accumulated options, as will be shown in a moment).

The previous discussion can be summarized as

Theorem 3.1. *If, prior to the collapse of the exchange rate upper bound $\bar{S}$, the international investor's shadow price of foreign currency and of the American call options on that currency with strike price $\bar{S}$, is high enough, then domestic households do not purchase new currency calls for some time before their maturity* •

Now, consider a household with a non-zero stock y^* of American calls on foreign currency. As follows from the third equation in (3.37), these calls are optimally exercised at rate δ^S satisfying the first order condition:

$$u_*^c\left(c, c^* + \vartheta(y^*)\frac{\delta^S}{p^*}\right) + \xi_c Q = (\xi_m \bar{S} + \xi_*)p^*$$

Therefore, as follows from the first equation in (3.37),

$$\frac{\partial \mathcal{H}^H}{\partial c^*} = [\xi_m(\bar{S} - S) + \xi_*]p^*$$

This partial derivative is negative if and only if $S - \bar{S} > \xi_*/\xi_m$. But, according to (3.36), for t prior to but sufficiently close to T, $\xi_*(t)/\xi_m(t)$ is close to

$$\vartheta(S_t - \bar{S})\left\{\frac{\xi_c(t)S_t}{\xi_m(t)p_t} - \bar{S}\right\} = \vartheta(S_t - \bar{S})\left\{S_t - \bar{S} - \frac{S_t u_c^c(t)}{\xi_m(t)p_t}\right\}$$

$$< S_t - \bar{S} \qquad\qquad (3.38)$$

The equality in (3.38) follows from the first order condition for the domestic consumption: $-\xi_m p + \xi_c + u_c^c = 0$, which can be rewritten as

$$\frac{\xi_c S}{\xi_m p} = S - \frac{S u_c^c}{\xi_m p}$$

The conclusion is that $c^* = 0$ is the optimal choice for times shortly before T. This is summarized as:

Theorem 3.2. *There exists a period of time $(T - \Delta, T)$ preceding the maturity of American call options on foreign currency, when the household's current value Hamiltonian $\mathcal{H}^H$ has the property*

$$\frac{\partial \mathcal{H}^H}{\partial c^*} < 0$$

This means that the optimal amount of the foreign good acquired by means of the foreign currency obtained in the spot market, c*, is zero. For every t ∈ (T − Δ, T), households cover their needs of imports by exercising $\delta_t^S > 0$ of the previously accumulated currency calls and exchanging the resulting foreign currency proceeds for imports •

To complete the story of the currency option market prior to the $\bar{S}$-bound collapse in the spot forex market, I need to establish positiveness of the $\mathcal{O}^*$-supply by the exporters. This is done in the next subsection.

Exporters' Option Writing Decisions

The exporter's problem must be modified to account for his writing of American calls on the foreign currency as well as the exercise of these options by the holders of long positions. Therefore, let us introduce an additional state variable, q_t^*, for times between 0 and T, to denote the position taken by FX in $\mathcal{O}^*$.

Further, it is convenient to keep track of domestic and foreign currency positions separately, so that there will be two state variables, q_t^m and q_t^0 instead of one, q_t^m, as above. Since R^S is the process of $\mathcal{O}^*$-exercise which is exogenous to FX (dR^S is the number of options per period exercised by H and INV), one can formulate three new state-transition equations for FX-problem:

$$dq^m = q^m(d\pi^m - dr^x) + Sq^0 dr^0 - q^b(dj + P^b d\pi^b)$$
$$- pv^c dt + P^b v^b dt + P^e v^e dt$$
$$- L^x(q^m, q^c; \varepsilon) dt - \zeta^x(\varepsilon) dZ + X^*\varepsilon^* dt + \bar{S}\vartheta(-q^*) dR^S \quad (3.39a)$$
$$dq^0 = -q^0 dr^0 - \vartheta(-q^*) dR^S + p^x\varepsilon dt \quad (3.39b)$$
$$dq^* = \vartheta(-q^*) dR^S - \varepsilon^* dt \quad (3.39c)$$

Here, ε^* is the amount of newly-written options per period. dr^0 is the rate at which the export revenue is being converted into domestic cash (it must be positive to enable the exporter to meet his obligations: cover operation costs, service the debt and pay out the dividends in the absence of new security issues). Laws of motion for q^c, q^b and q^e remain unchanged.

In the same way as in the households case, the exporter's life-cycle is divided by date T into two parts: during the first one, currency options may be used. During the second one, these options no longer exist, and the exporter's problem is identical to the one defined above, pp. 33–43. At date T, the remaining stock q_{T-}^* of $\mathcal{O}^*$ is exercised if in the money (that is if $S_T - \bar{S} > 0$). This means that

sector FX enters the after-T life with the bequest function:

$$V_T^x = V^x(q_T^m - \vartheta(S_T - \bar{S})\bar{S}q_{T-}^*, q_T^0 + \vartheta(S_T - \bar{S})q_{T-}^*, q_T^c, q_T^b, q_T^e)$$

where V^x is the value function of the infinite horizon problem. The optimization problem of FX is

$$\max_{\varepsilon, \upsilon} \mathbf{E}\left[\int_0^T e^{-[\theta]_0^t} H(q_t, \varepsilon_t, \upsilon_t)\, dt + e^{-[\theta]_0^T} V_T^x \right] \tag{3.40}$$

subject to (3.39) and the initial value of q (with $q_0^* = 0$). Naturally, with regard to the newly introduced variables, the definition of the instantaneous felicity function (aggregator) H must be modified compared to equation (3.11) to give

$$H(q, \varepsilon, \upsilon) = h(q^m, q^0, q^e) - h^a(\upsilon, \varepsilon^*) - \frac{\kappa_x}{2}|\zeta^x(\varepsilon)|^2$$

with

$$h^a(\upsilon, \varepsilon^*) = \frac{\kappa_e}{2}|\upsilon^e|^2 + \frac{\kappa_b}{2}|\upsilon^b|^2 + \frac{\kappa_*}{2}|\varepsilon^*|^2$$

Denoting by υ_* the shadow price of q^*, we dervive from (3.40) and the maximum principle that

$$\upsilon_*(T-0) = \frac{\partial V^x}{\partial q^m}(T)\vartheta(S_T - \bar{S})(-\bar{S}) + \frac{\partial V^x}{\partial q^0}(T)\vartheta(S_T - \bar{S})$$

$$= \{\upsilon_0(T) - \upsilon_m\bar{S}\}\vartheta(S_T - \bar{S}) \tag{3.41}$$

which is analogous to (3.36).

Another consequence of the stochastic maximum principle is the following expression for the partial derivative of the current value Hamiltonian $\mathcal{H}^x$ of problem (3.40):

$$\frac{\partial \mathcal{H}^x}{\partial \varepsilon} = \upsilon_m\left\{ -\frac{\partial L^x}{\partial \varepsilon} + (\sigma^m - r^{x1}) \cdot \left[\frac{d\zeta^x}{d\varepsilon}\right]^{\mathsf{T}} \right\}$$

$$+ \upsilon_0 p^x - \kappa_x \zeta^x \cdot \left[\frac{d\zeta^x}{d\varepsilon}\right]^{\mathsf{T}}$$

leading to the inverse supply function of exports:

$$p^x = \frac{\upsilon_m}{\upsilon_0}\left\{ L_\varepsilon^x + \left[\frac{\kappa_x}{\upsilon_m}\zeta^x - \sigma^m + r^{x1}\right] \cdot \left[\frac{d\zeta^x}{d\varepsilon}\right]^{\mathsf{T}} \right\} \tag{3.42}$$

For the newly introduced decision variable ε^* obtains

$$\frac{\partial \mathcal{H}^x}{\partial \varepsilon^*} = -\kappa_* \varepsilon^* + v_m X^* - v_*$$

meaning that the inverse $\mathcal{O}^*$-supply function is

$$X^* = \frac{v_*}{v_m} + \frac{\kappa_*}{v_m} \varepsilon^* \qquad (3.43)$$

This supply schedule (denoted by FX in Figure 3.2) meets demand provided the value v_*/v_m is not too big. As follows from (3.41), for t close to T the value $v_*(t)/v_m(t)$ is close to

$$\vartheta (S_T - \bar{S}) \left(\frac{v_0(T)}{v_m(T)} - \bar{S} \right) \leq \frac{v_0(T)}{v_m(T)} - \bar{S}$$

On the other hand, the supply equation (3.42) can be rewritten as

$$\frac{v_0}{v_m} = \frac{L_\varepsilon^x + [\kappa_x/v_m \zeta^x - \sigma^m + r^{x1}] \cdot [d\zeta^x/d\varepsilon]^\mathsf{T}}{p^x}$$

The right-hand side expression above is small enough provided the export price p^x (exogenously dictated by the world markets) is high enough. Therefore, Figure 3.2 showing the point v_*/v_m on the vertical axis below the highest possible demand level, depicts a feasible situation. This concludes the arguments that demonstrate the smoothing role of currency option markets for international trade at times of exchange rate regime breakdown. In other words, dampening an exchange rate regime collapse through the American calls on foreign currencies is, indeed, a viable scenario.

The trade dampening/smoothing can be traced down to the reservation price formation by H in the $\mathcal{C}^*$-market.

From the first equation in (3.37), after the substitution $Q = Sp^*/p$, follows the H-reservation price (that is demand schedule) expression

$$p^* = \frac{u_*^c}{S(\xi_m - \xi_c/p)} \qquad (3.44)$$

for the periods when H buy $\mathcal{C}^*$ directly with the currency obtained in the spot forex market. Therefore, this demand would be also valid any time in the absence of currency options. On the other hand, at times shortly before the expiration date T, when $\mathcal{O}^*$ are being exercised to purchase $\mathcal{C}^*$, the third equation in (3.37) renders the following expression for the reservation price of $\mathcal{C}^*$:

$$p^* = \frac{u_*^c}{S(\xi_m \bar{S}/S + \xi_*/S - \xi_c/p)} \qquad (3.45)$$

As was argued in connection with Theorem 3.1, at least during some short interval prior to T, the inequality

$$\frac{\xi_*}{\xi_m} < S - \bar{S}$$

is valid. The dynamics of ξ_c and ξ_m are independent of the method with which C^* is acquired (can be shown on the basis of the adjoint equation), and the same is true about the terminal values $\xi_c(T)$ and $\xi_m(T)$. Therefore, their current values are also the same with and without $\mathcal{O}^*$. Comparing (3.44) and (3.45), one concludes that the households' demand schedule under direct C^*-purchases lies below the one generated under the options-financed purchases (see Figure 3.3). Consequently, H consume more of C^* prior to T if these options exist.

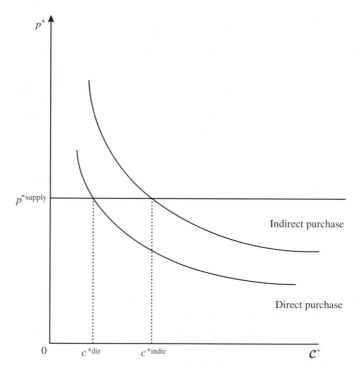

Figure 3.3 Equilibria in the imported-goods market with and without currency-call utilization

CONCLUSION

This chapter has described a model of exports, imports, production and consumption as the outcome of consumption/portfolio decisions of domestic and international investors and the producers in three sectors: consumption goods, exports and imports. As can be seen from the formulae for equilibrium prices and trade volumes, which are easily derived from the relevant supply/demand schedules, market equilibria are functions of the shadow prices of the agents. Some of them also depend on the current value of the exchange rate. A much more surprising result, however, is that they are seemingly independent of exchange rate movements. Parameters of the exchange rate process happen to cancel out from the supply and demand schedules. They stay present in the dynamics of the shadow prices, which represent a 'second-order' level of decision-making for optimizing consumers, investors and producers. In other words, in the world defined by the model, *increments* of the equilibrium prices and the exchanged commodity volumes are functions of the drift and diffusion of the exchange rate process. This should be taken into account when one starts to formulate a reduced form model for estimation purposes.

Another observation is the independence of the equilibrium of the drift parts of investment goods attrition/return rates: only the diffusion coefficients, that is, the risk factors contained in the investment goods and shocks in their returns, enter the formulae. This is in line with many results in theoretical finance, but seems to be a new observation in the present macroeconomic context.

Finally, the exchange rate regime shifts do not necessarily mean kinks or jumps in the equilibrium prices in the goods and asset markets. In the final section it was shown that the impending collapse of an exchange rate regime, specifically, a target zone, makes the agents hedge against the exchange rate bands breakdown by entering into currency option contracts with one another. On the one hand, a non-zero transaction volume in the currency option market does indicate the loss of credibility of the exchange rate bound acting as the strike price. The bound collapse is then a matter of self-fulfilling prophecies. On the other hand, agents' supply and demand schedules become smoothed-up at the times immediately prior and after the expiration date, because exercise of previously accumulated long positions lowers the effective price of the foreign currency used in international trade. The regime shift effects are thus dampened in comparison with the situation when option contracts are impossible.

Note

1.   This approach was discussed above, pp. 39–41.

Part II
Comparative Studies

4 Exchange Rate Policy and Output Growth in Transition Economies: The Experience of Bulgaria, the Czech Republic, Poland and Slovenia

Christos Papazoglou

INTRODUCTION

After a significant output decline during the early stages of transition, which primarily reflected the adverse initial conditions as well as the strong disinflationary policy stand, most transition economies moved into positive rates of growth. More specifically, by the end of 1994 the majority of the transition economies of Eastern and Central Europe recorded positive rates of growth that have been sustained up to the end of 1997. An important issue with respect to these output developments in the transition economies refers to the role of the exchange rate policies adopted by the countries in question. As a matter of fact, it represents an important aspect of exchange rate policy that has been somewhat overlooked. That is, while the relative merits of alternative exchange rate regimes regarding the stabilization process of these countries have been examined in detail, their effect on output growth has not received significant attention.

There is a considerable body of literature on the relative merits of alternative exchange rate arrangements that refer to market economies, either industrial or developing.[1] Although this literature provides valuable insights that are useful to transition economies, the unique features and problems of these economies imposed certain constraints that condition the workings of an exchange arrangement.[2] With respect to output performance in these countries, the impact of an exchange rate regime primarily runs through two main channels. The first one refers to the direct impact of exchange rate regimes on output which operates by affecting international price competitiveness of the economy in question. The

57

exchange rate influences both the demand for output by altering relative prices, and the supply by affecting production costs through its impact on the price of imported materials as well as on wage-setting behaviour. This is the conventional channel through which the exchange rate affects output in all market economies. The second channel, which is the indirect one, refers to the importance of the exchange rate policy to the disinflation process and is particularly vital to the case of the transition economies. That is, to the extent that the exchange rate policy has contributed to lower inflation in these countries it has indirectly caused higher economic growth.

The significance of the second channel draws from the conclusions of recent studies that have showed that lower inflation constitutes an important precondition for growth. Studies by Fischer (1993); De Gregorio and Fischer *et al.* (1993), (1996) for instance, advance arguments and provide evidence supporting the view that inflation is negatively associated with growth. To this effect, Bruno and Easterly (1995) and Easterly (1996), argue that growth cannot be sustained in when the annual rate of inflation is in excess of 40 per cent. With respect to transition economies of Central and Eastern Europe, a study by Fischer, Sahay and Vegh (1996) provides evidence establishing the negative relationship between inflation and growth in the particular countries. The study shows that for the majority of the transition economies growth began after or at the same year that inflation had fallen to moderate levels.[3] As a matter of fact, Bulgaria and Romania represent the only two countries of the region that moved into positive rates of growth while their respective inflation rates were at a three-digit level. On the other hand, however, these two countries constitute the only cases in which output growth was not sustained and as result it returned to negative rates.

The present analysis represents an attempt to examine the role of the exchange rate policy to output growth in specific transition economies. In particular, we shall consider the case of Bulgaria, the Czech Republic, Poland and Slovenia. We shall try to ascertain the importance of each of the two channels through which the exchange rate affects output developments in each country. In particular, we shall investigate the extent to which output growth in the above countries has come after inflation declined to moderate levels. To that effect, we shall also evaluate the connection between exchange rate policy, as well as other policy measures such as fiscal policy, and higher growth by examining the contribution of the former to lower inflation. In addition, we shall explore the impact of real exchange rate developments on output growth so that the importance of the direct channel is considered as well.

In the next section the experience of the four transition economies is examined with respect to the patterns of GDP growth, inflation and the real exchange rate, and their relation to exchange rate policy and other policy measures adopted in these countries. We then conduct a simple econometric analysis in order to empirically test for the importance of the two channels, together with other explanatory variables, through which the exchange rate affects output growth. As we shall

see for the purpose of the econometric analysis we shall include data from other transition economies so that the number of observations used becomes sufficiently large. Finally, we present some concluding remarks.

THE EXPERIENCE OF THE FOUR TRANSITION ECONOMIES

One could divide the transition period into two phases. The first phase refers to the initial stages of transition where stabilization and reform constitute the primary objectives of policy-makers. A common trend in all transition economies that characterizes this period is the falling trend in inflation and output. Assuming that stabilization occurs when inflation falls to moderate levels, that is around 40 per cent, the first phase ends as soon as such an objective is attained.[4] By the end of this period most countries start to have positive rates of growth and this manifests the close association between disinflation and growth. The success as well as the speed of the disinflation and reform programme during this first phase of transition largely determine the extent and sustainability of the economic recovery during the second phase.

In this section we examine the experience of each of the four countries during the two phases of the transition period. In particular, we trace out the time patterns of GDP, inflation, real exchange rate and fiscal policy in the four transition economies under consideration. As indicated, the influence of the exchange rate to growth is traced through its impact on the disinflation process on the one hand, and on real exchange rate developments on the other.

For each country there will be a corresponding set of four figures indicating the course of each of the four variables mentioned above. Note that the real exchange rate is given as an index of the real price of each domestic currency against the US dollar, and is expressed as the ratio of the foreign price, in domestic currency equivalent, to the domestic price. Thus, an increase in the index corresponds to real depreciation. The analysis extends until the end of 1997.

Poland[5]

In Poland, the transformation process started in 1990. The use of the exchange rate as a nominal anchor to break the emerging hyperinflation was the central element of the stabilization effort. Thus, after several devaluations the exchange rate was pegged to the US dollar on 1 January 1990. As Figure 4.1a indicates, the fixed exchange rate regime was successful in bringing down inflation. The first phase of transition actually finished at the end of 1992 when the inflation rate fell to 43 per cent. At the same time, output growth rates became positive during the same year (Figure 4.1b). The fall in inflation was sustained through a significant fiscal deficit reduction after 1992 as Figure 4.1c indicates.

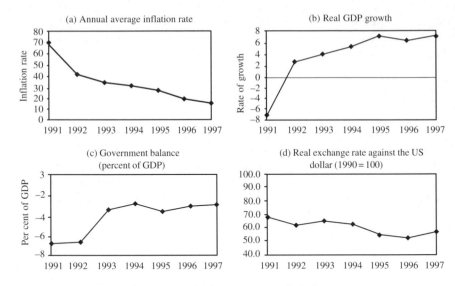

Figure 4.1   Poland: macroeconomic indicators

The commitment to peg the exchange rate, however, caused considerable real exchange rate appreciation and loss of international competitiveness which in turn led to current-account deficits and loss of international reserves, the index of the real exchange rate against the US dollar fell from 100 in 1990 to 70 in 1991, see Figure 4.1d. As a result, towards the end of 1991 the authorities replaced the pure fixed exchange rate with a pre-announced crawling peg. This change in the exchange rate policy constituted a gradual shift towards more growth-prone policies and signalled the start of the second phase of transition.

Poland constitutes a prime example of a country where the quick disinflation process, which relied on a nominal exchange rate anchor and was sustained through fiscal measures as well as successful reform programmes, led to early output growth. This output growth was sustained through necessary adjustments in the exchange rate policy that secured international competitiveness.

The Czech Republic[6]

The favourable macroeconomic starting conditions played a significant role in the early success of the former Czech and Slovak Federal Republic (CSFR). More important, however, to the success was the vigorous pursuit of stabilization policies comprising a pegged exchange rate and a restrictive monetary, fiscal and incomes policy. The success of this anti-inflation policy came rather quickly since the average inflation for 1992 was down to 11.1 per cent from 56.6 per cent in 1991

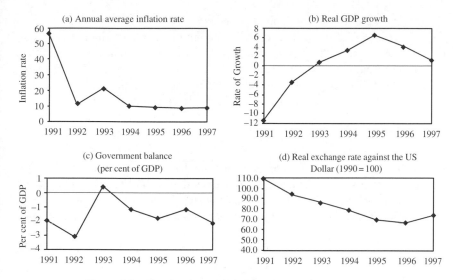

Figure 4.2   The Czech Republic: macroeconomic indicators

(Figure 4.2a). Moreover, the quick reorientation of exports to western markets together with the competitive advantage gained by the 50 per cent nominal devaluation of the exchange rate, which was engineered prior to the fixing, prevented a large real appreciation during the early stages of transition. The real exchange rate against the US dollar actually depreciated in 1991 as Figure 4.2d indicates.

The Czech Republic succeeded in stabilizing the economy very quickly, and, basically, since 1992 has entered the second phase of transition. As Figure 4.2b indicates, output growth started a year later, in 1993. In addition, by the same year the fiscal deficit was reduced significantly (Figure 4.2c). Thus, the Czech Republic constitutes a prime example of a country in which the quick fall in inflation, through exchange rate stability and drastic fiscal measures, led to an early output recovery.

Because of the fixed exchange rate regime, however, the economy experienced a continuing real appreciation of the exchange rate (Figure 4.2d) and a gradual deterioration of the current-account balance until 1996. The growth in output during the same period was exclusively due to domestic demand. In addition, the surge of capital flows, particularly since 1995, has been creating increasing strain on the central bank in the conduct of monetary policy.[7] As a result, in February 1996 the central bank decided to widen the exchange rate band from $+/- 0.5$ per cent to $+/- 7.5$ per cent aiming to introduce exchange rate risk in order to dissuade speculative capital flows and to allow the market to determine the appropriate exchange rate.

In 1996, the high and persistent current-account deficit was accompanied by a slow-down in economic performance which resulted in a deterioration of the fiscal

situation as well. These developments raised serious questions among investors about the sustainability of the exchange rate regime and led to a currency crisis in early 1997. The authorities reacted with a series of corrective actions among which the abandoning of the currency peg constituted a major measure. More specifically, the exchange rate was allowed to depreciate around 12 per cent of its previous central rate before being switched to a managed float system.

Slovenia[8]

Despite inherited structural problems and a difficult external environment, Slovenia was very successful in achieving macroeconomic stability. The almost compete lack of foreign reserves forced the Slovenian authorities to adopt a flexible exchange regime and to rely on tight monetary control in order to reduce the high rate of inflation.

Slovenia entered the second phase of transition in 1993. As shown in Figure 4.3a, by the end of that year inflation fell to moderate levels while output started recovering. Thus, consistent macroeconomic policies led to quick disinflation and early output growth. In addition, the exchange rate policy has mostly been managed to maintain competitiveness (Figure 4.3d) and sustain the export-led recovery. Indeed, in 1994 and 1995 the economy grew at a fast pace and this was primarily due to exports and investment growth.

In 1996 and 1997, economic growth did not accelerate, inflation declined only marginally, while at the same time there was a deterioration in the general

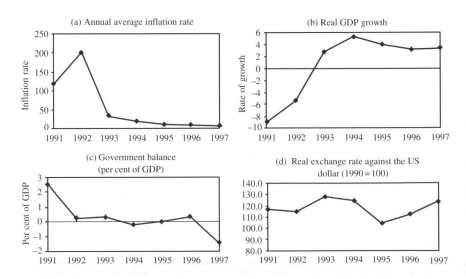

Figure 4.3   Slovenia: macroeconomic indicators

government balance (Figure 4.1c). Growth was mainly supported by external demand but, due to appropriate exchange rate policy and favourable international economic conditions, there was no deterioration in international competitiveness.

Bulgaria[9]

Bulgaria represents a prime example of a transition economy that is still in the process of stabilization. As a result, one could effectively argue that the country still remains in the first phase of transition. As Figures 4.4a and 4.4b show, inflation has always been well-above moderate levels, while output showed only modest increases in 1994 and 1995.

There have been two major stabilization programmes since the beginning of the transition process. The first one, at the start of the transition, had to rely on the curtailment of monetary growth to bring down inflation since the lack of sufficient foreign-exchange reserves had led the monetary authorities to adopt a flexible exchange rate regime. The persistence of large fiscal deficits (Figure 4.4c) placed an excessive burden on monetary policy to combat inflation. This led to significant real appreciation and further output decline. The fact that monetary and fiscal policy were not as restrictive eventually caused the exchange rate to depreciate rapidly. This led to a crisis in the foreign-exchange market in March of 1994. The dollar value of the lev fell 42 per cent while inflation soon accelerated.

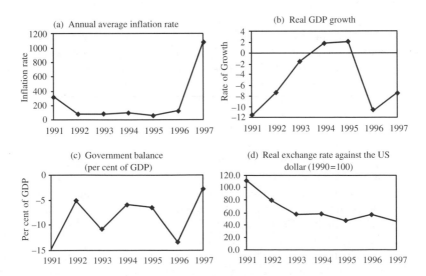

Figure 4.4   Bulgaria: macroeconomic indicators

These developments necessitated a tightening of fiscal, monetary and income policy. In addition, the recovery in exports growth, which was facilitated by the fact that there was no further deterioration in competitiveness, was one of the main reasons for the real output growth in 1994 and 1995. Nevertheless, the increase in output was not sustained. The persistence of inflation and the lack of far-reaching reform policies contributed to a loss of public confidence, which led to a major currency crisis in early 1996. As Figure 4.4 indicates, the economic performance of the Bulgarian economy in 1996 deteriorated sharply. As of February 1997, when the crisis ended, the lev had depreciated by about 4500 per cent leading, as a result, to a hyperinflation situation.

This crisis led to the second major programme of stabilization and structural reform, and the choice of the exchange rate as the nominal anchor constituted the central point of this new stabilization effort. This was manifested by the fact that a currency board arrangement was introduced in July of 1997. In 1997, as a result of this austerity programme, output declined even further while the fiscal deficit was considerably reduced.

EMPIRICAL ANALYSIS

In this section the previous analysis is taken a step further: more specifically, to test empirically whether inflation and the real exchange rate, together with other explanatory variables, have been important to output growth. That is, we use econometric analysis in order to ascertain the importance of the short-run determinants of growth in these countries. In addition, it must be pointed out that the single-equation model to be estimated does not represent the reduced form of some particular structural model, but rather it is used in order to provide results indicative of the relative importance of certain explanatory variables and in particular of those that stem from the exchange rate policy adopted.

The equation to be estimated is the following:

$$RGDPR_{it} = \alpha_i + \alpha_1 ERD_{it} + \alpha_2 FB_{it} + \alpha_3 RERD_{it} + \alpha_4 LCI91_{it} + u_{it}$$

where subscripts i and t index country and time respectively; $RGDPR$ is the average annual rate of real GDP growth; ERD is the standard deviation of the nominal exchange rate from the period (year) average; FB is the fiscal balance expressed as a percentage of GDP; $RERD$ is the percentage change in the real exchange rate *vis-à-vis* the US dollar; $LCI91$ is the log of per capita income in 1991, expressed in US dollars; and finally, u is the error term.

As we see in the above equation, the impact of inflation on growth is not considered explicitly. More specifically, it is introduced indirectly through the

incorporation of two macroeconomic policy variables that capture the extent of the anti-inflationary stand: the variable capturing the degree of stability in the nominal exchange rate regime, *ERD*, and the variable for the fiscal balance of the government, *FB*. Note, with respect to the exchange rate, that values closer to zero for *ERD* reflect greater exchange rate stability and as a result the empirical importance of the link between nominal exchange rate regimes and growth is revealed. Given the hypothesis that lower inflation leads to higher growth, we expect the variable for the exchange rate to have a negative sign and the fiscal balance variable to have a positive sign. That is, stabilization from high inflation has typically relied on a fixed exchange rate regime, while it is sustainable only if fiscal deficits are reduced.

The third variable captures the importance of international price competitiveness, which represents the direct channel through which the exchange rate affects output growth. The bilateral real exchange rate of each domestic currency against the US dollar is used as a common measure for all the transition economies involved. It is expressed in percentage terms and positive values correspond to a real depreciation. We expect this variable to have a positive sign since a real depreciation normally leads to higher output growth.

The last variable included is the log of the per capita income in these countries in 1991. This variable captures the initial income of the transition economies expressed in dollar terms, and provides a measure for the relative initial conditions of the transition economies. We expect lower initial income to be associated with higher growth rates.

To carry out the econometric analysis, we pooled cross-section and time-series data. In addition, in order to have a sufficient number of observations we expanded our sample by including three more transition economies of Central and Eastern Europe, that is Hungary, Romania and Slovakia. As a result, by pooling annual data for a total of seven countries for six years, 1992–97, we built a sample consisting of 42 observations.[10] Note that we assumed identical intercepts for all the countries involved.

The estimation results appear in Table 4.1 below. Equation 1 includes all the proposed variables, while in equation 2 the variable for the initial per capita income, *LCI91,* is dropped as statistically insignificant. The results suggest that countries which adopted policy measures that led to successful macroeconomic stabilization grew faster. Thus, countries that relied on exchange rate stability while, at the same time, being able to reduce fiscal deficits exerted a stronger effect on inflation and this led to higher growth. In addition, competitiveness, although it has a lesser impact on output than the previous two variables, is an important determinant of output growth since the real exchange rate appears to be a significant explanatory variable. Thus, countries that were successful in avoiding real exchange rate appreciation better facilitated the GDP growth.

Table 4.1   Empirical results

Variable	Equation 1	Equation 2
Constant	6.2	4.4
	(4.5)	(5.3)
ERD_{it}	−1.9	−2.2
	(−2.0)	(−2.5)
FB_{it}	0.61	0.72
	(4.7)	(4.1)
$RERD_{it}$	0.09	0.07
	(2.4)	(2.0)
$LCI91_{it}$	−0.0004	
	(−1.3)	
R^2	0.57	0.55
Adj. R^2	0.51	0.49
Probability value	0.00006	0.00005
Likelihood ratio	73.9	75.3
Total observations	42	42

Note: t-statistics appear in parentheses.

CONCLUSION

In this analysis the importance of exchange rates to output growth has been examined in four transition economies of Central and Eastern Europe. The analysis identifies two major channels through which the exchange rate affects output. The first, which is the conventional channel, operates through the real exchange rate and influences output by affecting international price competitiveness. The second operates indirectly since it affects output through its contribution to lower inflation. Recent evidence, which indicates that the disinflation process constitutes an important precondition for higher output growth makes this channel particularly significant for the transition economies.

   The experience of the four transition economies under consideration – that is Bulgaria, the Czech Republic, Poland and Slovenia – strongly suggests that both channels are important to output growth. This is particularly true with respect to the indirect channel. As we have seen, in the latter three countries output recovery started following successful efforts towards stabilization and structural reform. More specifically, output growth started during the same year or the year following the fall of inflation to moderate levels. On the other hand, countries that were not as successful in lowering inflation, such as Bulgaria in our sample, could not sustain output growth. In addition, the speed of the disinflation process affected the course of real exchange rate developments as well. That is, countries with

successful stabilization programmes prevented excessive real appreciation which, in turn, facilitated further the sustainability of the output growth.

In addition, the analysis suggests that a fixed exchange rate regime may be especially important to growth during the transition process. That is, to the extent that both channels through which the exchange rate affects output operate better under exchange rate stability, the latter may be more closely linked to output growth. In particular, by being successful in reducing inflation, a fixed exchange rate regime also prevents real appreciation and hence exerts positive influence on output growth through the direct channel as well. Note, however, that the analysis also indicates that the sustainability of stabilization is not possible unless the macroeconomic policies followed are in line with the objectives of the exchange rate policy. This is particularly true with respect to fiscal policy since it is clearly shown that smaller fiscal deficits seem especially important in reducing inflation and raising growth rates.

Finally, although not considered in the present analysis, the importance of structural reforms to growth must be mentioned. That is, the result that stabilization leads to higher growth in most cases also reflects the fact that it is accompanied by strong structural measures.[11] Hence, the link between exchange rate and growth may not have been as strong in cases where stabilization was not combined with structural reform.

Notes

1. See, for instance, Corden (1993), Aghevli, Khan and Montiel (1991) and Frenkel, Goldstein and Masson (1991).
2. An excellent analysis is provided by Borensztein and Masson (1993). See also World Bank (1996), Calvo and Kumar (1993) and Mecagni (1995).
3. In the analysis that follows, by a moderate inflation level we shall mean an annual rate of 40–50 per cent, as indicated by the above studies. See also Begg (1998).
4. See Begg (1998) and Bruno and Easterly (1995).
5. See Bruno (1992); Calvo and Coricelli (1992); Lipton and Sachs (1991); European Commission (various issues); World Bank (1995); OECD (1992c).
6. See OECD (1992a, 1997); Banerjee (1995); Bruno (1992); Aghevli, Borensztein and van der Willigen (1992); European Commission (various issues); World Bank (1995).
7. The inflow of capital reached US$ 8.4 billion by the end of 1995. See, *European Economy* (Supplement C, May 1996).
8. See OECD (1996); European Commission (various issues); World Bank (1995); and European Bank for Reconstruction and Development (various issues) and National Bank of Slovenia (various issues).
9. See OECD (1992d); European Commission (various issues); Bruno (1992); Bulgarian National Bank (various issues); World Bank (1995).
10. The data was located in the *Transition Report* (various issues) issued by the European Bank for Reconstruction and Development.
11. See Fischer, Sahay and Vegh (1996).

5 The Real Exchange Rate and the Output Response in Four Transition Economies: A Panel Data Study

Aleda Mitchell and Eric J. Pentecost

INTRODUCTION

The relationship between the real exchange rate and the level of output is an important and controversial issue for developing and transitional economies. The traditional literature suggests that a real exchange rate depreciation will lead to a rise in the demand for domestic output as the gain in competitiveness improves the trade balance, assuming that the sum of the import and export elasticities of demand exceed unity.[1] On the other hand, there are several theoretical reasons why, contrary to the traditional view, devaluation can be contractionary and generate a decline in economic activity. First, nominal devaluations can result in some contractionary pressures on aggregate demand, which could more than offset the traditional expenditure-switching effect. For example, a devaluation will raise the price level, generating a negative real balance effect (Alexander, 1952), which will in turn lower aggregate demand and output. Another channel through which devaluation can lower aggregate demand relates to its effect on income distribution. A devaluation can redistribute income from groups with a low marginal propensity to save to groups with a high marginal propensity to save, resulting in a decline in demand and output (see Krugman and Taylor, 1978). Furthermore, if the price elasticites of imports and export are sufficiently low, the trade balance expressed in domestic currency may worsen, generating a recessionary effect. Second, in addition to these demand-side effects there are a number of supply-side channels through which devaluation can be contractionary. For example, a devaluation may reduce aggregate supply because the increased costs of imported inputs reduce the demand for imported inputs and hence of domestic production (Hanson, 1983). Argy and Salop (1983) and Lizondo and Montiel (1989) also suggest that reduced profits in the non-traded sector, caused by the higher real costs of imported inputs, especially oil, lead to a contraction in output after a devaluation.

The empirical work on the effects of devaluation on output has been focused on developing economies. For example, Edwards (1986) undertakes a panel data study of 12 developing countries and concludes that any output contraction, following a devaluation in the short run, is more than fully offset in the long run by a rise in domestic output. Branson (1986), on the other hand, shows that devaluation has contractionary effects in the Kenyan economy. In the context of transitional economies, Halpern and Wyplosz (1997) have argued that the real exchange rate initially depreciates sharply, following liberalization, after which it appreciates. The problem is that it is not clear as to whether the subsequent appreciation amounts to a serious loss of competitiveness and hence of output, or whether the growth in productivity more than outweighs the extent of the appreciation.

In this chapter a reduced-form equation for output is derived from a set of structural equations denoting goods and money-market equilibrium and a cost-plus pricing model of the supply-side. The supply-side is chosen as a half-way house between a fully-administered price system, characteristic of centrally-planned economies, and a fully-flexible price system, which is more characteristic of the advanced industrial economies. This structure implies that the reduced form for output depends upon both demand and supply factors, such as the level of the money supply, the level of wages and the level of the real exchange rate. This reduced form relation for output is estimated for four transitional economies: Bulgaria, the Czech Republic, Poland and Slovenia over the sample period 1992:Q1 to 1997:Q2. The empirical model tested here enables us to distinguish between short-run and long-run effects of a change in the real exchange rate on the level of output. In contrast to Edward's study, we find that devaluations have contractionary effects upon output in both the short and the long run, although the long-run output effects are mitigated by some rise in output one year after the devaluation.

The structure of this chapter is as follows. The next section sets out a simple structural macroeconomic model, including the supply-side response to changes in the real exchange rate, based on an extended IS–LM framework, and derives the reduced form to be estimated. We then briefly consider the data set. The econometric methodology used is then explained with the results obtained from the estimation of the model over the panel data set. Finally we summarise the main findings, discuss the limitations of the analysis and offer some suggestions for future work.

THE MODEL

To investigate the supply-side response to changes in the real exchange rate a simple aggregate demand–aggregate supply (AD–AS) model is postulated whereby prices are determined as a mark-up on costs and the level of output is determined by

aggregate demand. Not withstanding the analysis in the introduction, the demand-side effects of a devaluation are assumed to have expansionary effects on output. In this model the traditional channel, whereby the devaluation improves competitiveness and the trade balance, is emphasized. The potential contractionary effects of devaluation are assumed to operate through the supply-side effects of devaluation on import prices and the cost of production. The result will be that the response of output to changes in the real exchange rate will depend upon whether the supply-side or demand-side effects of changes in the real exchange rate prevail.

The domestic money-market equilibrium condition is given as

$$m - p = \alpha y - \beta r \tag{5.1}$$

where m is the (log of the) money supply, p is the (log of the) domestic price level, y is the log level of output, and r is the nominal rate of interest. α and β are the income elasticity and interest-rate semi-elasticities of money demand respectively.

Goods market equilibrium is written as

$$y = -\delta(r - \pi) + \sigma q \tag{5.2}$$

where the supply of domestic output is equal to demand, which depends inversely on the real rate of interest defined as the nominal rate less the expected rate of inflation, π, and directly on the real exchange rate, $q = e + p^* - p$, where e is the (log of the) domestic price of foreign currency and p^* is the (log of the) foreign price level. If the Marshall–Lerner condition for a successful devaluation holds then $\sigma \geq 0$.

Solving (5.1) and (5.2) for y and r gives

$$y = \Delta^{-1}[\delta(m - p) + \beta\delta\pi + \beta\sigma q] \tag{5.3}$$

where $\Delta = (\beta + \alpha\delta) > 0$. Hence the level of output is directly related to the level of the real money stock, the expected rate of inflation and the real exchange rate.[2]

The supply side of the model is based on a simple linear production function of the form:

$$Y = \phi N \tag{5.4}$$

such that the level of output is directly related to labour input, N. From (5.4) the firm's average and marginal costs per unit are equal. Since average costs are predominantly wages, W, and the average product of labour is ϕ, the firm's costs per unit are given as W/ϕ. If prices are set as a constant mark-up, μ, on unit costs, then

$$P = \frac{(1 + \mu)}{\phi} W \tag{5.5}$$

In order to incorporate materials prices in the analysis, equation (5.5) is extended to include not only wage costs and the mark up but also the real or relative price

of raw materials, P_m/P. In equation (5.6) the parameter θ denotes the materials requirement per unit of output, and hence $(P_m/P)^\theta$ is the component of unit costs that comes from materials inputs. Thus we have

$$P = \frac{(1+\mu)}{\phi} W (P_m/P)^\theta \qquad (5.6)$$

Taking logs of (5.6) gives:

$$p = \kappa + w + \theta(e + p^* - p) \qquad (5.7)$$

where $\kappa = \log(1 + \mu)/\phi$, $\log W = w$, $\log P_m = (e + p^*)$ and $e + p^* - p = q$. Thus equation (5.7) includes the assumption that raw materials are purchased at world prices.

To close the model a process must be specified for inflation expectations. It is simply assumed that inflation expectations are formed regressively, such that the price level always adjusts towards the equilibrium price level, $\bar{p}$, according to equation (5.8), where γ is the speed of adjustment:

$$\pi = \gamma(\bar{p} - p) \quad \text{where } 0 \le \gamma \le \infty \qquad (5.8)$$

Thus inflation is rising if $\bar{p} > p$, falling if $\bar{p} < p$ and constant if $\bar{p} = p$. The equilibrium price level is assumed to be determined by the domestic value of the foreign price level, such that $\bar{p} = (e + p^*)$, and hence (5.8) can be written as

$$\pi = \gamma(e + p^* - p) = \gamma q \qquad (5.9)$$

Substituting equations (5.7) and (5.9) into the equation for aggregate demand, equation (5.3), gives the reduced form equation for output, which is

$$y = \Delta^{-1}[\delta\kappa + \delta m - \delta w + (\beta(\sigma + \delta\gamma) - \delta\theta)q] \qquad (5.10)$$

Since the determinant $\Delta > 0$, the expected signs are as follows:

$$\partial y/\partial w < 0, \qquad \partial y/\partial m > 0, \qquad \partial y/\partial q \gtrless 0$$

Thus a rise in money wages will raise unit costs and lower output. A rise in the money supply will lower interest rates, stimulate investment demand and raise output. The final partial derivative is, however, ambiguously signed. The effect of a rise in competitiveness on the level of output is ambiguous because of two opposing forces. A rise in the real exchange rate may raise the demand for domestic output both directly and indirectly. The direct effect operates through the increased competitiveness of domestic goods in foreign markets, which raises net exports.

The indirect effect works through the effect of real exchange rate depreciation on the real interest rate: a rise in the real exchange rate raises inflation expectations, which reduce the real rate of interest and so stimulates a rise in the demand for investment goods. On the other hand, a rise in the real exchange rate will lead to higher import costs, and hence production costs, that will tend to contract the supply of output. The net theoretical effect is therefore is strictly ambiguous.

The model does not explicitly allow for international capital flows, although to the extent that they impinge directly on the level of the spot exchange rate or the money supply they are effectively treated as an exogenous variable in the model. Under floating exchange rates a capital inflow is likely to lead to an appreciation of the domestic currency and hence *e* will fall and competitiveness will deteriorate. Alternatively, under fixed exchange rates a capital inflow will result in an increase in the money supply as the domestic authorities sell domestic currency to maintain the exchange rate peg. Under either type of exchange rate policy the effect of capital flows on output is captured by the reduced form parameters in equation (5.10).

THE DATA SET

The data set has been primarily collected from *International Financial Statistics* (*IFS*) for the Czech Republic, Poland and Slovenia.[3] For Bulgaria the data has been supplied by the Bulgarian national bank.[4] The data is quarterly from 1992:Q1 and for most variables ends in 1997:Q2 giving 22 observations on each country.[5]

The theoretical model has been constructed with minimal data requirements in mind. Thus the need is for data on real output, money-wage rates, the money supply and the real exchange rate. There does not seem to be much quarterly GDP data available and so we use the industrial production series from *IFS* (line 66). Data on money-wage rates is also taken from *IFS* (line 65). The money-supply data seems to be consistent across the countries, being from lines 34 or 35 of *IFS*. Given that there is little interest-rate data that is comparable across these countries, it seems preferable to assume that the interest rates are endogenously determined and the money supply exogenously controlled by the central banks. Since the four countries concerned each have some exchange rate flexibility, this is perhaps not a serious assumption. Consumer price data is consistent across the countries (line 64 in *IFS*). The nominal exchange rate is measured as the average market exchange rate. Two alternative measures of the bilateral, real exchange rate are employed for each country: the real price of the domestic currency against the US dollar and the German mark.

An initial analysis of the data suggests that there is a negative partial correlation between (the log of) the real exchange rate against the dollar and (the log of)

the level of industrial production. The correlation seems to be particularly strong for Poland and the Czech Republic with partial correlation coefficients of -0.92 and -0.75 respectively. Slovenia shows a lower correlation coefficient of -0.53, perhaps reflecting the floating exchange rate policy pursued by Slovenia. In terms of the proposed model this suggests that the supply-side effects may dominate the demand-side effects and that nominal appreciation can be associated with a rise in output, and need not be a problem for these economies' competitiveness.

ECONOMETRIC METHODOLOGY AND RESULTS

The estimation of equation (5.10) is not possible for each individual country since there is insufficient data; therefore a panel data method is employed, although this has the disadvantage that it is more difficult to ascertain the time-series properties of the data and to identify individual country effects.[6] Moreover, because output, wage rates and money-supply data are typically non-stationary time series we choose to estimate equation (5.10) in annual differences. In order, however, not to lose long-run information, we also include the lagged levels of the variables in the set of regressors. This procedure helps to ensure that the estimated residuals are stationary, so that our hypothesis testing is robust. The model tested is of the general form:[7]

$$
\Delta y_{it} = \beta_0 + \sum_{h=0}^{4} \beta_{1h} \Delta m_{it-h} + \sum_{h=0}^{4} \beta_{2h} \Delta w_{it-h} + \sum_{h=0}^{4} \beta_{3h} \Delta q_{it-h}
$$
$$
- \lambda (y_i - \delta_1 m_i - \delta_2 w_i - \delta_3 q_i)_{t-1} + \Gamma_i D_i + \Psi_t T_t + u_t \qquad (5.11)
$$

where $\beta_1 > 0$, $\beta_2 < 0$, $\beta_3 \gtrless 0$, $\lambda > 0$, $\delta_1 > 0$, $\delta_2 < 0$, $\delta_3 \gtrless 0$, u_t is the stochastic error term, Γ_i is a vector of coefficients on the set of country dummies, D_i (where i runs from 1 to 4) and Ψ_t is the set of coefficients of the period dummies, T_t, where, for example, T_1 takes the value of unity in period one and zero elsewhere. The expression in parenthesis denotes the error-correction term (see Engle and Granger, 1987) and the δ_i's are the long-run elasticities which measure the effect of changes in the explanatory variables on the level of industrial production. The number of lags, denoted by the subscript h, retained in the final model are empirically determined. The model in equation (5.11) can be re-parameterized as

$$
\Delta y_{it} = \beta_0 + \beta_{1h} \Delta m_{it-h} + \beta_{2h} \Delta w_{it-h} + \beta_{3h} \Delta q_{it-h} + \beta_4 y_{it-h}
$$
$$
+ \beta_5 m_{it-h} + \beta_6 w_{it-h} + \beta_7 q_{it-h} + \Gamma_i D_i + \Psi_t T_t + u_{it} \qquad (5.12)
$$

where $\beta_1 > 0$, $\beta_2 < 0$, $\beta_3 \gtrless 0$, $\beta_4 < 0$, $\beta_5 > 0$, $\beta_6 < 0$, $\beta_7 \gtrless 0$. In the long run (5.12) reduces to

$$y_i = \left(\frac{\beta_0 + \Gamma_i D_i}{\beta_4}\right) + \left(\frac{\beta_5}{\beta_4}\right)m_i + \left(\frac{\beta_6}{\beta_4}\right)w_i + \left(\frac{\beta_7}{\beta_4}\right)q_i \qquad (5.13)$$

where $\delta_1 = \beta_1/\beta_4$, $\delta_2 = \beta_5/\beta_4$ and $\delta_3 = \beta_7/\beta_4$. The estimated values of δ_i are given in Table 5.3.

The model given by equation (5.12) is estimated in three alternative versions: Model 1 (M1) without dummies; Model 2 (M2) with country dummies; and Model 3 (M3) with both country and period dummies. On the basis of variable exclusion tests the most appropriate model specification can be selected. Table 5.2 shows the results from the hypothesis tests on these various models. For both US dollar and German mark real bilateral exchange rate results, Model 3 (including both time and country dummies) is strongly preferred to both of the alternative specifications. Therefore Tables 5.1 and 5.3 only report results from the general model.

The dynamic results are presented in Table 5.1 with the implied long-run elasticities and country dummies from the most general model given in Table 5.3. Table 5.1 shows the results for the growth of output when the real exchange

Table 5.1   Alternative dynamic models

Dep. variable $\Delta_4 y$	1	2
Constant	2.094 (4.008)	2.065 (4.055)
$\Delta_4 m$	0.090 (1.481)	0.085 (1.376)
$\Delta_4 w$	−0.140 (−3.728)	−0.138 (−3.658)
$\Delta_4 q$	−0.985 (−3.208)	−1.014 (−3.230)
y_{-4}	−0.586 (−3.679)	−0.605 (−3.802)
m_{-4}	0.086 (1.316)	0.075 (1.139)
w_{-4}	−0.124 (−2.038)	−0.120 (−1.960)
q_{-4}	−0.689 (−1.878)	−0.687 (−1.960)
Group effects	Fixed	Fixed
Time effects	Yes	Yes
R^2	0.830	0.830
R^2 (adjusted)	0.706	0.705
F-statistic	6.68 [1.74]	6.66 [1.74]
Log-likelihood	158.154	158.079

Note: t-statistics in brackets; critical values in square brackets; column 1 results are for the US dollar bilateral real exchange rates, and column 2 are for the DM bilateral real exchange rates.

Table 5.2   Model selection tests

Hypothesis tests	1	2	$\chi^2_{0.05}$
M2 v M1	14.111	24.577	7.82 (3)
M3 v M2	66.054	58.869	30.14 (19)
M3 v M1	80.165	83.445	35.17 (23)

Note: The final column gives the critical values of chi-squared at 5 per cent with the appropriate degrees of freedom in brackets.

Table 5.3   Short-run and long-run coefficients and country fixed effects

Explanatory variables	#Short run	#Long run	*Short run	*Long run
$\Delta_4 m$	0.090		0.085	
$\Delta_4 w$	−0.140		−0.138	
$\Delta_4 q$	−0.985		−1.014	
m_{-4}	0.086	0.147	0.075	0.124
w_{-4}	−0.124	−0.212	−0.120	−0.198
q_{-4}	−0.649	−1.108	−0.687	−1.136
Constant	2.094		2.065	
+Bulgaria	0.402	4.259	0.446	4.150
+Czech Rep.	−0.086	3.427	−0.080	3.281
+Poland	−0.601	2.548	−0.663	2.317
+Slovenia	0.206	3.925	0.206	3.754

Note: # based on equation 1 in Table 5.1; * based on equation 2 in Table 5.1.

rate is measured against the US dollar (in column one) and against the German mark (in column two). Both equations give very similar results, explaining over 80 per cent of the variation in the growth of real industrial production, with the country and time dummies individually insignificant, but strongly significant in groups[8] and with all coefficients correctly signed.

The growth and the level of the money supply do have their expected positive effect upon industrial production, although this effect is statistically insignificant. This result was tested by an F-test on the exclusion restriction $\beta_1 = \beta_5 = 0$. This test gave an F-value of 1.157, that is less than the critical value of $F(2, 40)_{0.05} = 3.23$, confirming that the money supply is not an important determinant of the level or growth of industrial production. Money-wage rates are, however, an important determinant of the level of industrial production and its rate of growth, although the

coefficients are much smaller (less than one-tenth) than those for the real exchange rate in both the short and the long run.

The real exchange rate change is negatively signed in the short run, with a coefficient that is highly significant and close to unity. This indicates that in the context of this model supply-side effects dominate in the short run, such that any real appreciation of the real exchange rate leads to a rise in output. In the long run the supply-side effects continue to dominate,[9] although the long-run fall in output is partly offset by a positive effect of the real exchange rate on output after one year. To see this the dynamic adjustment equation from (5.12) takes the form:

$$y_{it} = 2.09 - 0.414y_{it-4} - 0.985q_{it} + 0.296q_{it-4} + \cdots \tag{5.14}$$

The idea that real depreciation (a rise in q) is negative in the short run and positive in the longer-run is consistent with low short-run elasticities of demand for exports and imports and J-curve effects. This is consistent with findings from developing countries like Jamaica (Rhodd, 1993) and Edwards' cross-section study of 12 developing countries for the period 1965–80. It is important to note that, in contrast to Edwards, the overall long-run effect is still negative and not neutral, but that the positive feed-through from the real exchange rate to output after a year partly curtails the negative impact of devaluation on real income.[10] This indicates that lower domestic inflation is vitally important if domestic industrial output is to grow, especially as the long-run elasticity of industrial production with respect to the real exchange rate is greater than unity.[11]

CONCLUSION

The theoretical model developed in this chapter is consistent with either a positive or a negative effect of the real exchange rate on domestic output, depending upon whether demand-side effects or supply-side effects dominate. The empirical results show the model to be robust with output responding inversely to real exchange rate changes, which is consistent with some previous studies of developing countries. The result, however, is in contrast with other findings that report a negative short-run effect and a positive long-run effect, in that although there is a positive effect of devaluation on domestic output after one year, the overall effect on output remains contractionary.

There are a number of shortcomings with the present analysis which mean that the relatively strong empirical results should, however, be treated with a little caution. First, the t-statistics have not been adjusted to allow for the fact that the sample contains overlapping observations due to the annual differencing procedure used. Such an adjustment is likely to reduce the statistical significance

of the estimated coefficients.[12] Second, because the data set includes only five years of data, the long-run effects may be unreliable as only a limited number of lags can be included in the estimated equation. A third potential limitation is the treatment of inflation expectations by a simple regressive process. A richer model might investigate alternative expectations-generating mechanisms, an extension that could be part of an improvement in the modelling of the short-run dynamics between the real exchange rate, inflation and the rate of growth of output. This, however, will only be possible when a long run of consistent time-series data is available on each sample country.

Notes

1. The Marshall–Lerner condition that the sum of the import and export demand elasticities exceed unity is only a necessary and not sufficient condition. If the devaluation is successful then incomes will rise which will in turn lead to a higher level of imports. For the trade balance to unambiguously improve, therefore, the sum of the demand elasticities must exceed unity (see Pentecost, 1993).
2. The public sector could also be included in (5.2), by the simple addition of real government expenditure, g. However for most of the countries in this sample there is no consistent data set for this variable.
3. The Polish partners also supplied data on industrial production that is unavailable from *IFS*.
4. In particular, Victor Zhaof has been particularly helpful. Other data on exchange rates and prices has been supplied by the Bulgarian partner.
5. There is, however, no quarterly data for the Czech Republic prior to 1993. For 1992 the relevant series were constructed on the basis of allocating two-thirds of the series to the Czech Republic and one-third to Slovakia.
6. See Pesaran and Smith (1995) for a discussion of the problems of estimating long-run relationships from dynamic panel data sets.
7. This reduced form is not dissimilar to that used by Khan and Knight (1981) and Edwards (1986).
8. The single exception is the country dummy for Slovenia in the equation for the German mark, which is statistically significant at the 10 per cent level.
9. For the real exchange rate against the US dollar the long-run coefficient is only significant at 10 per cent.
10. By comparing the sizes of the short-run and long-run coefficients in Table 5.3 we can see that the adjustment of output to real exchange rate changes is much faster than that of money wages. Some 89 per cent of the adjustment of output to the real exchange rate occurs within a quarter, compared with only 68 per cent for money-wage rates.
11. See also Pentecost (1998) in arguing for the maintenance of a fixed exchange rate in Ukraine.
12. However, when a quarterly model is estimated the empirical results are very similar, with the exception that the error-correction term ceases to be significant and the long-run effects therefore become unimportant.

6 The Exchange Rate, Prices and the Supply Response under Transition: A Simulation Study

Pavlos Karadeloglou with George Chobanov,
Aleš Delakorda, Wladyslaw Milo and Piotr Wdowinski

INTRODUCTION

Across the transition economies, both extensive liberalization as well as persistent stabilization efforts have been vital for improving economic performance. Liberalization involves freeing prices, trade and exit from state controls whereas stabilization means reducing domestic and external imbalances. An important issue related to liberalization and stabilization processes refers to the policy adopted for the determination of the exchange rate; that is, the choice of an appropriate exchange rate regime that would better serve these processes. The determination of an appropriate exchange rate is directly related to the objectives of the transition process. In particular, it influences the liberalization process by exposing domestic markets to world prices and the stabilization process through its contribution to external and internal balance.

One key question, when studying the path of the transition economies, is whether a fixed or flexible exchange rate is more effective and less costly in bringing down inflation. The latter being the most urgent objective of these economies. Experience shows that inflation has been reduced significantly under both fixed exchange rates (Czech Republic, Hungary, Poland) and flexible arrangements (Albania, Latvia, Slovenia). Several studies suggest, however, that although reducing fiscal deficits is crucial for disinflation under both arrangements, a fixed exchange rate can help to bring high inflation down more rapidly and at lower cost to growth. One reason is that the automatic exchange of foreign for local currency by central banks at a fixed rate allows enterprises and households to rebuild their real money balances more easily. Also, with flexible rather than fixed exchange rates, domestic authorities have complete discretion over monetary policy, so they have to tighten credit further to make their commitment to stabilization credible. Although a fixed rate

may thus be a useful policy instrument during the early stages of the stabilization process, at later stages of transition higher exchange rate flexibility may become a more desirable tool for successful achievement of the stabilization objective.

The double role of the exchange rate (as a stabilization and liberalization instrument) increased its importance as an effective means in completing the transition process, and as a result it became the central element in a number of studies. The large majority of these studies analyse the macroeconomic impact of the different exchange rate regimes. Some of these studies are more general in nature and, besides the pros and cons of fixed and flexible exchange rates, also focus on the macro performance under alternative exchange rate regimes; nominal and real exchange rates; speculative attacks and policies to deal with them; the sequencing of financial liberalization and deregulation; and the role of convertibility and exchange rate policy in the light of future EU membership. Such studies are provided by Mecagni (1995), Borensztein and Masson (1993), Bruno (1992), Nuti (1995), Rosati (1995), Ghosh (1995), Hrncir (1994), Sachs and Warner (1996), Selowsky and Martin (1996), Halpern and Wyplosz (1997), and Fischer *et al.* (1996). In addition, there are a number of studies devoted to the experiences of individual countries with exchange rate policies, see for example Saavalainen (1995), Halpern (1995), Vanags and Garry (1995), Oblath and Csermely (1994), Milo and Wdowinski (1995), Kokoszczynski and Durjasz (1995), Hrncir (1995).

In all the above-mentioned studies the role of the exchange rate as a means for economic recovery has been ignored. In fact, output has fallen dramatically in Central and Eastern European Countries (CEEC), one of the reasons being the disintegration of the eastern trade bloc, while the shift towards world market prices and trade in convertible currencies entailed huge price rises for previously subsidized energy and raw material imports especially from Russia. During the last two years, exports, a previously repressed activity, has been the major engine of growth in transition economies. However, overall, the European transition economies have been strikingly successful at opening their economies and reorienting their exports towards world markets. Despite early skepticism, many countries have been able to penetrate the 'quality barrier' to expanding exports to the West. Some have argued that foreign trade and exchange transactions should be liberalized more slowly than internal markets to lessen the initial decline in domestic employment and output. In the early stages of liberalization, producers in most countries have been shielded from foreign competition by heavily undervalued currencies, under both exchange rate regimes. Undervaluation also created a strong incentive to seek export markets. Thus a very interesting question could refer to the role of exchange rate policy in affecting output response, particularly for the exporting sector.

The studies listed above primarily examine the contribution of alternative exchange rate regimes to the stabilization process in various transition economies. While such an approach is primarily interested in the evaluation of the impact

of the various regimes on inflation and external competitiveness, they ignore the impact of the exchange rate, either direct or indirect, on the output growth of these economies. That is, they do not examine possible effects of alternative exchange arrangements on the supply response of these economies.

The objective of this chapter is to assess the contribution of the exchange rate policy to output growth within four transition economies – Bulgaria, the Czech Republic, Poland and Slovenia. We analyse the role of exchange rate policy in these four specific countries as each of them followed a different exchange rate regime during the transition process. Bulgaria and Slovenia have relied more on exchange rate flexibility by adopting a managed floating regime. That is, the exchange rates were basically determined by market forces while the degree of central bank intervention on the foreign exchange market has depended on the policy objectives of the policy-makers as well as on the availability of foreign reserves.[1] On the other hand, Poland and the Czech Republic preferred more exchange rate stability. More specifically, both countries started the transition process by adopting a fixed exchange rate system. The Czech Republic actually has a managed floating exchange rate system while Poland has shifted towards greater exchange rate flexibility by adopting a pre-announced crawling-peg system.

In the next section the model to be estimated is presented. We then present the estimation and simulation results of the country models, and in the final section offer some concluding remarks.

THE MODEL

There appear to be two major channels through which an exchange rate policy can affect output growth. The first represents the external channel of influence, since it captures the impact of exchange rate changes on external competitiveness. That is, it refers to exchange rate movements which, by raising or lowering the external value of the domestic currency, alter the relative price and profitability of domestically-produced goods and therefore production. The second channel, which represents the internal channel of influence, refers primarily to the effect of an exchange rate policy on wage-setting behaviour through its impact on inflationary expectations. The effect on wage determination, as well as that on imported intermediate goods, could exert significant influence on production costs generating a supply-side shock to the economy. Note that a flexible exchange rate regime operates mostly through the external channel since it relies on international competitiveness in order to impact on output by influencing the external position. A fixed exchange rate, on the other hand, operates primarily through the domestic channel by affecting domestic behaviour. Figure 6.1 is indicative of how the exchange rate affects output.

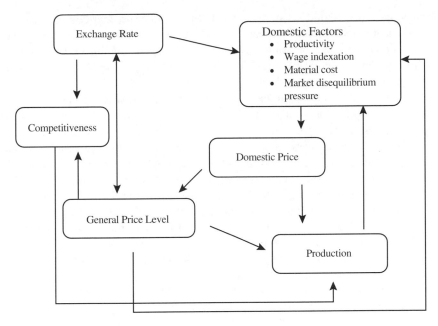

Figure 6.1   The interaction between exchange rate and output

In transition economies, the relative importance of these two channels in transmitting the impact of alternative exchange rate arrangements on output growth is conditional upon a number of factors, which reflect the specific features of these countries. Some of these features may be common while others could differ from country to country. Besides the degree of price liberalization as well as that of structural and institutional reform, these factors also refer to economic conditions which could range from the evolution of macroeconomic indicators to economic characteristics and the behaviour of specific sectors; the degree of wage indexation; the nature of shocks affecting the economy; the degree of discipline in fiscal and monetary policy; the availability of alternative policy instruments; the existence of an initial competitive edge, and so forth.

The interaction between exchange rate and output is examined in this chapter by modelling the two basic channels of transmission and incorporating the specific features of each transition economy. More specifically, a model for a small open economy that produces internationally-traded goods is used to examine the relationship between output growth, wage adjustment, competitiveness and exchange rate policy. The model includes two relations. The first is an output supply equation which consists of a production function for a sector which is assumed to be open to international competition. The assumption about the exchange rate regime

brings us to the second relation, which is that of international competitiveness defined as the relative price of traded goods. Given the exogenous international prices, domestic prices determine total competitiveness. The third relation refers to a wage-determination equation. The model thus determines output, the price level (competitiveness) and wages.

Output is assumed to be produced according to a three-factor production function, that is capital, labour and imported raw materials. We will also assume that firms are competitive profit-maximizers, to the extent that this is allowed by the price liberalization process (and that the capital is fixed in the short run). Labour and raw materials will be employed up to the point where their marginal revenue products are equal to their costs. According to the above description, GDP in the short run is negatively related to the real wage and the real price of intermediates and positively related to the capital stock. It is also positively related to real government expenditure. Moreover, for a given relative price of raw materials, product wages and competitiveness are negatively related. When wages go up, the relative price of the output falls and this is equivalent to a fall in competitiveness. If competitiveness is substituted in the output equation, then GDP is a positive function of competitiveness, government expenditure and the capital stock. The final equations to be estimated are the following:

$$y = f(k, (e + p^* - p), (p_m - p), g, t) \tag{6.1}$$

$$w - p = f((w - p)_{-1}, y, t) \tag{6.2}$$

$$p = f((w)_{-1}, y) \tag{6.3}$$

where y is output, k the capital stock, e is the exchange rate, p is the GDP deflator, p^* is the foreign price index, g the government expenditure, p_m is the price of raw materials, w is the nominal wage rate and t the time trend.

EMPIRICAL RESULTS

Estimation Results

The theoretical specification of the model presented above was modified, before being estimated, according to country specificities. While the estimation results were satisfactory for Bulgaria, Poland and Slovenia, as they took into account the main mechanisms of the exchange rate and its links with the economic activity and prices, the results for the Czech Republic were not promising. Negative wage and price correlation together with unclear influences of real activity on prices could not give a solid indication of the implications of the exchange rate on the activity.[2]

The estimated equations for the remaining countries include almost all of the explanatory variables in the basic theoretical model. Most of the variables have significant coefficients according to the standard *t*-test, nevertheless estimation results are not unanimous as to the sign of the exchange rate impact on production in the GDP equation. The real exchange rate has a positive sign both for Bulgaria and Slovenia, but its impact on GDP is negative in Poland. The above results should most probably indicate a different behaviour of exporters in these countries as well as an export diversification and differentiation as far as product and destination countries are concerned. The impact of the real wage rate on GDP is also different for Bulgaria and Slovenia, while it was not statistically different from zero for Poland. While the sign for Bulgaria is as expected, a positive sign for Slovenia indicates that at least in that stage the factor-substitution possibilities are extremely low in that country. Real interest rates and government spending have the expected sign for all countries. The real interest-rate elasticity for Poland is relatively high supporting the view of the high importance of investment activities in the country. The government spending elasticity is the lowest, indicating a small public investment multiplier. A special variable representing the absorption of the German economy is included in the Polish model, as most of the country's foreign trade is effected with Germany (see Table 6.1).

The wage equation is more or less consistent with the theoretical specification. For Bulgaria and Slovenia restricted equations were estimated while for Poland unrestricted estimation has shown that wages are fully indexed. Real wage changes are explained by productivity changes (proxied by GDP changes for Bulgaria and Slovenia), while it was not possible to use any market labour indicator due to its non-availability or unreliability of data (see Table 6.2).

Finally prices (consumer prices for Bulgaria and Slovenia, production price for Poland) are explained by wage movements representing domestic cost and exchange rate as a proxy for the imported inflation. The wage-rate elasticity accounts for about 0.3 in Poland and Bulgaria, a figure which is close to the share of the wage rate in the total production costs. In Slovenia the negative elasticity is supposed to be a specificity of that country. In fact, in Slovenia the positive causality between wages and prices is overshadowed by other influences. This country has started from high inflation rates but brought down successively in a very short period of time. The achievement of this target has more to do with the monetary and fiscal policy stance and bringing down inflationary expectations and less with the development of real wages, which did have a life of their own. Another fact relates to the functioning of the labour market based not on the neo-classical paradigm, but more on the power of various groups to negotiate and achieve their targets. The above may lead to a situation where falling inflation rates are observed together with rising wages (see Table 6.3).

Table 6.1   GDP equation[3]

	Poland[4]	Slovenia	Bulgaria
Constant	−6.38	5.93	1.90
	(0.68)	(0.95)	(0.17)
Real exchange rate	−0.17	0.13	0.02
	(0.17)	(0.07)	(0.02)
Real wage rate		0.38	−0.05
		(0.11)	(0.03)
Real interest rate	−0.29	−0.007	
	(−0.28)	(0.001)	
Government spending	0.12	0.38	0.7
	(0.05)	(0.08)	(0.03)
Capital			0.37
			(0.02)
German absorption	1.18		
	(0.08)		
Number of	−0.12		
Unemployed	(0.03)		
Time			0.009
			(0.0)
R^2	0.98	0.98	0.99
DW	2.21	2.84	0.69
SEE	0.014	0.01	0.03
Period	1991.4–1996.4	1993.1–1998.3	1991.05–1998.01

Simulation Results

The policy implications of the exchange rate as an instrument for economic recovery was investigated by simulating the estimated equation and carrying out a policy scenario in which the national currency is devalued by 5 per cent during the simulation period. Simulation results (Figures 6.2–6.4) confirm the results of estimated equations as to the impact of the exchange rate on GDP. A devaluation of the national currency could have positive effects on the economic activity only in Slovenia, while no impact on GDP is expected in Bulgaria and a negative impact is expected in Poland. In fact, exchange rate depreciation in Slovenia may increase GDP by as much as 1.2 per cent in 3–4 years time, while in the short run the GDP increase can reach 0.8 per cent. Although the boosting of economic activity is considered to be important, it should be mentioned that GDP is mostly increased due to real wage increases rather than to exchange rate depreciation, leading to a general conclusion which supports the ineffectiveness of the depreciation as a measure to boost economic activity.

Table 6.2 Wage equation

	Poland	**Slovenia**	**Bulgaria**
Constant	3.77	−1.97	0.67
	(1.71)	(3.87)	(0.25)
Prices	1.01	1.00	1.00
	(0.04)		
Prices$_{-1}$		0.56	0.79
		(0.22)	(0.067)
Wage$_{-1}$		0.56	0.79
		(0.22)	(0.067)
GDP		0.50	0.08
		(0.17)	(0.05)
Productivity	0.57		
	(0.22)		
Time		−0.001	
		(0.003)	
R^2	0.99	0.95	0.84
DW	1.36	2.03	2.39
SEE	0.045	0.02	0.12
Period	1990.1–1996.4	1993.1–1998.3	1991.05–1999.1

Table 6.3 Price equation

	Poland	**Slovenia**	**Bulgaria**
Constant	0.37	43.14	0.01
	(0.06)	(10.12)	(0.01)
Prices$_{-1}$	0.45	−1.61	
	(0.07)	(1.25)	
Wages	0.34		0.30
	(0.05)		(0.05)
Wages$_{-1}$		−1.61	
		(1.25)	
Exch rate* foreign price	0.17		
	(0.06)		
Exchange rate		0.72	0.66
		(1.74)	(0.04)
R^2	0.99	0.91	0.82
DW	1.45	1.99	1.74
SEE	0.016	0.34	0.06
Period	1991.1–1996.4	1993.1–1998.3	1991.5–1998.12

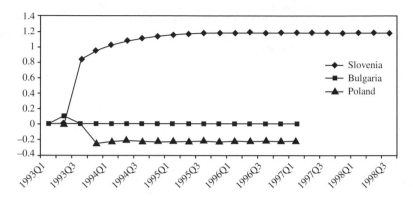

Figure 6.2   Devaluation by 5%, impact on GDP

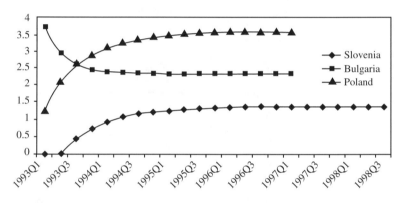

Figure 6.3   Devaluation by 5%, impact on wages

The profile of the inflationary pressures is different in each country. In Poland and Slovenia prices should stabilize to a higher level than the baseline by almost 4 per cent, while in Slovenia inflationary pressures, due to negative price-wage elasticity, will be very limited. Wages will also increase as a result of a price indexation scheme; real wages, however, would decrease in Poland and Bulgaria but increase in Slovenia due to high positive impacts of GDP increases on wages.

CONCLUSIONS

The objective of this chapter has been to investigate empirically the importance of exchange rate policies on economic activity in four Central and Eastern European

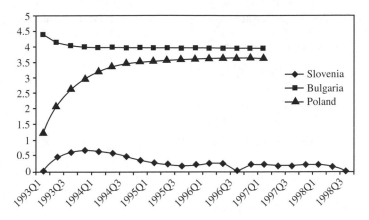

Figure 6.4   Devaluation by 5%, impact on prices

Countries, namely Bulgaria, the Czech Republic, Poland and Slovenia. The analysis was based on a traditional wage–price–GDP model in which the main explanatory variables of the economic activity are the production factor prices, the competitiveness and exogenous policy variables. To a certain extent adjusted versions of the model were estimated for the four countries of which three supplied acceptable results. The results for the Czech Republic being economically not acceptable and inconsistent with other studies were not considered.

The model was estimated for selected transition economies in an attempt to improve our understanding of the interactions of the exchange rate with the output supply and inflationary pressures. The results have shown that the effectiveness of the exchange rate for the boosting of economic activity is extremely limited. In Poland, a devaluation of the national currency might have had direct negative effects on economic activity. In Bulgaria, the initial positive effect had faded away by second-round negative impacts resulting from real wage rate increases. Finally in Slovenia, the overall impact of such a measure was marginally positive. However, the main impact results from the real wage increase, which acts positively on GDP in that country.

APPENDIX: RESULTS FOR THE CZECH REPUBLIC[5]

The estimation results of the model for the Czech Republic show a positive relationship of a weakening of the exchange rate with economic activity. However, in this equation a positive relationship of import prices with GDP is also reported. The real wage equation bears the influence of GDP but has a negative elasticity when the impact of the level of prices is concerned. Furthermore, the adjustment of the equation implies that the real wage

rate follows a slowing-down pattern after an overadjustment. Finally, while the sign of the interest rate and production cost is as expected in the price equation, both the real exchange rate and the wage rate have the wrong sign.

$$y = -0.39 - 0.18(w_{-1}/p_{-1}) + 0.81(e + p^* - p)_{-1}$$
$$\quad\;\; (0.24) \quad (0.09) \qquad\qquad\quad (0.40)$$

$$\qquad + 0.42 import\ prices + 0.22g + 0.09k$$
$$\qquad\;\; (0.16) \qquad\qquad\quad (0.16) \quad (0.04)$$

$$SEE = 0.047,\ R^2 = 0.62,\ DW = 2.24.$$

$$w - p = 0.18 + 0.04t - 0.17(w_{-1}/p_{-1}) - 1.68p + 0.52y$$
$$\qquad\;\; (0.12) \quad (0.01) \qquad (0.23) \qquad\qquad (0.96) \quad (0.29)$$

$$SEE = 0.062,\ R^2 = 0.95,\ DW = 1.76$$

$$p = 0.03 + 0.54p_{-1} + 0.19i_{-1} + 0.01(e + p^* - p)_{-1}$$
$$\quad\; (0.05) \quad (0.12) \qquad (0.09) \qquad\quad (0.08)$$

$$\qquad + 0.10 prod.\ cost_{-1} + 0.032w - 0.12w_{-1}$$
$$\qquad\;\; (0.03) \qquad\qquad\quad (0.027) \qquad (0.03)$$

$$SEE = 0.011,\ R^2 = 0.89,\ DW = 1.75$$

Where all variables are as previously defined.

Notes

1. Bulgaria has introduced the currency board system only in mid-1997.
2. These results are not included in the main paper but appear in the Appendix.
3. Standard errors in parenthesis.
4. Real exchange and interest rates are introduced with a 3-quarter lag.
5. Prepared by A. Derviz (Czech National Bank, Prague, the Czech Republic).

Part III
Country Studies

7 Price and Output Dynamics under a Currency Board: The Case of Bulgaria

George Chobanov and Eric J. Pentecost

INTRODUCTION

Bulgaria differs from the other transition economies considered in this book is that it has experienced the greatest exchange rate regime shift: from the most flexible, floating exchange rate system to the most rigid type of fixed-rate system – a currency board. From the start of the reform period in February 1991, when prices covering more than 70 per cent of retail turnover were liberalized and when administered prices increased fourfold, with the elimination of most subsidies, Bulgaria adopted a floating exchange rate regime. The exchange rate, however, quickly depreciated by 400 per cent, which fuelled inflation. In 1994 inflation was running at 96 per cent per annum and by 1996 had reached 122 per cent. With the advent of continued hyperinflation which exceeded 1000 per cent in 1997 and sharply falling levels of real output – about 7 per cent in 1997, following a 6 per cent fall in 1996 – the floating-rate system was replaced with a currency board regime on 1 July 1997. The Bulgarian currency board fixed the leva to 1000DM. This conveniently divides the period 1991–99 into two distinct sub-periods – the floating-rate period prior to July 1997, and the rigidly fixed exchange rate regime post-July 1997.

This switch of regime precludes any further econometric work to that under-taken in Part II, although it is possible to undertake some additional empirical work in order to compare the supply-side response of the Bulgarian economy under the currency board and floating exchange rate systems. This comparative empirical analysis is the subject of the next section. We then explain the rules and macroeconomic implications underlying a currency board system, and a stylized macroeconomic model of the Bulgarian economy with a currency board is then set out with a view to examining the stability and dynamic adjustment of the economy. Finally, we offer a brief conclusion.

EMPIRICAL ANALYSIS

Following the 'big bang' in February 1991 there was a sharp fall in economic activity in Bulgaria. Real GDP fell by about 23 per cent in 1991 and by a further 8–10 per cent in 1992 (Borensztein, Demekas and Ostry, 1993). This sharp decline in output is attributed to three main factors. First, the total volume of Bulgarian exports to the ex-CMEA area is estimated to have shrunk by about 66 per cent in 1991 and a further 15–25 per cent in 1992. Second, the shortage of raw material inputs, previously imported from the Soviet Union, adversely affected output, especially that of the large chemical and metallurgy sectors. A third contributory factor to the output decline was the compression of domestic demand resulting from the negative income effects of the trade and supply factors noted above, on top of which tight financial policies were pursued. Evidence of these policies is reflected in commercial banks' one-year lending rates in leva which stood at 58 per cent in 1993, rising to over 70 per cent in 1994. Since the establishment of the currency board in mid-1997, inflation has been reduced to about 8 per cent per annum and output is believed to have picked up, with some 2 per cent real growth between 1997 and 1998. Commercial bank lending rates were down to about 12 per cent per annum at the end of 1999 (Table 7.1).

The fundamental question of this section is how and to what extent is the output response in Bulgaria linked to the exchange rate regime. Table 7.2 shows the simple correlation coefficients between some of the key macroeconomic variables before and after the switch to the currency board in 1997. These partial correlation coefficients demonstrate two important features of the output decline under floating exchange rates: it was due primarily to supply-side shocks, hence the relationship

Table 7.1   Bulgarian macroeconomic statistics, 1993–99

	Lending rates (% per annum)	Money GDP growth (%)	CPI inflation (% per annum)	Real GDP growth (% per annum)	Real exchange rate (% per annum)	Unemployment (%)
1994	72.58	75.9	96	2	−8.93	12.4
1995	58.98	67.3	62	3	12.28	11.1
1996	123.48	98.8	122	−10	−13.95	12.5
1997	83.96	877.9	1062	−7	19.24	13.7
1998	13.3	26.2	19	7*	13.30	12.2*
1999	12.79	5.3	3	3*	1.48	–

Note: *denotes author's estimates. Other statistics from the IMF's *International Financial Statistics*. Note that column 4 is not the difference between columns 2 and 3. A rise in the real exchange rate denotes a rise in competitiveness.

Table 7.2   Macroeconomic correlation coefficients for Bulgaria

Period	Correlation Coefficient		
	Output–Inflation	Appreciation–Inflation	Appreciation–Output
1994–96	−0.865	−0.965	0.704
1997–99	0.592	0.765	−0.972

between prices and output is negative; and, secondly, the real appreciation of the Bulgarian leva worked to stimulate output. On the other hand, after the introduction of the currency board, these partial correlation coefficients change sign. That is output and inflation are positively correlated – indicative of the predominance of demand shocks – and real exchange rate appreciation works to reduce the growth of output. Thus, the supply-side response has been exactly the opposite under the currency board system than under the floating exchange rate system of the early 1990s.

Thus, although the Bulgarian currency board has had the effect of largely restoring price stability, a currency board regime does not offer stabilization of itself. In particular, it may also have the effect of curtailing output growth, as is suggested by the positive correlation between output and prices in the lower half of Table 7.2. This is particularly likely to be the case in transition economies where the liberalization process itself tends to result in some initial inflation as bottlenecks emerge in certain sectors due to the liberalization process advancing faster in some sectors of the economy than in others. This inflation is purely transitory and not a danger to longer-run stabilization objectives, although in the management of the currency board this may be difficult to distinguish from more persistent inflation. The theoretical model developed later in this chapter demonstrates the positive association between prices and output under a currency board regime.

THE CURRENCY BOARD SYSTEM

A currency board is an independent currency emission authority inside or outside of the Central Bank restricted by law with the following conditions:[1]

1. The exchange rate of the country's currency is fixed with respect to another stable currency (say the US dollar) called the reserve currency (or a set of stable currencies), but floating with the reserve currency in respect to all other currencies.
2. Absolute convertibility of the local and reserve currencies. This means that any amount of local currency could at any time be converted into the reserve currency. The reserve currency is a perfect substitute for the local currency.

3. The monetary base of the country is determined by its stock of international reserves converted into local currency at the fixed exchange rate.
4. The law forbids printing additional money for financing any kind of government budget deficit or discretionary fiscal policy.

A currency board enhances monetary credibility because of the direct link between monetary growth in a currency board country to that in a reserve currency country. Moreover, because the currency board only issues domestic money against foreign exchange at a fixed rate,[2] the money supply in the currency board country is related to the country's balance of payments position. To show this, the standard textbook money multiplier is given as $M^s = ((1+c)/(r+c))B$ where c is the public's average cash to deposits ratio, r is the banks cash reserve to deposits ratio, and B is the stock of base money or cash issued by the currency board. The currency board ensures that $B = FR$, where FR_T is the stock of foreign currency reserves at time T, which in turn depend on the past accumulation of foreign currency from balance of payments surpluses, such that

$$FR_T = \sum_{t=-\infty}^{T} (CAB_t + \Delta K_t) \tag{7.1}$$

where CAB is the current account balance and ΔK is the net private capital inflow. Thus the money supply is given as

$$M^s = \left[\frac{1+c}{c+r}\right]FR_T = \left[\frac{1+c}{c+r}\right] \sum_{t=-\infty}^{T} (CAB_t + \Delta K_t) \tag{7.2}$$

Since equation (7.2) is an identity, it follows that changes in the money stock can result from changes in the money multiplier or from the balance of payments. Suppose, for example, that the economy faces a fall in the demand for its exports. This leads to a deterioration in the current account that in turn reduces the money supply. As demand falls in the home country so may output and export prices, which will improve competitiveness and in turn restore the money supply. The crucial thing about this adjustment process is that it is automatic and the sterilization of reserve changes is not possible as it is under a standard fixed exchange rate regime.

One potential limitation of the adjustment mechanism is that with a fixed exchange rate changes in competitiveness and the terms of trade may only happen very slowly. This may cause greater disruption to domestic production and employment, than when there is some nominal exchange rate flexibility, which may serve to speed up the adjustment process. A second limitation is that the central bank's role as lender of last resort to the commercial banking sector is removed. In the case of Bulgaria, according to Article 33 of the Currency Board

Law, the Bulgarian National Bank (BNB) can refinance commercial banks in the case of systematic risk for the banking system. This refinancing, however, is only up to a preset limit, for a period not longer than three months and against a full collateral of gold, foreign convertible currency or other highly liquid assets.

TWO SIMPLE MODELS OF A TRANSITION ECONOMY WITH A CURRENCY BOARD

In this section a model of the aggregate goods and money markets is used to show the effect of a currency board on the evolution of prices and output. First we consider an exclusively demand-side model without a bond market, representing the early stages of the transition process. A labour market, with wage contracts following Calvo (1983) is then introduced to emphasize the importance of money-wage flexibility for macroeconomic stability with a currency board. Essentially, with sticky-goods market prices and underdeveloped financial markets, money-wage flexibility is required to ensure the stability of the economy in the face of autonomous shocks.

The Demand-Side Model

The supply of money under a currency board, as shown by equation (7.2), is equal to the past accumulation of foreign currency reserves multiplied by the money multiplier. To keep the model as simple as possible it is assumed that the money multiplier is unity and that there are no net private capital inflows. Therefore, the stock of levas depends only on past accumulated current-account balances. Equation (7.3) gives the continuous time equivalent of (7.2) where $\Delta K_t = 0$ and the money multiplier is unity:

$$m = \bar{m} + \int_{t=-\infty}^{T} (CAB)\, \partial t = \bar{m} + \int_{t=-\infty}^{T} [\eta(\bar{y} - y) - \tau(p - q - e)]\, \partial t \quad (7.3)$$

Equation (7.3) also postulates that the current balance surplus depends directly upon the difference between domestic income and absorption, $\bar{y} - y$, and the real exchange rate, $e + q - p$, where e is the domestic price of foreign currency and q is the foreign price level. The parameter τ, is the Marshall–Lerner condition, which is expected to be greater than zero if devaluation is to improve the trade balance. The rate of increase of the domestic money supply is obtained by differentiating equation (7.3) with respect to time to yield:

$$\dot{m} = \dot{m}^* = \eta(\bar{y} - y) - \tau(p - q) \quad (7.4)$$

Equation (7.4) says that the rate of growth of the domestic money supply, $\dot{m}$, is identically equal to the rate of growth of the foreign reserves, $\dot{m}^*$, which in turn is determined by the trade balance, where the exchange rate is fixed and normalized to unity.

The real side of the model is represented by two equations: one for domestic demand and another for inflation. Domestic absorption is written in log-linear terms as

$$y = \bar{g} + \delta(m - p) \tag{7.5}$$

where $\bar{g}$ is the exogenous level of government spending. Hence domestic absorption depends directly on public sector spending and the term $m - p$ represents the real balance effect or wealth effect on consumption.

The actual level of prices in a transition economy is a mixture of administered prices and market prices, which makes it difficult to model. On the other hand, the general level of prices tends to rise directly with the excess demand for goods and services, reflecting in part the availability of money balances. Hence we choose to model the rate of inflation rather than the level of prices, which can be represented as

$$\dot{p} = \lambda(d - y) \quad 0 < \lambda < \infty \tag{7.6}$$

The steady-state solutions for prices and money are easily obtained by setting $\dot{p} = \dot{m} = 0$. From equation (7.4) the log of the domestic price level is equal to q, the foreign price level, in equilibrium. This is a feature of a currency board arrangement. From equation (7.6) the supply of output $\bar{y}$ is equal to the level of demand ($y = \bar{y}$). The steady-state solution for the money supply is therefore

$$m = \bar{q} + \frac{\bar{y} - \bar{g}}{\delta} \tag{7.7}$$

Thus the money supply unambiguously falls with government spending and rises with output, but the price level is unaffected by the domestic economy being tied to the foreign price level.

Substituting (7.5) into the dynamic equations for money-supply growth and the rate of inflation gives

$$\begin{bmatrix} \dot{m} \\ \dot{p} \end{bmatrix} = \begin{bmatrix} -\eta\delta & \{\eta\delta - \tau\} \\ \lambda\delta & -\lambda\delta \end{bmatrix} \begin{bmatrix} m \\ p \end{bmatrix} + \begin{bmatrix} -\eta\bar{g} + \eta\bar{y} \\ \lambda\bar{g} - \lambda\bar{y} \end{bmatrix} \tag{7.8}$$

The stability conditions are:

$$Det = \delta\lambda\tau > 0 \tag{7.9}$$

$$Tr = -(\eta + \lambda)\delta < 0 \tag{7.10}$$

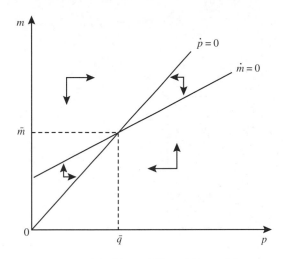

Figure 7.1 The stability of the model

These conditions are unambiguously satisfied suggesting that the model is convergent.

The dynamic system (7.8) is illustrated in Figure 7.1. The $\dot{m} = 0$ locus may have a negative or positive slope in (m, p) space. The greater the price elasticity of exports and imports the more likely is a negative slope, whereas the stronger the expenditure effects the more likely is a positive slope. Thus a fall in domestic prices will induce a higher equilibrium money supply if the gain in competitiveness and the increased net exports exceeds the increase in domestic demand, thereby giving a negatively sloped $\dot{m} = 0$ locus. On the other hand, if the domestic demand effect is stronger than the competitiveness effect, the money supply locus will have a positive slope. Given the typically low price elasticities in Bulgaria and other transition economies, Figure 7.1 shows the slope of the $\dot{m} = 0$ locus to be positive. The slope of the $\dot{p} = 0$ locus is equal to unity.

This system can be used to consider two alternative shocks. First, a rise in the long-run level of output, brought about by supply-side efficiency gains, resulting in turn from the liberalization process.[3] Secondly, from a rise in the foreign price level, q.

In Figure 7.2 the effect of a rise in the level of output shifts both schedules (as does a cut in government spending). The rise in output will generate a trade balance surplus directly as home production replaces foreign production. This in

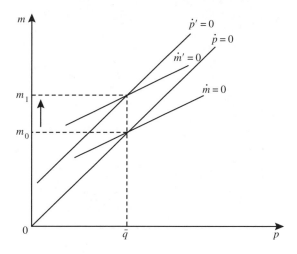

Figure 7.2   A rise in output (or fall in government spending)

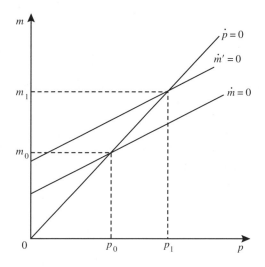

Figure 7.3   The dynamics of a foreign price rise

turn leads to a higher money supply that augments aggregate demand restoring the price level to its initial level.

Figure 7.3 shows the effect of a rise in the foreign price level. This shifts the trade balance equilibrium schedule upwards as domestic production becomes more competitive, which raises the money supply. The higher money supply then raises

consumption and aggregate demand, which in turn leads to a rise in the price level. In the final equilibrium the domestic price level is higher in line with the foreign price level.

The Model with a Supply-Side

The principal shortcoming of the model of the previous section is that there is no behavioural treatment of the supply-side. This is perhaps characteristic of a country in the early stages of transition, but as the liberalization proceeds and the supply-side becomes more established on market lines then wages need to be brought into the picture. In this section an alternative dynamic model is set out to capture this possibility.

The principal difference lies in the treatment of the dynamics. Combining equations (7.4) and (7.6) gives a single dynamic equation for real money balances, where the direct effect of prices on the trade balance and aggregate demand are excluded for simplicity, so that $\tau = 0$. Thus the dynamics of real money balances, h, are given as

$$\dot{m} - \dot{p} = \dot{h} = (\lambda + \eta)(\bar{y} - y) \tag{7.11}$$

Thus the growth of real money balances, $\dot{h}$, depends on the excess supply of output, which is equivalent to the trade balance surplus and where the speed of adjustment is a combination of the responsiveness of the money stock to the trade balance and the responsiveness of prices to excess demand.

The other dynamic equation is for the growth of real wages and can be derived from the multi-period overlapping wage contract due to Calvo (1983). Following the exposition of Scarth (1996), let w_t denote the log of all wages contracted in period t and let ρ be the proportion of contracts that are of one period duration, $\rho(1 - \rho)$ the proportion of contracts that are of two period duration and so on. This implies that p_t the overall wage index is

$$p_t = \rho[w_t + (1 - \rho)w_{t-1} + (1 - \rho)^2 w_{t-2} + \cdots] \tag{7.12}$$

Assuming constant returns to scale, the marginal product of labour equals the real wage rate. Units can be chosen so that the marginal product of labour is unity so that $p_t = w_t$. The money wage in each period, w_t, is set with a view to the expected (actual) price that will materialize in each of the various periods in the future and to the state of market pressure in all future periods; that is, $w_t = p_t + \sigma(y - \bar{y})_t$ where $\sigma(y - \bar{y})_t$ denotes the state of market pressure. Applying this to all future periods where the weight given to each period depends on the number of contracts

that will run for each period, yields

$$w_t = \rho[p_t + (1-\rho)p_{t+1} + (1-\rho)^2 p_{t+2} + \cdots]$$
$$+ \sigma\rho[(y-\bar{y})_t + (1-\rho)(y-\bar{y})_{t+1} + (1-\rho)^2(y-\bar{y})_{t+2} + \cdots] \tag{7.13}$$

Writing (7.13) one period forward, multiplying the result by $(1-\rho)$ and subtracting (7.13) from the result gives

$$w_{t+1} - w_t = \pi(w_t - p_t - \sigma(y-\bar{y})_t) \tag{7.14}$$

where $\pi = \rho/(1-\rho)$, which in continuous time becomes

$$\dot{w} = \pi(w - p - \sigma(y-\bar{y})) \tag{7.15}$$

Subtracting $\dot{p}$ from both sides of (7.15), defining x as the real wage rate and using (7.6) gives

$$\dot{w} - \dot{p} = \dot{x} = \pi(x - \sigma(y-\bar{y})) - \lambda(y-\bar{y})$$
$$= \pi x + (\pi\sigma\phi + \lambda)(\bar{y} - y) \tag{7.16}$$

This is an expression for the rate of change in the real wage rate, which depends directly on the level of the real wage rate, and inversely on the level of excess demand in the goods market.

The dynamic system is now given by substituting for y in equations (7.11) and (7.16) to give

$$\begin{bmatrix} \dot{h} \\ \dot{x} \end{bmatrix} = \begin{bmatrix} -\delta(\eta+\lambda) & 0 \\ -\delta(\psi+\lambda) & \pi \end{bmatrix} \begin{bmatrix} h \\ x \end{bmatrix} + \begin{bmatrix} -(\eta+\lambda)\bar{g} + (\eta+\lambda)\bar{y} \\ -(\psi+\lambda)\bar{g} + (\psi+\lambda)\bar{y} \end{bmatrix} \tag{7.17}$$

where $\psi = \sigma\pi\phi$. This dynamic system is inherently unstable since the determinant, Δ, is given as

$$\Delta = -\delta\pi(\eta+\lambda) < 0$$

The only way this system can be stable is if there is a saddle-path solution. Such a solution, however, requires a free variable that is able to jump discretely to put the model on a unique stable path. Given that money, output and prices are all slow-moving variables, the only candidate for a jump variable is the money-wage rate. By assuming that the money-wage rate can jump at a moment in time – such as when a new set of wage contracts are signed – the model can give a stable solution.

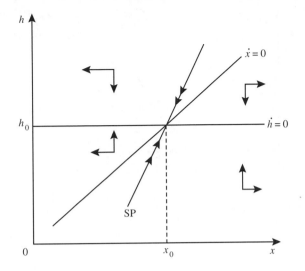

Figure 7.4 The stability in the supply-side model

This is shown in Figure 7.4 where the $\dot{h} = 0$ locus is horizontal since real money balances are independent of the real-wage rate. The real wage equilibrium schedule, on the other hand, has a positive slope since a higher level of real money balances are associated with higher output, through a trade balance surplus, and the higher production leads to higher real wages through labour market pressure. Figure 7.4 gives the direction arrows, showing the model to be unstable unless on the stable arm denoted by SP. Shocks to the system can now be analysed as they were in the demand-side model.[4]

A cut in government spending (or a rise in the long-run level of output) will raise both the money-market equilibrium line and the constant real-wage line. The new equilibrium will be reached by an initial downward jump in the money-wage rate, since rational agents will anticipate a fall in public spending (or rise in output) to reduce prices. This will stimulate the demand for output and raise the real money supply through a balance of trade surplus. Note in Figure 7.5 that initially the real-wage rate falls below its long-run level – that is it overshoots the final equilibrium at C moving from point A to point B – due to the stickiness of prices and output in the model. It is also important to note that a cut in aggregate demand had the effect of raising output in this model because of its effect on the supply-side through the money wage. This is potentially important for Bulgaria, since reducing state spending without liberalizing the supply-side will not lead to output growth.

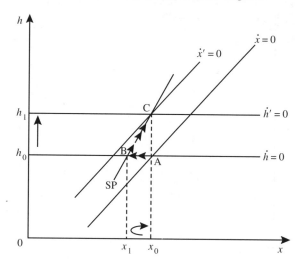

Figure 7.5　The effect of a rise in output due to the liberalization of production

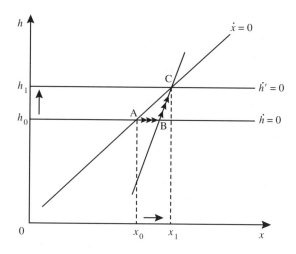

Figure 7.6　A trade balance shock

An exogenous trade balance shock – such as a rise in the foreign price level – leaves the constant real-wage schedule unaffected, but causes the real-money balance locus to shift up. Figure 7.6 shows that the real-wage rate initially jumps, from point A to point B, but undershoots its final equilibrium level at x_1. The higher foreign price level initially raises the money supply which in turn stimulates demand and domestic prices. The money wage jumps because wage-setters

anticipate the higher foreign prices feeding through into higher domestic prices and a higher demand for domestic output.

This model with supply-side dynamics assumes, crucially, that the labour market always clears as money wages are flexible to bring about market clearing at each point in time. Without flexible money wages the model would become unstable, as goods market prices and output are only sluggish in their response to shocks. The policy implication is that sharp falls in money-wage rates may be essential from time to time if the model is to reach a stable equilibrium, given the degree of stickiness apparent in other prices.

CONCLUSIONS AND POLICY IMPLICATIONS

The Bulgarian currency board has produced relatively low and stable inflation rates. Table 7.1 shows that monthly inflation was less than 2 per cent per month during 1998 and only 3 per cent per annum in 1999. The currency board has therefore been particularly effective at eliminating the hyperinflation of 1997. This is vitally important for the liberalization and modernization of the economy where relative prices are to serve as important signals in the determination of the allocation of resources.

It has also been demonstrated that the currency board regime has reversed the correlation between inflation and output growth. Under a floating-rate system inflation and growth were negatively correlated, whereas under a currency board they are positively correlated. Therefore curtailing domestic inflation is likely to also involve curtailing economic growth. This problem is the principal rationale for the need for flexible labour markets, without which output declines may be exaggerated rather than damped.

Notes

1. For a theoretical introduction to currency boards see Osband and Villanueva (1993) and Humpage and Melntire (1995).
2. In the case of Bulgaria, Article 30 of the Currency Board Legislation says that the National Bank is obligated to respond to any requirement of buying and selling on the territory of the country of German marks for Bulgarian levas at spot exchange rates which are not allowed to deviate from the officially determined exchange rate by more than 0.5 per cent, including any kind of commissions and costs for the client.
3. Note that in this case a rise in output is analytically equivalent to a cut in government spending.
4. The steady-state values for x and h are identical to the steady-state values for p and m in the demand-side only model.

8 Exchange Rates and the Supply Response in the Czech Republic: Is PPP a Relevant Rule for Assessing the Equilibrium?

Vladimir Benacek

INTRODUCTION

The functioning of the Eastern European economies received much attention after their changeover to markets after 1989. The peculiarities in the subsequent development in these countries posed several new empirical issues to be theoretically explained. The problem of finding the equilibrium real exchange rate (RER) and exchange rate stability in these economies has remained one of the most resilient features to solve. Contrary to traditional experience in dealing with exchange rate adjustment, many of these countries, after sharp devaluations of their currencies to the level of market equilibrium, went through a long period of real appreciation. Both the economic policy-makers and the theorists were then not able to get an equivocal agreement in the interpretation of these developments. It became apparent that many rules that functioned satisfactorily in stable economies, became of ill-advice for economies in transition or for economies undergoing a fast industrial restructuring. The Czech case is a prime example of how the exchange rate could behave in the most unexpected way. Table 8.1 shows the basic indicators relevant for the assessment of the RER and the evolution of the environment influencing the RER.

The Czech economy transforms over 55 per cent of its GDP through exports, and for such an economy the exchange rate becomes a macroeconomic variable of fundamental importance. The point of departure from the central planning to free markets in 1990 was marked by a devaluation of 114 per cent. Though the ensuing pass-through to inflation was sharp, it took full four years until the RER returned to the pre-devaluation level. In the following four years (1995–98) the nominal exchange rate both to the German mark and the US dollar remained unperturbed

and practically equal to their rates in December 1990, while the aggregated CPI inflation rate scored an additional 39 per cent during 1995–98. The influence of both adverse determining factors (the inflation and the RER appreciation) notwithstanding, the Czech trade performance during the whole period of 1990–98 showed an unparalleled growth.

Figure 8.1 (p. 108) illustrates the basic developments at issue. The problems to clarify are as follows:

(a) What is the optimal level of devaluation at the beginning of transition?
(b) Is the prolonged RER appreciation a sustainable development compatible with growth or is this tendency detrimental to the performance of domestic industries?
(c) Is the path of fundamental RER equilibrium above or below the empirical trajectory of RER?
(d) Is the RER development converging quickly to the equilibrium RER or will that tendency be prolonged to a long run?
(e) Is the measure of RER based on the consumer price index (CPI) or the producer price index (PPI) a meaningful concept for the economic policy in countries with highly dynamic real (that is non-monetary) changes?

The aim of this chapter is to empirically test the past behaviour of Czech producers, exporters and importers, and their foreign trade response to exchange rates adjusted to purchasing power parity (PPP) differentials in various countries. The results of the test are important for drawing implications about the validity of the PPP rule in a country in transition. If the tests reject the validity of the PPP hypothesis, then relative price levels are not a primary factor relevant for the real behaviour of economic agents in international trade, and trade competitiveness must be described by variables other than relative prices. An alternative interpretation of the real exchange rate is attempted at the end of the chapter.

The relevance of real exchange rate appreciation is outlined in explaining the specific aspects of growth in transition economies. Instead of concentrating only on the real growth of GDP (in constant domestic prices), as is followed in the standard economics of comparative international studies, equal attention should be given to the RER appreciation.

PROBLEMS WITH REAL EXCHANGE RATE MEASUREMENT IN A TRANSITION ECONOMY

In the past two decades the concept of real exchange rate was developed in order to distinguish between nominal (monetary or price) phenomena and the real

Table 8.1   Selected macroeconomic indicators for the Czech Republic, 1989–99

Indicator	1989	1990	1991	1992	1993	1994	1995	1996	1997	1998	1999[g]
Nominal GDP[a]	524.5	579.3	749.6	846.8	1 002.3	1 148.6	1 348.7	1 532.6	1 680.5	1 798.0	1 836.0
Real GDP[b] % annual change	4.5	−1.2	−14.2	−6.6	+0.6	2.7	6.4	3.9	1.0	−2.7	−0.1
Productivity of labour,[b] 1990 = 100%	100.4	100.0	90.7	87.2	88.9	90.3	94.3	96.9	98.5	98.1	99.2
Real wage, 1990 = 100	98.2	100.0	73.7	81.2	85.7	92.8	100.7	109.2	112.6	111.2	114.7
Real output of industry,[b] 1990 = 100%	103.6	100.0	77.7	69.5	65.8	67.2	73.0	77.7	81.2	82.6	80.4
Real output in industry,[b] %	2.4	−3.5	−22.3	−10.6	−5.3	+2.1	8.7	6.4	4.5	1.6	−3.4
Producer price annual inflation, %	1.2	16.6	54.8	9.9	13.1	5.3	7.2	4.4	5.7	2.2	3.4
Consumer price annual inflation, %	1.9	10.0	57.9	11.1	20.8	10.0	7.9	8.6	10.0	6.8	2.5
Share of savings on GDP, %	n.a.	n.a.	36.7	27.4	27.3	30.1	34.1	35.5	33.9	32.2	30.0
Share of investment on GDP, %	32.5	28.7	19.2	25.0	27.7	30.1	34.9	38.0	36.7	33.5	32.6
Average wage per month in $	212	195	142	163	199	239	308	357	337	388	39.5

107

Rate of unemployment, %	0.0	0.8	4.1	2.6	3.5	3.2	2.9	3.5	5.2	7.5	10.0
Exports (incl. services)[c]	16 401	13 833	12 576	13 860	18 952	21 086	28 181[f]	29 870[f]	29 679[f]	32 943[f]	34 116[d]
Imports (incl. services)[c]	15 482	4 611	11 187	15 860	18 466	21 978	30 016[f]	33 824[f]	32 537[f]	35 465[f]	34 595[d]
Current-account balance[c]	292	−721	356	53	456	−787	−1 369	−4 292	−3 156	−1 822	−1 058
Nominal exch. rate (Kc/$), average	15.1	18.3	29.5	28.3	29.2	28.8	26.6	27.1	31.7	32.3	34.6
Nominal exch. rate (Kc/DM)			17.8	18.1	17.6	17.7	18.5	18.1	18.3	18.3	18.9
Real exch. rate DM (PPI), 1990 = 100%	100.0	124.8	125.8	119.3	101.6	98.7	97.5	90.3	87.6	82.9	82.0
Share of OECD on exports,[e] %	38.1	45.0	55.8	68.5	69.9	71.4	76.8	74.2	75.1	77.0	78.0
Exports to EU 12[c] (goods)	3 423	3 407	4 020	5 402	6 509	7 704	9 406	9 114	13 545[f]	15 100	17 200
Imports from EU 12[c] (goods)	3 412	3 895	3 530	6 108	6 717	8 326	11 747	13 236	16 767[f]	18 300	18 000

Sources: Statistics of the Czech National Bank (1993–99), Czech Statistical Office (1993–99).

Notes: [a] billion Kc, nominal; [b] billion Kc, until 1992 constant prices of 1984, since 1993 constant prices of 1994; [c] million US dollars; [d] provisional figures for trade; [e] without trade with Slovakia; [f] new methodology, including processing traffic and leasing; [g] provisional data of March 2000.

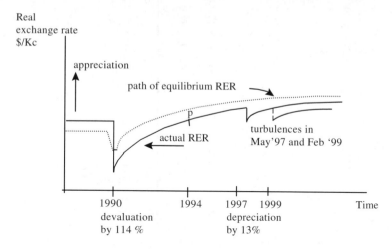

Figure 8.1 The stylized facts describing the hypothetical trajectory of the Czech real exchange rate

conditions. Once an indicator as simple as the real exchange rate becomes a fundamental variable, one should be certain of its meaning the same in all economic circumstances.

The practice in the real equilibrium exchange rate is to a large extent ruled by PPP (purchasing power parity) in its absolute or relative forms. This is due to the crucial role of relative prices (foreign P^*/ domestic P), usually measured as the CPI or PPI, in the most common indicator of RER.[1] (For a review of RER and PPP issues see Rogoff, 1996. Many economists have expressed doubts as to whether PPP can be applied to economies in transition, and Halpern and Wyplosz, 1997 have recently provided the most persuasive empirical argument.) Generally speaking, this problem is valid in all economies with extensive factor reallocation, production fluctuation and quality changes.

Firstly, it can be doubted whether the transition economies have a meaningful measure of inflation. A large portion of the price changes is misleadingly interpreted as 'inflation', instead of taking them as representing a change in quality or image (or even an introduction of new products). Therefore, the difference between the changes in foreign and domestic price levels can be grossly misleading leading giving rise to improper expectations and incorrect policy conclusions. Similarly the statistics of relative foreign to domestic prices (P_i^*/P_i) by products i (as used for the PPP or the real exchange rate estimation) can be misleading because there is an attempt to compare horizontally or even vertically differentiated products. As was analysed by Fontagne, Freudenburg and Pindy (1998) the quality and the

market structure became essential characteristics of modern trade. This means that with PPP there is often a danger of comparing physical products, which are not perfect substitutes. As argued by Isard (1977), pricing of differentiated products fails the arbitrage test and thus the relationship between exchange rate and relative prices is often statistically insignificant.

Since the transition economies generally do not satisfy this condition, and given their high degree of specialization in intra-industrial products of low quality,[2] their index of the aggregate price level in nominal dollar terms must therefore also be misleading. In comparing two economies, each of which is at the opposite corner of the quality competition, the PPP method in fact attempts to solve the problem by transforming the quality competition into mere price competition. The price-level divergence between a transition and a stabilized EU economy can thus lead to wrong conclusions if one mechanically applies criteria suitable for highly integrated economies with a comparable product mix. For example, one can come to incorrect policy implications about the sustainability of the current exchange rate. Also the estimates of GDP per capita, both in nominal dollar terms and PPP dollar terms, can thus be difficult to reconcile. The catch-up scenarios based on PPP values per capita may lead in such cased to an elusive optimism.

Secondly, price differentials are not the only important variables. A change in the exchange rate can be measured either in nominal terms or in real terms: the former can be caused either by devaluation (in a fixed regime) or by a market fluctuation (in a float regime); the latter, on top of the nominal exchange rate changes, also includes the changes in the relative prices levels, such as the inflation differentials between two countries or the different developments in the price levels between domestic tradables and non-tradables. Unfortunately, the problem of exchange rates is far from being determined by only these variables. Its equilibrium value is also determined by the level of relative productivity growth, relative wages, terms of trade, fiscal spending, tariff and non-tariff barriers, changes in consumers' tastes, capital account disequilibrium, and so on.

As a result, exchange rate policy cannot be neutral to alternative policy instruments and alternative states of the remaining real determining variables. As pointed out by Drabek and Brada (1998), there are also many economic policies, alternative to exchange rate changes, that lead to analogous impacts on the behaviour of economic agents. These policy instruments or adjustment variables may be autonomous from price-level differentials. A nominal exchange rate can therefore be in equilibrium with a whole set of real exchange rates (for example based on given PPI), provided there is an adjustment through various complementary or competing policy instruments or other real autonomous variables. This is a different approach to reasoning than the traditional one, where the given RER (that is, the given price inflation) is compatible with only one nominal exchange rate. As Eichengreen (1988) and Hsieh (1982) confirmed, the RER has a higher

explanatory power in macroeconomically stabilised economies and economies with harmonized economic development.

ECONOMETRIC TESTS OF PRICE DIFFERENTIALS AND TRADE PERFORMANCE UNDER ABSOLUTE PPP

Even though many reservations can be raised against the universal validity of the price-deflated RER, one cannot avoid an intuitive feeling that the relative prices must matter, however relative and partial this concept may be. We can question its relevance only if the empirical evidence is in direct conflict with its theoretical reasoning. Therefore, let us now test a central hypothesis of RER: that the magnitude of dollar-price differentials between two countries is in a direct relationship with the intensities of exports and imports.

The index of a relative price differential between Czechia (CZ) and the United States (US), as her trading partner, is given by the exchange rate deviation index (ERDI) related to the nominal exchange rate ($E_{Kc/\$}$) of koruna (Kc) to Dollar ($\$$), and the relative (weighted average) prices of two countries measured in their respective domestic currencies:

$$ERDI_{Kc/\$} = E_{Kc/\$}(P_{US}^{\$}/P_{CZ}^{Kc}) \tag{8.1}$$

Because the term in brackets is the exchange rate in absolute PPP terms, we can derive from it an alternative formula:

$$ERDI_{Kc/\$} = E_{Kc/\$}/E_{Kc/\$}^{PPP}$$

ERDI remains the same if we use both alternative exchange rates for the calculation of GDP per capita in nominal dollars or in PPP dollars:

$$ERDI_{Kc/\$} = y_{CZ}^{\$ \text{ in PPP}}/y_{CZ}^{\$ \text{ nominal}}$$

where y is the Czech (CZ) GDP per capita in US$ – in international PPP dollars and in nominal dollars, respectively. This is an expression which can be applied to international statistics collected by the World Bank or OECD. By using these statistical resources we can compute the Czech ERDI for all other currencies. For example, to obtain the ERDI of Kc to German DM (that is, between CZ and Germany DM), we can apply the formula:

$$ERDI_{Kc/DM} = (y_D^{\$}/y_D^{\$ PPP})(y_{CZ}^{\$ PPP}/y_{CZ}^{\$}) \tag{8.2}$$

Indices of ERDI quantify the price level differentials between Czechia and the respective countries i (respectively their currencies).

If the theory of absolute PPP is valid, then Czech exports should be directed to countries where ERDI is high – to Switzerland, Denmark and Germany; and imports should be targeted on low-price countries, such as Egypt, India, China or Slovakia. Czech trade with the former should be in surplus and in deficit with the latter.

The basic hypothesis for testing is given as follows:

$$X_{it} - M_{it} = a_1 + b_1 ERDI_{it} + \varepsilon_{it} \tag{8.3}$$

where a and b are coefficients of regression, and ε_{it} is a random variable; X and M are Czech exports and imports; $i = (1, 2, \ldots 30)$ are indices of countries (30 main Czech trading partners covering 98 per cent of all Czech turnover of trade), or their currencies, respectively; and $t = (1993, 1994, 1995$ and $1996)$.

Table 8.2 offers all necessary data for an empirical testing of Czech trade with her 30 most important partners during 1993–96. $ERDI_i \neq 1$ means that the $E_{Kc/i}$ is not in parity with the price level in country i. $ERDI_i > 1$ implies an 'undervaluation' of the nominal (market) exchange rate of koruna to the currency of given country i. ERDI is thus the coefficient of 'correction' to the level of PPP. If $0 < ERDI_i < 1$ then an 'overvaluation' of the nominal exchange rate of koruna relative to the currency of given country i is signalled. The economic meaning of the above test centres around the validity of the theory of absolute PPP. If the ERDIs of the koruna differed from 1 in both directions, and if the reality would have behaved in accordance with our hypothesis, then the expected coefficients of equation (8.3) should be $b > 0$ and $a < 0$.

Our tests by using least-square regressions both for pooled data for all four years, as well as for annually separated estimations, finished with one uniform conclusion: the relative price levels were relevant for the determination of the Czech trade flows because the null hypothesis for the coefficients has been rejected. The results for the estimation based on 120 observations were as follows:

Statistics	a_1	b_1
Coefficients	3009.0	−2129.0
t-statistics	2.9	−4.5
Probability of 0 hypothesis	0.004	0.000
R-squared $+ R^2$-adj.	0.149	0.142

However, these results are in conflict with the expected signs. Since the test for both the heteroscedasticity and autocorrelation of residuals were in order, the negative slope of b and the positive intercept indicate that the assumption of absolute PPP must be rejected. Figure 8.2 shows the data and the fitted line. The

Table 8.2 The exchange rate deviation index and balance of trade of Czechia

Country	ERDI 1993	ERDI 1994	ERDI 1995	ERDI 1996	Balance of trade, mil. CZK				Index of RCA in trade: $(X-M)/(X+M)$			
					1993	1994	1995	1996	1993	1994	1995	1996
Austria	3.47	3.04	2.56	2.56	−6 028	−4 486	−8 517	−4 981	−0.1152	−0.0700	−0.1012	−0.0609
Belgium	3.24	2.76	2.31	2.33	−794	−2 591	−4 294	−3 532	−0.0717	−0.1786	−0.2002	−0.1576
Brazil	1.56	1.48	1.37	1.37	−521	−874	−1 262	−2 008	−0.3713	−0.3807	−0.3589	−0.4946
Bulgaria	0.88	0.68	0.60	0.56	1 232	1 421	1 530	1 201	0.6087	0.6375	0.6145	0.4948
Canada	2.86	2.26	1.86	1.75	−1 070	−416	−562	−760	−0.2997	−0.1386	−0.1603	−0.1915
Denmark	3.95	3.33	2.85	2.86	−1 106	−1 174	−1 875	−2 451	−0.1898	−0.1716	−0.2107	−0.2506
Egypt	0.53	0.48	0.42	0.54	4 151	3 349	1 905	2 087	0.9105	0.9020	0.7974	0.7034
Finland	3.51	2.83	2.38	2.51	−846	−2 789	−3 090	−4 801	−0.2171	−0.4130	−0.3758	−0.4936
France	3.24	2.92	2.41	2.70	−4 119	−5 085	−11 871	−14 633	−0.2184	−0.1967	−0.2822	−0.3009
Germany	3.17	3.17	2.78	2.70	4 814	13 059	3 481	−11 354	0.0246	0.0573	0.0081	−0.0259
Hongkong	2.32	2.31	2.03	1.92	1 306	1 342	−879	−138	0.2571	0.2466	−0.1897	−0.0239
Hungary	1.50	1.50	1.30	1.27	3 539	5 956	4 237	3 085	0.2577	0.3813	0.2679	0.1702
China	0.65	0.52	0.43	0.44	5 094	−417	−3 043	−6 176	0.5327	−0.0780	−0.3775	−0.6138
India	0.65	0.59	0.49	0.47	464	242	531	16	0.1895	0.0812	0.1410	0.0035
Italy	3.06	2.55	1.94	1.97	1 465	−2 090	−14 229	−24 768	0.0399	−0.0492	−0.2496	−0.3865

113

Japan	4.21	4.00	3.63	3.45	−4 628	−5 897	−8 012	−10 362	−0.5473	−0.5344	−0.5197	−0.6658
Malaysia	1.03	1.01	0.87	0.83	−500	−686	−955	−1 490	−0.6793	−0.7029	−0.5987	−0.6816
Netherlands	3.24	2.99	2.44	2.45	−1 322	−2 130	−3 906	−4 839	−0.0672	−0.0936	−0.1246	−0.1641
Poland	1.28	1.13	1.05	1.06	1 071	3 552	7 526	10 751	0.0539	0.1280	0.1721	0.1962
Romania	1.13	1.04	0.69	0.69	728	994	1 135	1 532	0.5741	0.6054	0.5996	0.6331
Russia*	1.26	1.24	1.01	1.13	−19 641	−19 987	−33 040	−37 036	−0.3625	−0.3863	−0.4966	−0.4959
S. Korea	2.21	1.92	1.72	1.60	−1 295	−2 308	−2 176	−3 673	−0.6181	−0.7379	−0.5201	−0.5969
Singapore	2.66	2.69	2.38	2.24	347	−188	1 379	418	0.1946	−0.0917	0.2703	0.1237
Slovakia	0.83	0.83	0.69	0.90	17 064	6 778	579	12 767	0.1151	0.0533	0.0036	0.0813
Spain	2.89	2.33	1.90	1.85	1 767	−694	−2 896	−5 344	0.2357	−0.0833	−0.2474	−0.3784
Sweden	3.99	3.26	2.60	2.70	−1 696	−2 679	−3 974	−4 406	−0.2528	−0.3033	−0.3152	−0.3157
Switzerland	4.35	3.76	3.18	3.32	−3 932	−3 812	−5 283	−6 266	−0.3053	−0.2537	−0.2580	−0.3072
Turkey	1.08	1.31	1.01	0.92	2 704	1 208	244	318	0.5232	0.3228	0.0698	0.0691
U. Kingdom	2.86	2.50	1.93	1.94	1 287	−1 436	−7 029	−13 452	0.0597	−0.0595	−0.1616	−0.3103
Ukraine	1.34	1.16	1.38	1.06	−449	486	175	1 241	−0.0712	0.0700	0.0150	0.1133
USA	2.82	2.46	2.03	1.97	−4 353	−5 447	−11 592	−12 879	−0.2398	−0.2359	−0.3449	−0.3376

Note: *Russian trade without oil and natural gas.
Source: Capek (1997); The World Bank (1997); and the Czech Statistical Office *Yearbooks*, 1995–98.

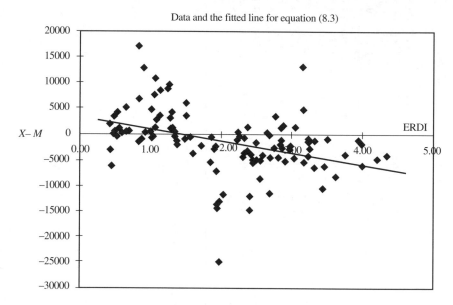

Figure 8.2   Balance of trade as a function of ERDI

discrepancy between the expected relationship and the reality is obvious and cannot be explained solely by data contamination or a few overshooting outliers.

Since our hypothesis was rejected, the results can be interpreted as direct evidence that both the theory of absolute PPP and the theory of real exchange rate based on relative prices are not valid if applied to the Czech trade in its years of transformation. The conclusion could be made even stronger: there was an evident tendency to a reversal of the theoretical relationship – the higher prices were abroad, the more imports were targeted from that country and lesser exports could be placed in such a country.

However, if we accept a hypothesis that ERDI is an index of a gap in quality, goodwill, marketing, ability to differentiate or a lack in market power, then there will be no paradox in our results. The higher that foreign prices are (relative to our prices), the higher is the foreign quality and thus the more attractive are those goods as our imports. Also, countries with a high demand for quality have a low demand for our inferior goods, and thus our exports must be weak. These products, on the other hand, can be sold in large quantities in countries with low quality standards – for example, in countries where they have lower price levels than our price level. High intra-industrial exchanges between countries with unequal standing in quality may bias towards a misleading interpretation of these flows. These are not exchanges of similar products, which would be close substitutes,

but a trade in highly differentiated non-substitutable and non-competing products, sold on different (parallel) markets. Both the PPP estimate of the GDP or the PPP-based estimate of the real exchange rate do not offer a reliable point of departure for the explanation of dynamics in such countries.

ECONOMETRIC TESTS OF TRADE PERFORMANCE UNDER RELATIVE PPP

We have seen that the equilibrium exchange rate approximated by a function of the relative gap between nominal domestic and foreign prices (that is, by the PPP in its absolute form), may not, in some cases, be a rule to be followed. In our case it led to a controversial conclusion that the more undervalued was the nominal (market) exchange rate (relative to relative prices), the higher was the deficit in the balance of trade. From it one could derive an absurd (and false) prescriptive inference that the balance of trade deficit could be improved by an exchange rate appreciation. The correct inference would be that the balance of trade could be improved if the quality improved – that is, if domestic prices increased because of gains in quality, that would cause the exchange rate to appreciate. Therefore the relative price changes can matter and we should test their relevance.

Actually, our previous test has not dealt with a case of how PPP behaves in its weaker (relative) form. For example, there may still exist a standard positive correlation between a change in the exchange rate (which thus shifts relative prices between and inside countries) and trade performance. That means, we have to test whether PPP is valid in its relative definition. The concept of ERDI can be transformed into the relative version of PPP by dividing equation (8.1) for time t by the same expression for time $t - 1$:

$$ERDI_i^t / ERDI_i^{t-1} = (E_i^t / E_i^{t-1})(P_i^t / P_i^{t-1})/(P_{CZ}^t / P_{CZ}^{t-1}) \qquad (8.4)$$

where i is a list of countries (trading partners), CZ indicates Czechia and $t = (1994, 1995, 1996)$. The right-hand side of the equation is the price-deflated formula for the real exchange rate of the Czech koruna individually tailored to each trading partner i with a one-year lag.

Let us therefore test a hypothesis that the annual changes in the Czech trade balance by countries i is a function of the real exchange rate developments in the given year t relative to $t - 1$:

$$(X_{i,t} - M_{i,t}) - (X_{i,t-1} - M_{i,t-1})$$
$$= a_2 + b_2(ERDI_{i,t}/ERDI_{i,t-1})100 + \varepsilon_i \quad t = (1994, 1995, 1996) \qquad (8.5)$$

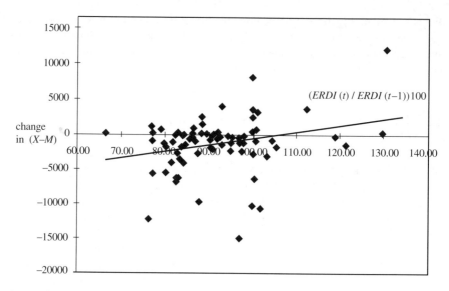

Figure 8.3   Change in the balance of trade as a function of the changes in real exchange rates

Its interpretation is as follows: the higher is the real exchange rate depreciation in the year t relative to $t - 1$, the more internationally competitive the Czech exports to the given country i should be. An opposite development should be expected in imports from i. Thus, after the real exchange rate appreciation, net exports to i should decrease in the given year t relative to the balance in the previous year. Slope b_2 is thus expected to be positive, provided the relative PPP is valid. The results for the estimation based on 90 observations were as follows (see equation (8.5) and Figure 8.3):

Statistics	a_2	b_2
Coefficients	−9853.00	92.46
t-statistics	−3.20	2.75
Probability of 0 hypothesis	0.002	0.007
R-squared + R^2-adj.	0.080	0.069

Though the estimated signs are correct this time, the decreased statistical significance of coefficients, and especially, the very low R-squared do not encourage the presumption that the relative PPP hypothesis is a concept which might have a dominant role for the explanation of the changes in trade flows, as the literature assumes on that issue. Though it is evident that appreciation had some negative

influence on Czech net exports, it definitely has not been able to explain why in the majority of cases a significant appreciation had only a marginal impact on the Czech balance of trade. In our case, the effective change of ERDI (real appreciation) was by 29 per cent in a mere three years, which hardly any country could bear. In 1997 it resulted in a 13 per cent effective depreciation, but in 1998 the nominal exchange for DM recovered close to the level of 1996. We can therefore come to a hypothesis that the convergence of relative price levels between transient countries and developed countries (that is, the decreasing trend in ERDI) can be taken as a factor with an uncertain relationship for the explanation of trade flows, especially if the inflation differential is small. It is evident in the Czech case that the pressure of the exchange rate appreciation was to a large extent balanced by some other factors.

We can also observe that neither the unit labour costs (or dollar wages) nor the relative prices between traded and non-traded commodities evolved during 1993–96 in a way that would compensate for the worsening of the CPI-based RER. They all revealed a clear tendency for real exchange rate appreciation. Actually, there may be cases in the world economy when all alternative indices of RER appreciate, and the balance of trade is not sensitive to these adverse changes (as was also revealed by Halpern and Wyplosz, 1997). Though the relevance of the PPP doctrines is paramount in cases of hyperinflation, the inflation differential of 3–8 per cent between a transient economy and a stabilized market economy may escape the PPP rule.

REAL (FUNDAMENTAL) AND NOMINAL (MONETARY) CHANGES

How can we explain that a country may become so insensitive to an adverse RER pressure on her trade competitiveness? The real worsening of the Czech balance of trade did occur, but only in 1996 and 1997. That means it happened with a lag of approximately three years and this response was not very strong. What kind of buffers and countervailing factors could there have been which would explain this behaviour? Our explanation is that there were specific circumstances, specific for a transition economy, which cushioned the impact of RER appreciation on the performance of trade:

- The fall in profits and a decrease in the recoupment of depreciation (that is, in lower cash-flow, see Benacek et al., 1997).
- The bailouts of the National Bank, Ministry of Finance and the Fund of National Property which helped in financing the trade indebtedness.
- Rising indebtedness of exporting firms and firms competing with imports to banks, suppliers, tax authorities and the social security fund.

- The financing of the trade deficit by the surplus of the capital account due to increasing inflows of foreign productive capital (FDI).
- A rapid development of non-traded services, the prices of which were artificially low (often subsidized). This kind of RER appreciation has only a mild impact on the decrease in competitiveness of the traded sector.
- Terms-of-trade improvements, especially from the side of rising export prices, which imply quality and gains in the market position.
- Productivity improvements.

The first three 'cushions' can be coined as financing through unproductive debts, which only postpone the crisis of adjustment. Of course, not all enterprises or sectors had to solve the challenge of RER appreciation with the above measures of a 'slow extermination'. For many of them (but especially for those with FDI – see Benacek, 1999) the main instrument for eliminating the impact of RER appreciation was their growth, quality, price and productivity improvements.[3] The last two factors are closely related to 'fundamentals' and their influence can be opposite to the influence of monetary factors.[4] While the monetary inflation under a fixed exchange rate definitely decreases the competitiveness of exports, the 'inflation' caused by changes in quality will increase competitiveness.

What is even more important, is that while a pure monetary inflation can have an expected elasticity in the (real) exchange rate depreciation of unity, an alleged inflation caused by improvements in quality should in fact appreciate the real exchange rate. Therefore, the relationship between differentials in inflation and the exchange rate should not have a constant elasticity of one, provided the given backward country is narrowing the gap in the GDP per capita (in US$) between her and the developed economies. At some low level of the differentials in inflation, this elasticity may even change sign. The RER is a composite indicator in which both the monetary and the real (fundamental) elements exert their partial and invariant influence.

One can argue that the reason for rather reluctant conclusions in our previous empirical tests was that the models were incorrectly specified. In measuring the trade imbalances $X_i - M_i$ the differences in the turnover of trade were disregarded. Thus the estimates could have been biased by the trade imbalances of a few large countries. A theoretically purer approach would be if the net exports were weighted – for example by a turnover of trade:

$$\left((X_{it} - M_{it})/(X_{it} + M_{it})100 = a_3 + b_3 * ERDI_{it} + \varepsilon_{it}\right) \tag{8.6}$$

Values of the weighted net trade index range in the interval $\langle -1, 1 \rangle$. The higher is ERDI, the higher should be the expected net weighted exports. The coefficient b_3 should again be positive, provided the PPP hypothesis is valid (see equation (8.6) and Figure 8.4).

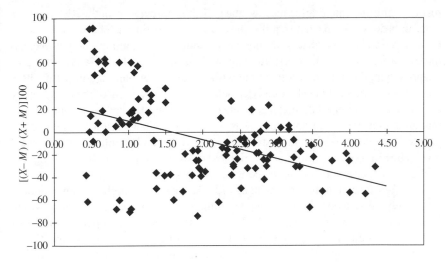

Figure 8.4   Net exports weighted by the turnover of trade taken as a function of ERDI

Statistics	a_3	b_3
Coefficients	26.4	−16.40
t-statistics	4.16	−5.72
Probability of null hypothesis	0.000	0.000
R^2	0.217	0.211

Unfortunately, this alternative did not provide any new insights to our previous estimates. It confirms that the differences in relative price levels between countries matters, though the supply response was negative – in contradiction with our expected sign. The reversal of our hypothesis was even stronger than in the test of equation (8.3).

ERDI and the importance of relative price levels (as built-in underpinnings of RER), remains an exceptionally controversial variable for the explanation of the behaviour of both Czech exporters and importers. They often behaved in a direct contradiction to the behaviour of those exporters on foreign markets where the conditions of product homogeneity, their perfect substitutability and perfect competition were valid. Or, what was more characteristic, their behaviour was indifferent to wide-ranging differentials in relative prices in their partner countries. We can explain it by assuming that higher foreign prices were not acting as an opportunity cost for Czech exporters and thus their existence was more relevant for the decision-making of Czech importers than for Czech exporters.

Therefore we can argue that price differentials between countries have their equilibrium level reflecting the gaps in quality and productivity. If the progress in

restructuring and catching-up narrows the gap, the appreciation of the RER can take place in order to attain a new equilibrium. One must distinguish between a change in fundamentals and a change in monetary conditions. A gain in competitiveness through a favourable change in fundamentals is associated with a narrowing of the price gap, and thus it is compatible with 'inflation'. A gain in competitiveness through a competitive devaluation is associated with a widening of the price gap by mere monetary manipulation. An opposite effect can be achieved by a 'competitive' real appreciation due to an inflation as a monetary phenomenon. A permanent parallel combination of an intensive convergence in fundamentals with a modest divergence in monetary (nominal) variables makes the impact of the resulting real exchange rate appreciation on the competitiveness of trade uncertain.

It is often forgotten that the changes in RER for a small highly-open economy are closely correlated with the changes in the terms of trade. Some authors (see Kenen, 1994, p. 357) even explicitly define the RER as the reciprocal of the terms of trade. It would be more appropriate for small open economies in transition if their RERs were adjusted also by the changes in the index of terms of trade. For example, if the Czech RER was appreciating by 6 per cent each year and the terms of trade were improving steadily by 4 per cent, then the pressure on the nominal exchange rate to depreciate would be much smaller than one would infer from the differentials in international inflation.

CONCLUSIONS

We have found out in this chapter that empirical evidence does not support a hypothesis that the dynamics of trade of former advanced centrally-planned economies was not as sensitive to differentials in international price levels as it was expected for standard market economies. This observation seems to be valid at least during the early stages of economic transition. Neither the absolute PPP and ERDI, nor the relative PPP and RER, have been found to be reliable indicators reflecting the space for real manoeuvring in the allocation of production for both exports and import replacements. International relative price differences in such an environment become an elusive concept often based on a superficial comparison of some simple time series. With the exception of hyperinflation, these indicators are not a good rule for defining an equilibrium exchange rate. In the same manner that a nominal ER higher than ER adjusted to the PPP level cannot be interpreted as a sign of currency undervaluation, one cannot automatically interpret the higher 'inflation' at home (relative to abroad) as a sign of worsening in the competitiveness of domestic products. The exchange rate policy and also the expectations of exporters and importers should be based on additional information related to the development in real variables.

Our argument can be generalized and made even stronger. As the doctrine of absolute PPP is nearly completely irrelevant for the quantification of export competitiveness of a country in transition, so one cannot rely on the doctrine of relative PPP. Since the most common indicator of the real exchange rate with relative CPI or PPI deflators is just an extension of the theory of relative PPP, one must be aware of its monetary (nominal) nature. Its meaning for an advancing economy in transition can be very different than for developed, stabilized and mutually well-adjusted economies. For example, a real exchange rate appreciation (due to higher 'inflation' at home in the segment of traded commodities) cannot in some be circumstances interpreted as a worsening of the competitiveness of exports. Just the opposite interpretation may hold: increased domestic prices in traded goods can reflect an improvement in external competitiveness, due to changes in quality, image, marketing techniques or gains in market power. If the gain in competitiveness is even more than proportional to the increase in price, the seemingly appreciated RER may in fact disguise its real depreciation. The results suggest that not only the statistics of inflation, but also the changes in quality, goodwill, market structure, terms of trade, productivity in tradables and non-tradables sectors, factor endowments, savings and capital account flows should be considered in the assessment of the equilibrium exchange rate.

Notes

1. In order to avoid the trivialization of the problem one should mention that there are other definitions of the RER which attempt to include alternative variables into the estimate: domestic prices of tradables to non-tradables, relative dollar wages, relative unit labour costs or debt-adjusted RER. Nevertheless, none of them is a complex indicator which would stand alone in all circumstances. All of them are based on an implicit assumption that the law of one price and the homogeneity of products are a valid rule behind all exchanges of tradables.
2. The research by Aiginger (1996a) has disclosed that the price competition in homogenous products and the quality competition in differentiated products present two different aspects of competition that should not be intermixed. In the next study, Aiginger (1996b) disclosed that the quality differentials between tradables of CEECs and EU countries are very high.
3. For example, 10 per cent of Czech exports is now realized by Skoda-VW car sales. In a mere six years, the productivity in this company reached the top European level and the quality of assembled parts shot up from preponderantly C-level (in 1992) to 99 per cent of A-level in 1997. The giant tyre company Barum-Continental increased its productivity 10-fold in nine years, etc. According to Pomery (1997) similar patterns can be observed in approximately a half of Czech exports.
4. Here one should mention that the fundamental approaches to RER have recently tested a wide range of alternatives. Let us mention the studies by Williamson (1994), Stein and Allen (1995), and Clark and MacDonald (1998).

9 Exchange Rate and the Price Response in the Czech Republic

Jan Hošek

INTRODUCTION

In mainstream economic theory, the exchange rate is considered to be a policy tool which may (among others) serve to support the supply-side of the economy and to solve the problems with the current account deficit. Namely, a devaluation makes domestic goods more competitive in foreign markets, thus stimulating domestic production in export-oriented branches, either via higher profits of producers or via higher foreign demand if exports are offered for lower prices (measured in foreign currency). In case producers have temporarily limited production capacity, they may compensate the higher supply to the foreign market by lowering quantities oriented to the domestic market. This will (in the case of non-perfect competition in this market) increase domestic prices of affected commodities. In addition, such devaluation makes imports more expensive (in domestic currency) and the domestic demand is supposed to switch to domestically-produced substitutes. Domestic firms that compete with foreign suppliers in the domestic market face a higher demand for their goods, which enables them to expand production or raise prices or most probably both, thus increasing their profits. As can be clearly seen, the likely positive real supply response of domestic firms will most probably be accompanied by a positive price response, the size of which is negatively correlated with the real supply response. The price increase is limited by zero (when the domestic supply will react purely by real expansion) on the one hand, and on the other hand by the extent to which the domestic currency was depreciated (in a hypothetical case when all traded goods are internationally tradable and domestic producers do not expand real quantities and raise prices only, for example, when they operate at their short-run potential output). In the long run the causality reverses. The rise in the domestic price level is reflected in wages and increases the input cost of domestic producers lowering their competitiveness again and offsetting (at least a part of) the real supply response. The real supply response is empirically investigated in a separate paper (Hošek, 1999).

122

In this chapter the impact of the change in the exchange rate into domestic prices[1] is going to be empirically estimated in the environment of a small open economy in transition. Since it is difficult to draw any conclusion about a long-run relationship between these two (and possibly other) macroeconomic variables (due to short time-series available, and structural changes that are continuously underway), our goal is to obtain, at least, a short-run relationship. We will draw on the theoretical framework in Hošek (1997). In the Czech Republic, goods and services with, in some way, administered prices constitute about 20 per cent of the consumer basket. The change in the regulation results in an immediate impulsive increase in the consumer price index (CPI). This price shock, however, is not compensated by an appropriate increase in disposable income. Thus, consumers that are temporarily constrained by their budget have to lower their consumption for several periods. If the demand for goods with non-administered prices is elastic, and the supply-side has (at least a somewhat) monopolistic structure, the negative demand shock should result in a price decrease (or rather a slow-down in inflation) of the items with non-regulated prices. This effect, of course, is temporary and will gradually disappear with continuously increasing disposable income of households.

The exchange rate is added as another explanatory variable to the above-described framework, and some other macroeconomic variables that are commonly hypothesized to influence the price level either by their change or their level (not to get biased parameters due to missing explanatory variables) are also included. Since there can be different impacts of selected variables on inflation in different groups of the consumer basket, we will investigate those groups separately and consolidate the particular results to obtain the summary effects.

We start by setting up the empirical specification of the equations to be estimated. The estimation technique is then discussed, as are some data issues. Finally we discuss the results and simulate a 10 per cent devaluation shock to see its dynamic impact on the inflation of consumer prices.

THE EMPIRICAL MODEL

We construct a linear single-equation model that will connect price changes to changes or levels of macro- and microeconomic variables that are commonly assumed to directly influence the rate of inflation, or can at least serve as proxy variables for forces that cannot be measured directly. Due to quite a large number of possible explanatory variables and short time-series of yearly data, we will make use of monthly seasonally unadjusted data.

The explanatory variables, as suggested by the theory, can be divided into those predominantly influencing the demand-side (disposable income), the supply-side (variables influencing the cost of the production), or both (interest rate,

unemployment rate, wages) in the price-setting market mechanism. Since the Czech Republic is a small open economy, the exchange rate also has to be taken into account as one of the key variables. Another criterion to divide the explanatory variables is whether the change in the price level is caused by their changes (exchange rate, income) or levels (real interest rate, unemployment rate).

In our simple single-equation model there is a possibility that some explanatory variables may not be independent from each other. This multi-collinearity may cause some technical problems with estimation. A more severe problem of the single-equation model is the possible non-independence of some explanatory variables and regression residuals,[2] which may cause the estimated coefficients to be biased and inconsistent. Especially, the real interest rate could be such a variable. On the other hand, the different periodicity (inflation to be explained is expressed as monthly relative changes of the price level, whereas the real interest rate is computed from yearly changes of the prices) could mitigate this problem. The econometric techniques employed, however, will help to remove the danger of biased coefficients.

One of the special features of the selected theoretical model is that it takes into account the influence of change in the regulation of administered prices on the short-run dynamics of the overall price level. Namely, a *change in the regulation* of some prices (which causes an immediate increase of those prices) should exert, under the assumption of non-substitutability of regulated goods, a temporary income effect causing in return a *slower increase* of prices of non-regulated goods in subsequent periods (Hošek, 1997). Theoretically, due to the binding budget constraint of consumers, the price increase of a regulated good should be totally offset by slower inflation in the group of non-regulated goods, thus having no impact on the total inflation rate in the medium run and no clear impact in the long run. The temporarily higher living cost can be taken into consideration in wage negotiations, resulting most probably in higher wages and thus higher overall inflation in the future. It would be interesting to investigate the role of savings that may serve to bridge the temporary lack of income for 'smooth' consumption. A lower rate of savings, or even dis-savings, could moderate the impact of the income effect on prices of non-regulated goods. Unfortunately, the measurement of savings is very unreliable, making any investigation of monthly data impossible.

If we do not consider the permanent income hypothesis and the role of wealth in consumption behaviour, the aggregate demand for non-regulated goods is determined primarily by the income of households. Since the higher demand induces higher prices in our model, we expect a *positive* disposable income elasticity of prices.[3]

The change in the exchange rate should serve as a proxy for the change in the marginal cost of traders (imported goods from the consumer basket), as well as of producers (imported raw materials and intermediate goods). For producers,

however, the total impact of a change of the exchange rate on prices is even more severe since a depreciation of the exchange rate will make imported investment goods necessary for production more expensive. Theoretically, there is even a possibility that with depreciation exporting domestic firms can charge lower prices in foreign currency, meet the possible increase in foreign demand and ration the supply to the domestic market which would again contribute to the price increase at the domestic market. However, since the domestic demand is, for the vast majority of domestic firms, more important than the foreign demand, the last hypothesis seems to be implausible. More probable is the possibility that due to the higher prices of imported goods some domestic firms will raise their prices to convert part of their increased competitiveness into profits. Thus, we should be expecting a tight *positive* relation between the exchange rate and domestic prices.

Most imports of consumer goods are accounted in deutsche marks whereas most imported raw materials are paid in US$. Since both exchange rates can influence the overall price level with a different dynamics, the change in the exchange rate is included in the model separately for those two important currencies.

Interest rates have a very complicated effect both on the demand- and the supply-sides. As to the demand-side, higher interest rates can contribute to higher savings on the one side, and to higher disposable income[4] on the other. Concerning the supply-side, part of the interest paid goes to fixed costs, but if current production is financed by short-term credit this interest can be assumed to be part of the marginal cost. It will be impossible to discriminate between particular effects of the interest rate in our simple model. There will also be a long-run impact of interest rates on prices. Higher real interest rates induce lower investment and lower future supply. This will increase either the price level in the future, or, more probably, deteriorate the trade balance in the future. Long-run effects, however, are difficult to study with our short time-series of yearly data when, in addition, the problem is complicated by the fact that the economy undergoes a transition period. There also exists a reverse causality in the price–nominal interest mechanism that, in general, increases nominal interest rates in periods with higher inflation. This is why we use real interest rates in our model. A natural question can be raised at this point as to how the real interest rates are computed. From the two limiting cases (that is, rational expectations and pure adaptive expectations) we prefer the second, which means that people know that they are not able to form correct expectations about future inflation and thus they demand interest rates that will cover their losses due to inflation in the past. For firms, it is almost impossible to compute some general real interest rate since it differs in different industries and sectors of the economy according to producer price inflation in a particular industry. Moreover, some firms can borrow abroad at foreign interest rates (but also, thereby, facing the exchange rate risk). Thus, there is no clear impact of interest rates to be expected,

yet monetary theory suggests a *negative* relationship between prices and interest rates in the short run.

Unemployment is another variable commonly assumed to play a role in the price-setting process. In our case, the short-run Phillips curve should indicate a *negative* relationship between the inflation rate and the rate of unemployment. Higher unemployment means lower dynamics of wage increases, perhaps lower total income as well, and higher savings or lower consumption of those who are afraid of becoming unemployed.

In addition to the above explicitly listed macroeconomic variables, there exist other forces that influence the dynamics of prices in the short and long run. The long-run effects are summarized as constant in the model, causing the price indices to show a trend. This trend can be explained by the existence of other, not explicitly expressed, effects, either domestic or foreign, that contribute to the price increase and are relatively stable (at least in the short run). Some of those factors can be called 'structural' impulses (as opposed to monetary impulses) that cannot be identified separately but may be connected to the transition period.

The seasonal or specific effects can be approximated by dummies (for example, legislative changes like VAT introduction) or by seasonal dummies (regular January price increases, as suggested, for example, by the 'menu cost' theory; or a decrease of food prices in July, when the new crop comes to markets). Other shocks that influence the monthly inflation for longer than one month are modelled by a (seasonal) ARMA (autoregressive moving average) process applied to the residuals.

MODEL SPECIFICATION

In the consumer basket there are different groups of goods, the price development of which is more or less similar, but the impact of monetary policy measures and other macroeconomic fundamentals on inflation can differ across those groups as to both its scope and its dynamics. This is why we decompose the complete basket into four groups according to the division adopted by the Czech National Bank (this division is discussed later in greater detail). The group of administered prices is assumed to have an exogenous price development set by central and local authorities. The rest of the goods with non-administered prices are then further divided into the sub-groups of non-tradable goods, tradable non-food and food items. The general empirical specification of the model for the last three groups (the time index omitted) is

$$p_i = C_i + \alpha_i p_{reg} + \beta_i di + \chi_i IR$$
$$+ \delta_i er + \phi_i UN + \varphi_{ij} D_j + u_i \qquad (9.1)$$

where p_i represents the weighted monthly percentage change of the price index in the group i (tradable, non-tradable and food). (Other variables are defined below.) For weighing, the actual variable weight[5] of the group in the total index for a given month is used. The reason for using weighted variables is, first, that in this way inflation can be simply interpreted as a value in percentage points by which the specified group contributes to the total inflation, thus enabling us to mechanically add the partial effects of particular explanatory variables to get the total effect on the overall inflation. Second, the variable weights of particular groups change in time. The variable weight (the normalized product of the fixed weight and the price index) of the group of items with administered prices (its trend more precisely) grows due to the higher growth of prices in this group whereas the other variable weights go down. Thus, we can expect the same percentage change of price in this group to have a different effect on other groups in different periods.

Similarly, p_{reg} stands for the weighted monthly percentage change of the price index in the group of items, prices of which are set by administrative measures.

The percentage change in disposable income, di (computed as a difference of logarithms) is derived from the series monitored by the Czech National Bank on the basis of income and expenditure of households. The money income consists of wages, social receipts and other revenues. The money expenditure is composed of expenditure for goods and services, taxes, social and health insurance contributions and other charges. The difference of those two groups constitutes the disposable income of households. The resulting value is then slightly corrected by the transaction change of financial assets and liabilities of households. This comprises changes in deposits and loans in local and foreign currencies, the balance of securities purchases and sales, changes in cash and changes in insurance technical reserves of life and retirement insurance.

Another short-term variable with an immediate effect on inflation is the (percentage) change in the exchange rate, er. Rather than employ the effective exchange rate index for the Czech Republic, the bilateral exchange rates of the krona against the deutsche mark (CZK/DM) and against the US$ (CZK/US$) are used as these are the most important currencies for Czech foreign trade. The reason for using these two exchange rates separately is that most imports of consumer goods are accounted in DM, whereas most raw materials are imported for US dollars. We can thus hypothesize that the former exchange rate will influence the demand-side more, while the latter can increase the cost for suppliers. Moreover, the time dynamics of both effects can differ.

The level of the real interest rate, IR, is a kind of a variable, which is assumed to influence inflation by its level, not by its change. The nominal interest rate on mid-term time deposits is used as the representative interest rate that consumers react to, either by increasing their savings or consumption. By subtracting a 12-month

inflation rate from this monthly average interest rate we get the real interest rate according to the adaptive expectations hypothesis (see above).

UN stands for the unemployment rate as announced by the Ministry of Labor and Social Affairs. There are also two seasonal dummies, D_j, used in the specification of the equations, and a constant term C which summarizes the trend in the price level, caused by forces not explicitly included in the regression equation that are more or less stable.

THE ESTIMATION TECHNIQUE

Due to the lack of long-run time-series our objective is to build at least a short-run model, which would describe the short-term behaviour of inflation and its reaction to the changes in the exchange rate. We expect a change in our explanatory variable in a given month to influence the inflation for a longer period than is one month. Thus we have chosen a dynamic regression model, in the econometric literature known as the ARMAX model (see for example, Greene, 1997). This time-series model enables a very general dynamic specification both for the explanatory and dependent variables. In addition, the disturbance is allowed to have a dynamic structure of its own. The general specification of the ARMAX model is

$$C(L)y_t = \alpha + B(L)x_t + D(L)\varepsilon_t \tag{9.2}$$

where $C(L)$ defines the AR(p) part, that is the autoregressive behaviour of the dependent variable, and $D(L)$ is the MA(q) or moving average part for regression residuals. For the lag structure of explanatory variables, $B(L)$, we have to use such a pattern that will be able to simulate the appropriate dynamics of the impact of a shock in the explanatory variable on the dependent variable. We can assume that the shock caused by the change in the exchange rate will show up in inflation in several consecutive months after the shock, and its influence can grow for some period and then decrease again until it vanishes completely. This is why the 'Polynomial Distributed Lag' method (PDL) is chosen. The principle of this method (Almon, 1965) is based on using several (and possibly many) lags of the explanatory variable (in our case we can invert the explanation in the sense that the explanatory variable – exchange rate – influences several future values of the variable to be explained – price level). Not to lose as many degrees of freedom as is the number of lags of the explanatory variable, the method restricts the lag coefficients to lie on a polynomial of some reasonably small degree. In addition, this restriction says that the impact should be continuous in consecutive months. Technical

issues related to the estimation of the PDL model are discussed in greater detail in Appendix 9.1.

Decomposition of the Consumer Basket

For the basic decomposition of the complete basket of consumer goods we use the rules agreed upon between the Czech Statistical Office (CSO) and the Czech National Bank (CNB). Based on the list of 'regulated' items that are excluded from the basket when the CSO computes the so called 'net inflation', we create our group of administered or regulated prices. This group is assumed to have an exogenous price development.[6] Appendix 9.2 contains the list of items in this group as of 1998. The codes that specify the method of price regulation of the items have the following meaning:

A   items with maximum price;
Aa   maximum prices are set centrally by the Ministry of Finance;
Ab   maximum prices are set locally by local authorities;
B   prices of items in this group can grow only on the basis of a
     documented increase in input costs;
C   fees and charges set by law.

The main changes to this group in the past include deregulation of coal prices since 1 May 1994, and of liquid and motor fuels since 1 January 1997. Some other changes have been implemented, but their total weight is negligible.

The rest of the goods with non-administered prices were then further divided into the sub-groups of non-tradable goods, tradable non-food and food items. Based on these definitions (and taking into account the main changes in regulation in the past), consistent time-series of indices for particular groups were computed starting with December 1993. In a slightly artificial way, the main groups' indices were prolonged to start in January 1990. For details, see Appendix 9.3.

ESTIMATION RESULTS

The final form in which the model has been estimated is summarized in equations (9.3)–(9.5). For the group of non-tradable, non-regulated items the specification with the following estimated coefficients has been selected:[7]

$$p_{nt} = 0.14 - 0.08 p_{reg(-1 \text{ to } -7)} + 0.03 di_{(-1 \text{ to } -7)}$$
$$- 0.026 IR + 0.03 er_{DEM(-1 \text{ to } -5)} + 0.15 D_{Jan} \tag{9.3}$$

This equation explains about 80 per cent of the variability in prices of non-tradable goods, using 13 explanatory variables (including estimated coefficients for chosen degrees of polynomials restricting the lag structure of some variables and the twelfth-order moving average process, MA(12)). Even though the data is available since 1990, the estimation period was shortened so that it starts only after the separation of the former Czechoslovakia in January 1993.[8] The residuals from the regression are modelled as a twelfth-order moving average process. The seasonal moving average term is −0.88. This cannot be explained by ordinary seasonality but rather by some seasonal effects that are normally randomly distributed. Thus, if at some time some seasonal effect draws the inflation down, since it is more favourable than normal, it is probable that the next year it will be less favourable than normal and will increase the price level by almost the same amount.[9]

The coefficient in which we are most interested is the exchange rate elasticity of the price level. In the group of non-tradables we should not expect this elasticity to be high, since there is no direct link between the change in the exchange rate and inflation in the short run. Still, the price level in the non-tradable group is affected by the exchange rate via possible material inputs from abroad in the short and medium run, and through the labour cost, which is principally set in the tradable sector and which through the labour market is transmitted to the non-tradable sector. This is a long-run effect that is probably not reflected in our model.

The other group, tradables without food, has a different specification from the previous group:

$$p_{tr} = 0.30 - 0.02p_{reg(-1 \text{ to } -4)} - 0.04UN + 0.06er_{DEM(0 \text{ to } -5)} \qquad (9.4)$$

As expected, the total influence of the exchange rate on prices in this group is higher than in the previous group.[10] On the other hand, as domestic prices are set predominantly by the world price level or by domestic competition, the short-run demand effects of income are negligible and are substituted by the rather longer-run effect of unemployment.

Finally, prices of food can be modelled by the estimated equation:

$$p_{food} = 0.42 - 0.60p_{reg(-1 \text{ to } -4)} + 0.10di_{(-1 \text{ to } -8)}$$
$$- 0.08IR + 0.6er_{DEM(-1 \text{ to } -5)} - 0.75D_{Jul} \qquad (9.5)$$

Since most of the food items are tradables, the quite high elasticity to the exchange rate is natural. On the other hand, we can observe a high income elasticity of prices (also due to the income effect of the deregulation) which could be interpreted as follows. When people have lower incomes and are forced to lower their consumption, they cut their food consumption at first (not the quantity, of course, but the

quality). While for non-tradables the January dummy could have reflected a menu cost, because some producers or shops only change prices once a year and January is the beginning of the year, here the seasonal dummy is probably related to agricultural production and regular seasonal price decreases with a new crop coming to the market.

As was pointed out above, we can simply add the particular effects in the groups to get the summary effects on the overall price level:

$$p = 0.86 + (1 - 0.70)p_{reg} + 0.13di - 0.04UN - 0.11IR$$
$$+ 0.15er + 0.15D_{Jan} - 0.75D_{Jul} \tag{9.6}$$

Thus, a 1 percentage point change in the exchange rate will (*ceteris paribus*) increase the domestic price level (as measured by the CPI) by 0.15 per cent in the horizon of about half a year, when the influence culminates two or three months after the devaluation shock (and vice versa for the revaluation).

Even though the model is specified as a short-run model for changes, it also gives some mid-term equilibrium values. For example, if the natural rate of unemployment is fixed at 6 per cent and the real interest rate is 2 per cent, then, *ceteris paribus*, the equilibrium annual inflation rate is 4.2 per cent. We can hypothesize this to be non-monetary 'structural' inflation that cannot be cut down by monetary policy without extremely high costs of disinflation. Since for a country in transition one cannot expect the model parameters to be constant, it is rational to expect this value to go down in the future. The econometric method used in this chapter cannot account for structural changes and gives the results as average values for the period under consideration. To obtain variable parameters we should employ dynamic estimation methods such as the Kalman filter or bootstrap methods.

SIMULATION EXERCISE

In the previous section, the exchange rate elasticity of prices was quantified to be about 0.3. This means that a 1 per cent change in the exchange rate (other variables being constant) causes the overall price level to change by 0.3 per cent in the same direction (increase in the exchange rate means depreciation) in the short run. If the monetary policy (represented in the model by the scenario of nominal interest rates) reacts neither to the exchange rate change nor to the subsequent inflation increase, one of the explanatory variables in the model, namely the real interest rate, is changed (decreases with devaluation). Thus, in the case of a passive monetary policy, the impact of the exchange rate on the price level is much higher.

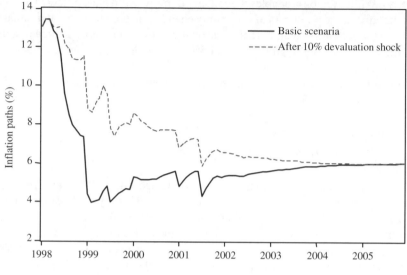

Figure 9.1   Simulation time profile

For illustration we simulate a 10 per cent devaluation impulse and compare the resulting inflation to the inflation path without the shock. The results are graphically shown in Figure 9.1.

Until March 1998, the actual data are used for all variables. In the base case the exchange rate is fixed after this date, whereas in the other case a 10 per cent step devaluation is simulated in April 1998, the exchange rate being held fixed again after that date. Other explanatory variables are simulated, being the same in both variants. The example simulates the dynamic impact of the exchange rate shock on the price level for a subsequent period of several years. As we can see, the CPI inflation rate starts to diverge after the devaluation, reaching its peak difference after about 12 months. Then, both inflation rates start to converge to each other again. For the simulated period, the price level increased by more than 11.7 per cent in comparison to the basic case. Thus, the model predicts the impact of the devaluation on prices to last several years and to increase the price level by more than was the extent of the original exchange rate shock.

The explanation is as follows. The devaluation causes the price level to increase by 3 per cent in the short run.[11] With the passive monetary policy (meaning constant nominal interest rate), however, the real interest rate begins to decrease, causing another increase in the inflation, followed by another drop in real interest rates and so forth until the inflation and real interest rates converge to an

equilibrium. Unfortunately, the coefficient for the real interest rate is crucial in this simulation. In recent periods the estimated coefficient (the impact of the real interest rate) grows. This implies the convergence of real interest rates and inflation to take more time. Another consequence is that a small change in nominal interest rates leads to a big change in real interest rates. As a result, the long-run impact of depreciation within a framework of constant nominal interest rates is enormously big, suggesting that the model is not able to simulate the long-run impact of a change in the exchange rate. On the other hand, the simulation of depreciation in the framework of constant real (adaptive) interest rates delivers only the extent of the short-run impact in the horizon of about half a year.

CONCLUSION

This chapter quantifies the influence of the main macro- and microeconomic factors that affect the price level in the Czech Republic in the short and medium run. For a small, open and transitional market economy the exchange rate was identified as one of the most important variables that directly affects the domestic price level. In reaction to the change in the exchange rate, prices alter for about six consecutive periods with the maximum response three months after the exchange rate shock. The estimated summary (short-run) exchange rate elasticity of the price level changes quite a lot during the period under consideration. Until March 1998 the average coefficient has been estimated to be about 0.3. As could have been expected, the most affected was the group of food items followed by other tradable items. The exchange rate shock, though, was also transmitted into the group of non-tradables.

The recent data, however, brought about large changes of the exchange rate that were not accompanied with appropriate swings in the price level. Thus, the model estimates the short-run exchange rate elasticity of the price level for the current period to be about 0.15. The largest drop can be observed in the group of food items, which could be attributed to the increasing competition in this market segment in the current period of economic recession. The import prices converted into foreign currency suggest that during the period with currency appreciation foreign firms charge higher prices, and vice versa, to smooth price swings on the domestic market. This fact has a natural explanation. With the appreciation of the koruna, domestic consumers become relatively richer compared to foreign consumers. Foreign firms can either take advantage of the fact that for the same price in foreign currency they can sell their products cheaper in koruna, thus expanding their market share, or they can have higher

profits by increasing their prices in foreign currency. The opposite holds for depreciation.

APPENDIX 9.1   PDL MODEL ESTIMATION, SOME TECHNICAL ISSUES

There are several technical problems with the estimation of the polynomial distributed lag (PDL) model. First, how to choose the degree of the polynomial, and secondly, how many lags of the explanatory variable are needed in the model specification. One simple procedure is to estimate a lot of regression equations, gradually decrease the number of lags and/or degree of the polynomial in successive equations, and choose the one with the highest adjusted R^2. With some provision, one can admit this criterion as a decision rule and in practice it is often used. A more rigorous approach is to test hypotheses about the polynomial degree and the number of lags.

Testing a degree of the polynomial consists of a comparison of the unrestricted model with the restricted one (having one degree lower polynomial) based on the classical F-test. Since we have to carry out a sequence of such tests before a decision can be made, it is necessary to progressively increase the critical value of the test statistic to maintain the same level of significance.

Even more problematic is the decision about the correct number of lags. We choose some maximum number of lags and regard this model as unrestricted. Then, based on the F-test again, we test the hypothesis that the last lag is equal to zero. If we cannot reject this hypothesis, we test another hypothesis that the last two lags are zero, and so on. This method has to be used with caution since neither the true significance value nor the distribution of resulting estimates has been derived yet (Greene, 1997). Based on this method, one can decide only when it gives unambiguous results. The reason is that, in fact, we do not estimate original models, that are nested, but transformed models with different numbers of lags that have quite different artificially constructed regressors.

In practice, fitting the polynomial with a higher than correct degree leads to inefficient estimation, because if the coefficients lie on the true polynomial of degree p, then they lie on polynomials of degree $p + 1, p + 2, \ldots$ as well. However, fitting the polynomial with too low a degree has the same consequence as applying invalid restrictions. Estimating the lag length is again more complicated, but in general it is true that a higher number of lags does not bias the results since the weights of redundant lags should approach zero (under the condition that the degree of the polynomial is sufficient). In general, we can adopt the rule saying that we need higher degree of the polynomial if we use higher numbers of lags, whereas we can use a parabola or even a line if the number of lags is between 4 and 8.

In addition to the above-mentioned restrictions, the PDL method may employ another set of restrictions. Namely, we can require one or both ends of the polynomial (at lags -1 and $n + 1$) to approach zero. In our case it seems reasonable to request the impact of the exchange rate shock to start from zero and diminish after some time. Thus, we could use a restriction at both ends of the polynomial. However, some authors do not recommend this approach since it can warp the trajectory of the polynomial inside the requested interval. As an alternative to the PDL, we can also use the Shiller lag method, which is the generalization of the PDL method in that the lag coefficients are considered to be random variables.

APPENDIX 9.2

Subdivision of the Consumer Basket (as of January 1998)

COICOP	ITEM	KATEG.	Weight9093	Weight9499
3111	NET RENT PAID BY TENANTS IN TENEMENT FLATS	Aa	11.84	16.53
3311	PAYMENTS FOR SERVICES IN TENEMENT FLATS	B		2.49
3312	PAYMENTS FOR SERVICES IN COOPERATIVE FLATS	B		1.13
3313	WASTE LIQUIDATION AND OTHER SANITARIAN SERVICES	B	0.29	2.74
3331	WATER SUPPLY	B	0.37	9.87
3411	ELECTRIC ENERGY FOR HOUSEHOLDS	Aa	16.05	25.25
3421	NATURAL GAS FOR HOUSEHOLDS	Aa	4.08	9.59
3422	LIQUIDIZED CARBOHYDROGENS	B	2.17	1.46
3443	HEAT ENERGY FOR HOUSEHOLDS	B	11.85	30.17
5111	MEDICAMENTS PRESCRIBED BY DOCTOR	Aa, B	0.26	0.37
5112	DRUGS SOLD FREE OF PRESCRIPTION	Aa, B	1.80	3.20
5131	ORTHOPEDIC ARTICLES	Aa, B	0.00	0.13
5133	DENTAL REPLACEMENTS	Aa, B	0.28	0.78
5211	GENERAL PRACTITIONERS SERVICES	Aa, B	0.08	0.84
5221	DENTISTS SERVICES	Aa, B	0.00	0.42
5231	MEDICAL LABORATORY ANALYSES	Aa, B	0.00	0.14
5241	OPTICIANS SERVICES	Aa, B	0.00	0.36
5311	BALNEAL TREATMENT	Aa, B	1.02	0.50
5411	PERSONAL SICKNESS INSURANCE	C	6.85	34.78
6241	LAWFUL MOTOR VEHICLE LIABILITY INSURANCE	C		4.10
6241	PARKING FEE	Ab		0.17
6311	URBAN TRANSPORT SERVICE	Ab	3.79	7.72
6312	TAXI SERVICE	Ab	1.25	0.29
6321	BUS TRANSPORT	B	5.33	6.90
6322	RAILROAD TRANSPORT	Aa	2.60	2.08
7222	BROADCASTING AND TELEVISION	C	5.08	8.16
8341	FARE FOR PUPILS AND STUDENTS	B		1.78
10311	POSTAL SERVICES	B	2.72	1.16
10321	TELEPHONE	Aa	4.97	7.61
10322	TELEGRAPH	B		0.12
10511	FINANCIAL SERVICES	C	0.38	0.35
10611	OTHER SERVICES NOT CLASSIFIED ELSEWHERE	C		2.03
	Total weight		109.22	183.22

Non-Regulated Items

COICOP	ITEM	Weight9093	Weight9499
1111	RICE	1.06	1.29
1112	FLOUR	2.33	3.67
1113	BREAD AND PASTRY	13.72	20.80
1114	CONFECTIONERY AND DURABLE PASTRY	13.36	12.27
1115	PASTE PRODUCTS	1.00	1.61
1116	OTHER CEREALS AND CEREAL PRODUCTS	2.24	1.89
1121	FRESH BEEF	10.71	8.81
1122	FRESH VEAL	0.09	0.42
1123	FRESH PORK	19.39	14.68
1124	FRESH OR FROZEN POULTRY	8.21	8.80
1125	EDIBLE BOWELS	1.20	2.24
1126	SMOKE-DRIED PRODUCTS	33.67	33.88
1127	TINNED MEAT	6.68	2.73
1128	OTHER SORTS OF MEAT (FRESH, FROZEN, CHILLED,...)	0.16	1.80
1131	FISH (FRESH, CHILLED, FROZEN)	1.46	2.78
1132	SMOKED FISH	0.66	0.78
1133	TINNED FISH AND OTHER FISH PRODUCTS	1.61	2.72
1141	FRESH MILK	6.07	13.00
1142	PRESERVED MILK	2.01	2.00
1143	OTHER MILK PRODUCTS EXCEPT CHEESE PRODUCTS	9.11	11.58
1144	CHEESE PRODUCTS	6.58	11.86
1145	EGGS AND EGG PRODUCTS	4.63	7.07
1151	BUTTER	11.63	7.86
1152	MARGARINE	1.98	5.65
1153	EDIBLE OILS EXCEPT OLIVE OIL	2.95	2.84
1154	OLIVE OIL	0.00	0.71
1155	OTHER SORTS OF FAT	1.08	0.74
1161	FRESH FRUIT FROM THE TEMPERATE ZONE	3.41	5.88
1162	FRESH SOUTHERN FRUIT	7.97	10.81
1163	DRIED FRUIT AND NUTS	2.13	1.82
1164	PRESERVED AND FROZEN FRUIT	2.47	0.53
1171	FRESH VEGETABLES	6.17	7.94
1172	PULSE	0.24	0.84
1173	PRESERVED AND FROZEN VEGETABLES	2.76	1.92
1181	POTATOES	2.71	3.30
1182	POTATO PRODUCTS	0.94	1.62
1191	SUGAR	4.80	5.39
1192	COFFEE	16.24	6.81
1193	TEA	1.53	1.96
1194	COCOA	0.42	0.73
1195	CHOCOLATE AND CHOCOLATE CONFECTIONERY	10.30	5.77
1196	NON CHOCOLATE CONFECTIONERY	4.62	2.09
1197	JAM, MARMALADE, HONEY AND SIRUPS	4.39	3.63
1198	ICE	3.46	3.15
1199	OTHER FOOD	6.63	5.75
1211	ALCOHOLIC BEVERAGES	8.06	6.21
1221	BEER	15.00	13.01
1222	VINE	10.59	7.54
1223	SPIRITS	18.29	8.65
1311	CIGARETTES	27.81	37.10
1321	CIGARS	0.00	0.09
1322	TOBACCO	0.09	0.08
2111	TEXTILE MATERIALS	6.70	3.50
2121	MEN'S WEAR	14.26	13.91
2122	LADIES' WEAR	17.92	23.44
2123	CHILD'S WEAR	10.36	6.37
2124	MEN'S UNDERWEAR AND NIGHT-WEAR	8.84	6.43
2125	LADIES' UNDERWEAR AND NIGHT-WEAR	8.09	5.35
2126	CHILD'S AND NURSE-CHILD'S UNDERWEAR AND NIGHT-WEAR	4.36	4.31
2131	FASHION ACCESSORIES	2.02	2.03
2132	TEXTILE HABERDASHERY	4.53	2.19
2141	CUSTOM-MADE NEEDLEWORK AND CLOTHING REPAIR	1.61	1.41
2142	GARMENT LENDING	0.00	0.07
2211	MEN'S FOOTWEAR	7.18	6.09
2212	LADIES' FOOTWEAR	4.19	9.50
2213	CHILD'S AND NURSE-CHILD'S FOOTWEAR	10.37	5.30
2221	FOOTWEAR REPAIR	0.41	0.98
3211	PRODUCTS FOR COMMON FLAT MAINTENANCE	6.76	3.81
3221	SERVICES FOR COMMON FLAT MAINTENANCE	1.01	1.81
3311	SERVICES RELATED TO LIVING IN TENEMENT FLATS	0.00	2.49
3312	SERVICES RELATED TO LIVING IN COOPERATIVE FLATS	0.00	1.13
3321	INSURANCE RELATED TO HOUSING	1.07	2.55
3442	FUEL WOOD AND OTHER SOLID FUELS	0.39	0.36
4111	FURNITURE	22.89	10.18
4112	FLAT EQUIPMENT AND DECORATION	2.42	5.01
4121	CARPETS	6.45	2.27
4122	OTHER GROUND-CLOTHES	3.70	1.51
4131	FURNITURE REPAIR	0.88	0.92
4211	FLAT TEXTILE	4.00	2.36
4221	BED- AND TABLE-LINEN	2.58	5.82
4231	TEXTILE MATERIAL FOR BED-LINEN	2.04	0.27
4241	BED-LINEN FABRICATION	0.57	0.20
4311	BOILING AND HEATING APPLIANCES	0.90	5.12
4312	WASHING AND DISHWASHING MACHINES	3.84	2.94
4313	REFRIGERATORS AND DEEP-FREEZERS	7.06	3.98
4314	CLEANING EQUIPMENT	1.52	0.77
4315	SEWING-MACHINES	1.10	0.39
4321	SMALL HOUSEHOLD ELECTRIC APPLIANCES	2.64	2.47
4331	NON-ELECTRIC HOUSEHOLD ACCESSORIES	1.17	0.45
4341	HOUSEHOLD APPLIANCES REPAIR	0.85	1.57
4411	GLASS DISHES	7.06	2.80
4412	KITCHEN DISHES AND TOOLS	3.48	4.94
4511	ELECTRIC TOOLS	0.72	1.61
4521	TOOLS AND DIVERSE ACCESSORIES	9.91	3.34
4611	CLEANSERS	5.86	12.45
4612	OTHER HOUSEHOLD GOODS	16.68	3.10
4621	HOUSEHOLD SERVICES	0.00	1.06
4631	LAUNDRY AND DRYCLEANER'S SERVICES	1.41	1.10
4632	OTHER HOUSE CARE SERVICES	0.01	0.50
6111	AUTOMOBILES	35.87	21.42
6121	BICYCLES	1.78	4.38
6122	MOTORBIKES	0.76	0.26
6211	SPARE PARTS AND ACCESSORIES FOR CARS	6.28	4.57
6212	SPARE PARTS AND ACCESSORIES FOR BIKES AND MOTORBIKE	0.00	0.74
6222	OILS AND LUBRICANTS, AUTO-COSMETICS	1.17	0.98
6231	CAR REPAIR AND MAINTENANCE	5.80	5.98
6232	BIKES AND MOTORBIKES REPAIR AND MAINTENANCE	0.00	0.18
6323	AIRCRAFT TRANSPORT	1.53	0.33
6331	TRUCK TRANSPORT	0.42	0.56
7111	TV SETS AND VIDEO RECORDERS	18.74	9.97
7112	RADIO SETS, TAPE DECKS AND OTHERS	5.01	3.03
7121	CAMERA SUPPLIES	1.00	1.18
7131	PERSONAL COMPUTERS	0.29	1.74
7132	TYPING MACHINES AND CALCULATORS	0.56	0.53
7141	OTHER INVESTMENT GOODS FOR CULTURE CONSUMPTION	0.97	0.81
7151	TOYS	4.68	5.45
7152	SPORTING GOODS	6.36	3.69
7161	DEVICES FOR PICTURE AND SOUND RECORDING	7.44	5.19
7171	FLOWERS AND FLOWER PRODUCTS	3.33	3.75
7172	FARMING AND PLANTING EQUIPMENT	1.55	3.72
7181	LEISURE EQUIPMENT REPAIR	0.94	1.41
7211	CULTURE SERVICES	2.85	3.74
7212	SPORT ACTIVITIES	0.27	2.14
7213	RECREATION IN ABROAD	3.88	13.10
7214	INLAND RECREATION	1.44	8.24
7221	OTHER RECREATION AND CULTURE SERVICES	5.72	4.56
7311	BOOKS	4.17	5.30
7321	NEWSPAPERS AND JOURNALS	9.27	9.64
7331	STATIONERY	3.20	2.20
8111	PRE-SCHOOL AND BASIC EDUCATION	1.97	3.02
8121	HIGH SCHOOL EDUCATION	0.15	0.98
8131	UNIVERSITY EDUCATION	0.00	0.17
8141	LANGUAGE AND OTHER EDUCATION	0.26	1.98
8211	HIGH SCHOOL TEXT BOOKS	1.99	1.15
8311	SCHOOL BOARDING	5.51	7.00
8321	OTHER SUPPLEMENTARY EDUCATIONAL SERVICES	0.00	0.81
8341	OTHER SUPPLEMENTARY EDUCATIONAL SERVICES	0.95	1.78
9111	SOUPS	1.66	1.28
9112	MAIN MEATY DISHES (WITHOUT VEGETABLE)	18.35	9.31
9113	MAIN NON-MEATY DISHES	0.77	2.04
9114	MAIN NON-MEATY DISHES	5.47	1.56
9115	OTHER DISHES AND REFRESHMENTS	10.63	2.17
9121	NON-ALCOHOLIC BEVERAGES	4.01	3.22
9122	ALCOHOLIC BEVERAGES	37.36	8.94
9211	DINNERS AND SUPPERS (MENU)	10.27	14.74
9221	OTHER DISHES IN CANTEENS	2.30	1.33
9222	BEVERAGES IN CANTEENS	2.95	1.31
9311	HOTEL ACCOMMODATION	0.62	0.60
9321	NON-HOTEL ACCOMMODATION	0.62	0.74
10111	HAIRDRESSER'S AND PERSONAL CARE SALONS	2.86	5.63
10121	ELECTRIC APPLIANCES FOR PERSONAL CARE	0.38	0.87
10131	COSMETIC AND TOILET ARTICLES	23.09	20.04
10211	JEWELRY AND WATCHES	6.43	5.56
10221	PERSONAL ACCESSORIES	5.55	3.84
10222	OTHER GOODS	2.21	1.59
10322	TELEGRAPH	0.08	0.12
10411	SOCIAL CARE WITH ACCOMMODATION	1.86	0.00
10421	SOCIAL CARE WITHOUT ACCOMMODATION	0.17	0.17
10611	OTHER SERVICES	3.45	3.53

Non-Tradable Items

COICOP	ITEM	Weight9093	Weight9499
2141	CUSTOM-MADE NEEDLEWORK AND CLOTHING REPAIR	1.61	1.41
2142	GARMENT LENDING	0.00	0.07
2221	FOOTWEAR REPAIR	0.41	0.98
3221	SERVICES FOR COMMON FLAT MAINTENANCE	1.01	1.81
3311	SERVICES RELATED TO LIVING IN TENEMENT FLATS	0.00	2.49
3312	SERVICES RELATED TO LIVING IN COOPERATIVE FLATS	0.00	1.13
3321	INSURANCE RELATED TO HOUSING	1.07	2.55
4131	FURNITURE REPAIR	0.88	0.92
4241	BED-LINEN FABRICATION	0.57	0.20
4341	HOUSEHOLD APPLIANCES REPAIR	0.85	1.57
4621	HOUSEHOLD SERVICES	0.00	1.06
4631	LAUNDRY AND DRYCLEANER'S SERVICES	1.41	1.10
4632	OTHER HOUSE CARE SERVICES	0.01	0.50
6231	CAR REPAIR AND MAINTENANCE	5.80	5.98
6232	BIKES AND MOTORBIKES REPAIR AND MAINTENANCE	0.00	0.18
6331	TRUCK TRANSPORT	0.42	0.56
7181	LEISURE EQUIPMENT REPAIR	0.94	1.41
7211	CULTURE SERVICES	2.85	3.74
7212	SPORT ACTIVITIES	0.27	2.14
7214	INLAND RECREATION	1.44	8.24
7221	OTHER RECREATION AND CULTURE SERVICES	5.72	4.56
7311	BOOKS	4.17	5.30
7321	NEWSPAPERS AND JOURNALS	9.27	9.64
8111	PRE-SCHOOL AND BASIC EDUCATION	1.97	3.02
8121	HIGH SCHOOL EDUCATION	0.15	0.98
8131	UNIVERSITY EDUCATION	0.00	0.17
8141	LANGUAGE AND OTHER EDUCATION	0.26	1.98
8211	HIGH SCHOOL TEXT BOOKS	1.99	1.15
8311	SCHOOL BOARDING	5.51	7.00
8341	OTHER SUPPLEMENTARY EDUCATIONAL SERVICES	0.95	1.78
9111	SOUPS	1.66	1.28
9112	MAIN MEATY DISHES (WITHOUT VEGETABLE)	18.35	9.31
9113	MAIN NON-MEATY DISHES	0.77	2.04
9114	MAIN DISH GARNISHES	5.47	1.56
9115	OTHER DISHES AND REFRESHMENTS	10.63	2.17
9121	NON-ALCOHOLIC BEVERAGES	4.01	3.22
9122	ALCOHOLIC BEVERAGES	37.36	8.94
9211	DINNERS AND SUPPERS (MENU)	10.27	14.74
9221	OTHER DISHES IN CANTEENS	2.30	1.33
9222	BEVERAGES IN CANTEENS	2.95	1.31
9311	HOTEL ACCOMMODATION	0.62	0.60
9321	NON-HOTEL ACCOMMODATION	0.62	0.74
10111	HAIRDRESSER'S AND PERSONAL CARE SALONS	2.86	5.63
10322	TELEGRAPH	0.08	0.12
10411	SOCIAL CARE WITH ACCOMMODATION	1.86	0.00
10421	SOCIAL CARE WITHOUT ACCOMMODATION	0.17	0.17
10611	OTHER SERVICES	3.45	3.53

APPENDIX 9.3   EXPLORING THE CONSUMER BASKET
IN GREATER DETAIL

There were 1117 items in the consumer basket in 1990 that were divided according to their use into four groups: food, non-food commodities, public catering and services. The basket was step by step reduced to 849, 812 and 804 goods representatives in 1992, 1993 and 1994. All these periods used constant weights with the base of January 1989 = 100. In 1995 the number of representatives dropped further to 762, and the new system of Classification of Individual Consumption by Purpose (COICOP) was adopted. Ten new groups have been created to be more comparable with the European Union classification, namely: food, clothing, housing, household, medical care, transport, leisure, education, public catering and accommodation, other goods and services. At the same time, the weights of the individual representatives have been adjusted to better reflect changes in the actual consumption and thus in the consumer basket. December 1993 has been taken as the new base for the price indices.

Since some items from the old basket were missing in the new basket and, in reverse, some new items were introduced into it, there was no possibility to insure compatibility between both groups of data (this means before and after January 1995) at the level of individual representatives. The solution, which the Czech Statistical Office (CSO) had adopted, was to aggregate the individual representatives into 192 partially aggregated groups according to the COICOP. This means that all the individual representatives having the same last two digits of the six-digit code have been grouped into one item. The indices with the new base in December 1993 started to be officially published from January 1995. The Czech Statistical Office, however, also computed retrospectively the price indices in the new classification for 1994. For the period before 1994 (when the COICOP classification had not yet been introduced) the new groups were created in a rather *ad hoc* way when one tried to find a corresponding old representative to every new individual representative, though one did not insist on one-to-one correspondence.[12] We took over this division of the basket with some small changes[13] and judged every item as to whether it is regulated (whether its price is set by market forces or by administrative intervention[14]) and whether it is internationally tradable or not. Based on these criteria every item was filed into one of the following groups. Appendix 9.2 contains a list of items in particular groups as of 1998; and in the group of administered prices codes that specify the method of price regulation of the item are included:

A   items with maximum price;
Aa   maximum prices are set centrally by the Ministry of Finance;
Ab   maximum prices are set locally by local authorities;
B   prices of items in this group can grow only on the basis of
        documented increasing input costs;
C   fees and charges set by law.

As noted earlier in the chapter, the main changes to this group in the past have included deregulation of coal prices since 1 May 1994, and of liquid and motor fuels since 1 January 1997.

There are only 10 purely regulated items in the group of centrally-regulated commodities (Aa, C). The price of those commodities changed in only a few jumps, but to a great extent, and the aggregated weight of this group is 59/101 before/after 1995. The rest of this group

includes 22 items that are not purely regulated (we shall call them items with guided prices), but their prices are to a great extent not determined by the market. The weight of this remainder is 109/158.

The remaining representatives in the consumer basket were gathered into a group of *non-regulated items*, which covers 161 items with an aggregated weight of 832/742. This group was then further divided into 114 *tradable items*[15] with a total weight of 665/590 and 47 *non-tradable items* with a weight of 167/152.

Variable Weights

For the computations the aggregated price indices are transformed into differences of logarithms to (approximately) express percentage changes. Both groups of the index series (that is, before and after 1993) are consolidated to have a common value 12/93 = 100 and to this date they have fixed weights as mentioned above.[16] With the different price developments in different aggregated groups, the current weights in the basket change. One can expect that a 1 percentage point change in the price index of regulated goods will have a different impact on non-regulated goods at different times when the variable weight of regulated goods in the consumer's basket changes (grows). To avoid this problem we adjust the indices through weighing by their current weights. The dependence between weighted variables can be interpreted as follows: 'What consequent percentage change in the total price index will cause a 1 per cent change of the total index purely due to the increase of regulated prices?' The advantage of this form is that the resulting estimated parameter represents the elasticity of the price level to its previous increase due to the change in regulated prices. The other plus is that the inflation in particular groups, weighted by the variable (actual) weight can be simply interpreted as a value in percentage points by which the group under consideration contributes to the total inflation. This enables us to simply add up the partial effects of individual explanatory variables in sub-groups to get the overall effect on the total inflation.

This approach, of course, will not remove another very severe problem, namely the continuous substitution of items in the consumer's basket as a reaction of the representative consumer to relative price changes. The Statistical Office takes this substitution into account now and then by changing fixed weights of the representatives according to actual consumption. Any continuous adjustment is out of the question, since it would be extremely messy.

Notes

1. As a measure of domestic prices, the CPI was adopted. This index, as a natural measure of the cost of living, is mostly used as a criterion in wage-setting negotiations between employers and unions, thus having a direct impact on production costs at the supply-side of the economy.
2. In other words, this means that some random shock to the economy causes a change in the dependent variable (inflation) and at the same time it changes the value of some 'independent' explanatory variable.
3. Wages constitute a predominant part of disposable income. On the supply-side they represent the cost of production. However, if firms increase wages in relation to labour

productivity, there is no reason to reflect higher wages into higher prices. To avoid the multi-collinearity problem, we will not consider wages explicitly in the model.

4. Unlike in the USA and other developed countries, in the Czech Republic mortgages and purchases of durable goods on consumer credit are not yet ordinarily used. This is why households have more money in their saving accounts than are their liabilities. Higher interest rates then lead to higher disposable income of households thus having no restrictive impact on their demand.

5. Fixed weight multiplied by the price index and normalized so that all item weights sum up to one.

6. Some people would argue that exogeneity is to strong assumption, since there must be some relation between regulated prices and the overall price level. I argue that in the short run this long-run relationship is not binding, especially not in a transition economy when a different rate of price changes in the group of regulated items leads to the common market price structure.

7. The variable subscripts $(-i$ to $-j)$ refer to the number of lags estimated in the polynomial, where the reported coefficient is the sum of all of these coefficient lags. In the following specifications only significant coefficients from the general model are included.

8. Still, the macroeconomic development in this year is influenced by the shock of the separation. This is why we use the data from this period only to form moving averages or to get necessary lags for lag polynomials and the MA(12) process.

9. It is always difficult to identify the factors that cause the ARMA process, but considering the AR and MA terms in the regression improves the quality of estimators (see Box Jenkins, 1984).

10. In the model for the whole period the exchange rate CZK/US$ was also included. Its impact was significant with the two-month lag. The most important raw material which is imported for US dollars is oil. Since the domestic refineries did not reflect the world prices of oil into gasoline prices immediately, and they were the price leaders on the domestic market, the lag of two months seemed reasonable. In more recent periods, however, the behaviour of refineries changed; world oil prices are reflected into domestic prices of gasoline almost immediately and the model is not able to discriminate between the influence of separate currencies. Thus, the exchange rate CZK/DM alone is a good proxy for the changes of the effective exchange rate.

11. This is the coefficient that we obtain if the model is estimated for the period until March 1998. Recent data signal a large drop of this elasticity to about half of the previous number.

12. Every such aggregated representative has two weights in the consumer basket. Till December 1993 it is the constant weight (and thus the base) of January 1989, afterwards December 1993 is taken as a base with corresponding constant weight. In this way, processed time-series show up a significant downward jump in January 1994. The new groups have been created with respect to these weights for the appropriate period. Only then parts of the resulting series before January 1994 were shifted downwards to have the same base December 1993 = 100 (and not January 1989 = 100). Thus we obtained continuity but violated consistence of new time-series in the sense that the weights of new groups do not sum up to one before January 1994. We do not expect this to cause severe problems in the estimation.

13. Our division consists from 193 groups in being better able to separate goods with administered prices from non-regulated items. Thus we had to divide the group 6241xx ('other services connected to the motor vehicles operation') into two groups,

separating the 'lawful motor vehicle liability insurance' from the other items in the group.

14. Administrative interventions influencing price also include changes in excise tax, charged with some particular goods. For the purpose of this study those interventions have been neglected.

15. This subdivision is perhaps the most controversial point of this section, since it is purely subjective and also variable in time.

16. The consolidation of both periods required shifting the first-period series to have the value of 100 in December 1993. Due to the different development of particular partially aggregated groups, different shifts of particular time-series were necessary and the fixed weights for the first period (used later for further aggregation) had to be adjusted correspondingly.

10 Economic Performance in Poland under Fixed and Flexible Exchange Rate Regimes

Piotr Wdowinski and Bas van Aarle

INTRODUCTION

During the last decade, Europe has experienced a remarkable increase in the integration of economic, political and social structures. In the European Union, this process of integration culminated in the Economic and Monetary Union (EMU). EMU formally started on 1 January 1999 with the replacement of national currencies by a common currency, the euro, and the replacement of national monetary policy autonomy by a common monetary policy implemented by the European Central Bank (ECB). The introduction of the euro and the so-called Eastern Enlargement of the EU – first outlined in the Treaty of Copenhagen in 1993 and further developed in the EU Council Meeting in Madrid in 1995 and the recent Agenda 2000 – offers economies in transition in Central and Eastern Europe (CEEC countries) the possibility to embark upon a process of integration and convergence that should lead in the end to their accession into the current EU 15.

A comprehensive overview of macroeconomic design in Poland during the period 1990–98 is given by Durjasz and Kokoszczynski (1998) and Gomulka (1998). The adjustment in monetary and fiscal policy, exchange rate management and capital mobility are analysed. Since October 1991 the exchange rate policy of a pre-announced crawling peg is in place which seeks to strike a balance between containing inflationary pressure and to maintain competitiveness. Both the rate of crawling and the bandwidth have been adjusted several times to adjust to changes in nominal and real developments in the Polish economy. An important issue in this period has been the increasing capital inflow with considerable repercussions for monetary and exchange rate management. Foreign direct investment and net portfolio investment led to recent surges in capital flows and reserve accumulation. Successive liberalization of capital in and outflows also contributed to larger capital flows. Sterilization attempts were ineffective and abandoned in 1995 when exchange rate and interest-rate policy were instead explicitly directed at containing

capital inflows. Since 1997 the current-account balance turned into a deficit given a strong surge in consumption and investment and only a modest export performance. Throughout the period the fiscal policy has been mildly expansionary with fiscal deficits around 2.5–3.0 per cent of GDP.

Poland's way towards the EU will have a strong effect on its present and future macroeconomic policies and vice versa. In particular, we will focus on the effectiveness of two polar types of exchange rate management – fixed and flexible exchange rates – for Poland during adjustment towards the EU. The two exchange rate regimes differ significantly in the transmission of monetary and fiscal policies conducted in Poland and of macroeconomic disturbances in the EU into the Polish economy. Therefore, the choice of the exchange rate regime of the zloty versus the euro will be of crucial importance for the Polish economy during its convergence process. The policy of the fixed zloty/euro exchange rate would imply, for example, a drastic move from the current exchange rate policy that prescribes a target zone for the zloty against a basket of major currencies. Assuming the euro to be strong, pegging the zloty to the euro – if credible – will provide monetary discipline that is likely to provide considerable benefits. That was experienced earlier by small EMS countries while pegging their currencies to a strong deutsche mark. Inflexibility in case of asymmetric shocks, domestic policy impulses and disturbances in the EU are likely, however, to bring considerable adjustment costs to the Polish economy at the cost side. Since it is very likely that the Polish economy will operate under the fixed exchange rate regime in the future, we regard the flexible exchange rate regime as an opportunity exchange rate system.

This chapter studies the problem of a macroeconomic policy in a transition economy – Poland – that considers future accession into the EU and EMU. We analyse the most important interactions between the Polish and EU economies and the impact of a further integration and convergence process. To analyse the implications of a given policy we propose a stylized model of the Polish economy. Especially, the relations for the demand for goods and the balance of payments all include parameters for a transition economy. The parameters enable us to analyse the effects of the macroeconomic policies and foreign shocks on the development of output, prices and the exchange rate within a framework of the transition process. The effects of macroeconomic policies are studied where the focus is on three traditional macroeconomic policy instruments: (i) fiscal policy, (ii) monetary policy and (iii) exchange rate management. Moreover, we analyse effects of interactions between the Polish economy and the EU economy. We study macroeconomic policy dilemmas that are likely to arise during the adjustment process towards entrance into the EU and EMU.

The analytical solution of the model allows for simulation analysis. Different scenarios can be defined: alternative monetary and fiscal policies, as well as shocks to foreign interest rate, prices and demand. The chapter is structured as follows: in

the next section we present the model, followed by a description of the results of the simulation. Finally we summarize the main results of the analysis. The Appendix provides some details on the solution and stability of the model in the cases of fixed and flexible exchange rate regimes.

A STYLIZED MODEL OF THE POLISH ECONOMY

To study the effects of alternative economic policy regimes and the interaction with the EU on macroeconomic adjustment of the Polish economy, we use a model that is an extension of the standard Mundell–Fleming model. This type of model has been widely used in macroeconomic policy analyses and there exists a vast literature on these types of models.[1] A comprehensive theoretical study of a typical transition economy within a framework of the Mundell–Fleming type of model is given in Papazoglou and Pentecost (2001) where the emphasis is put into the real sector, the absence of well-functioning capital markets with only minimal asset choice. Mitchell and Pentecost (2001) develop a theoretical model to investigate supply-side responses to changes in the real exchange rate and test it empirically for four transitional economies: Bulgaria, the Czech Republic, Poland and Slovenia.

The model developed below assumes that there are two countries, a domestic country, Poland, which has the zloty as its domestic currency, and the foreign economy, the EU, that has adopted the euro as its single currency.[2] Given our focus on macroeconomic adjustment and policy design in Poland, the usual small-country assumption is adopted in the sense that the effects of the Polish economy on the EU economy are neglected and the focus is directed on the effects of the EU on the Polish economy. Below we describe the structure of the model.

Total demand for domestic goods in the Polish economy is assumed to be a function of domestic income, the real interest rate, government consumption, competitiveness relative to the EU economy, and real demand in the EU economy:

$$y^d = \zeta y - \sigma r + \delta g + \alpha c + \beta y^* - \rho y \qquad (10.1)$$

where y denotes real output; r, the real interest rate; g, real government consumption; c, competitiveness; and y^* real EU demand (which can be proxied by the sum of output and imports). ζ reflects the multiplier process and ρ the imports leakage. Supply of goods is elastic and output is therefore demand-determined in the short run. In our analysis all variables except the interest rate are in logarithms and refer to deviations from equilibrium (whose values have been normalized to zero for convenience). The model therefore characterizes the short-run business-cycle fluctuations induced by macroeconomic shocks and policy impulses. In a long run, the economy returns to its equilibrium which is independent of monetary and fiscal shocks and the type of exchange rate management.

Money-market equilibrium is given by the following LM schedule:

$$m^s - p = \kappa y - \lambda i \tag{10.2}$$

where m^s denotes nominal money supply; p, the domestic output price index; and i, the nominal interest rate.

The money supply M^s consists of two components: credit provided by the Central Bank to the domestic banking sector, D, and foreign reserves of the Central Bank, F:

$$M^s \equiv D + F \tag{10.3}$$

Since the economy is assumed to operate alternatively in the fixed or floating exchange rate regime, the analysis is based *de facto* on two models. These models differ with respect to the balance of payments equation. This equation is crucial in the model since it enables us to characterize alternative regimes of the zloty/euro exchange rate. In a fully flexible exchange rate system both the domestic and foreign component of the money supply are exogenous. Consequently, the money supply is exogenous as well and can be fully controlled by the monetary authorities to meet macroeconomic objectives. In a fixed exchange rate system, the money supply is endogenous because monetary authorities need to intervene and match any *ex ante* excess demand or supply in the foreign exchange market. A fixed exchange rate, therefore, implies a serious restriction on the flexibility and autonomy of monetary policy.

For simplicity, we assume that initial foreign exchange reserves are equal to one and that the initial shares of D and F in the money supply are equal to θ and $(1 - \theta)$, respectively. Redefining (10.3) in terms of deviations from a steady state implies therefore

$$m^s = \theta d + (1 - \theta)f \tag{10.4}$$

In a system of flexible exchange rates, foreign exchange reserves remain constant, implying $f = 0$ and an exogenous money supply.

The balance of payments equation in a system of fixed exchange rates is the following:

$$S\dot{F}^* = \pi(i - i^* - E(\dot{s})) + \alpha c + \beta y^* - \rho y \tag{10.5}$$

where S is the nominal zloty/euro exchange rate and i^* is the EU interest rate. E denotes the expectation operator. Changes[3] in reserves in terms of euros, $\dot{F}^*$, equal the sum of the capital and current-account balances. The capital account is assumed to be a function of the expected differential in capital returns

(see Frenkel and Rodriguez, 1982). The current-account balance, on the other hand, is a function of competitiveness as well as foreign and domestic income. In general, the balance of payments equation is the following:

$$S\dot{F}^* = \psi((i - i^* - E(\dot{s})), c, y^*, y) \tag{10.6}$$

Because the left-hand side of (10.6) is expressed in levels and not in logs, we have to log-linearize it around the steady state. After simple calculations we derive the final form of the balance of payments equation expressed in terms of deviations from the steady state:

$$\dot{f}^* = \frac{\psi_1}{S_0 F_0^*}(i - i^* - E(\dot{s})) + \frac{\psi_2}{S_0 F_0^*}c + \frac{\psi_3}{S_0 F_0^*}y^* - \frac{\psi_4}{S_0 F_0^*}y \tag{10.7}$$

where ψ_1, ψ_2, ψ_3 and ψ_4 are partial derivatives of a function ψ with respect to interest differential, competitiveness, as well as foreign and domestic income respectively. S_0 and F_0^* stand for the initial values of the zloty/euro exchange rate and foreign reserves, respectively. Recall that $\psi_1 = \pi$ where π stands for the degree of capital mobility: $\pi \to \infty$ implies perfect capital mobility and $\pi = 0$ the case of financial autarky. For simplicity we assume that $\psi_2 = \alpha$, $\psi_3 = \beta$ and $\psi_4 = \rho$ as well as $S_0 = 1$ and $F_0^* = 1$. Then we have

$$\dot{f}^* = \pi(i - i^* - E(\dot{s})) + \alpha c + \beta y^* - \rho y \tag{10.8}$$

In the case of a fixed exchange rate regime, (10.8) simplifies since $E(\dot{s})$. For convenience, we also assume that $s \equiv \bar{s} = 0$. Then the balance of payments simplifies to

$$\dot{f}^* = \pi(i - i^*) - \alpha(p - p^*) + \beta y^* - \rho y \tag{10.9}$$

In the case of the flexible exchange rate regime, the change in reserves equals zero. Accordingly, any surplus (deficit) in the capital account must be matched by the deficit (surplus) of the same size in the current account. No change in reserves ($\dot{f}^* = 0$) implies that the balance of payments equation takes the form:

$$\pi(i - i^* - E(\dot{s})) = -(\alpha c + \beta y^* - \rho y) \tag{10.10}$$

Free floating keeps the balance of payments in equilibrium. It means that monetary authorities do not intervene and official reserves do not change. This serves as a definition of the floating exchange rate zloty/euro. According to (10.10) and perfect foresight assumption we have

$$\dot{s} = i - i^* + \frac{\alpha}{\pi}(s - p + p^*) + \frac{\beta}{\pi}y^* - \frac{\rho}{\pi}y \tag{10.11}$$

It should be pointed out that in the case of perfect capital mobility ($\pi \rightarrow \infty$) in the flexible exchange rate regime, current account changes become insignificant in the determination of the exchange rate. In that case interest parity

$$E(\dot{s}) = i - i^* \tag{10.12}$$

holds approximately. Perfect capital mobility that implies uncovered interest parity is in other words a special case in our model.

A Phillips curve type relation links inflation and output fluctuations:

$$\dot{p} = \nu y \tag{10.13}$$

The parameter ν plays a very important role in the model. It stands for all the institutional factors that determine the level of short-run price stickiness in the economy. As such, it will be a major element that determines the speed of adjustment towards the long-run equilibrium of the economy. A low value of ν implies a prolonged adjustment path along which the economy adjusts only at a slow pace.

Finally, we need to define competitiveness, the real interest rate and the formation of exchange rate expectations. The competitiveness of the domestic economy is defined as the real exchange rate based on output prices

$$c \equiv s - p + p^* \tag{10.14}$$

in which p^* denotes the EU price level. The real interest rate is defined as a difference between the nominal interest rate and *ex post* inflation

$$r \equiv i - \dot{p} \tag{10.15}$$

In the case of a flexible exchange rate regime, we assume rational exchange rate expectations. In the absence of uncertainty this implies perfect foresight and therefore

$$E(\dot{s}) = \dot{s} \tag{10.16}$$

In the presence of price rigidities, exchange rate adjustment serves as an important adjustment mechanism when the economy is hit by shocks. Exchange rate flexibility therefore plays an important role in the adjustment towards equilibrium. In a long run, there is complete price adjustment and the model displays neo-classical features, that is neutrality with respect to monetary and fiscal shocks, both under flexible and fixed exchange rates.

The model is assumed to reflect the main features of the Polish economy in transition. This is done by introducing selected model parameters with an empirical background from econometric studies. On this basis we make the following

assumptions concerning the current structural parameters of the Polish economy: (i) depreciation of the zloty has a relatively small positive impact on exports growth, that is the parameter α is small; its positive value, however, means that the Marshall–Lerner condition is satisfied; (ii) the Polish economy is a highly import-consuming one, that is the parameter ρ is relatively high; and (iii) prices are sticky in the short run, that is the parameter ν is small. Moreover, in a longer-run perspective it is expected that capital controls will weaken in Poland. It is very likely, however, that even then financial assets will not become perfect substitutes. It means that in a long run there will be a small but positive and declining risk premium. Capital controls in our model are characterized by the value of π as noted earlier. A low value of π indicates rather tight capital controls and a high value a more liberal regime of capital controls.

MACROECONOMIC DISTURBANCES AND POLICY IMPULSES IN POLAND: A SIMULATION APPROACH

The effects of pursuing different macroeconomic policy strategies can be traced by the use of numerical simulations of the model. There are several control variables and many macroeconomic scenarios can be analysed, for example different domestic monetary and fiscal policies as well as foreign shocks to demand, output price and interest rate in the EU.

In Table 10.1 we give the values of the structural parameters of the model that we assume in the simulation analysis. The dynamics and stability of the system is a function of the structural parameters. In the case of our particular set of model parameters, the floating exchange rate regime is saddlepoint-stable and the fixed exchange rate regime is globally stable.[4] Figures 10.1–10.4 show the adjustment paths of several important variables that result from a shock to the Polish economy. Solid lines indicate the adjustment process in the fixed exchange rate regime and dashed lines indicate adjustment in the flexible exchange rate regime. The panels display the following variables: (a) output prices, (b) the zloty/euro exchange rate, (c) foreign reserves denominated in euros, (d) real output, (e) the real zloty/euro exchange rate, (f) the nominal interest rate, (g) the capital account, (h) the current account, and (i) the balance of payments. The variables p, s, y and c are expressed in logs. The nominal interest rate i is expressed in terms

Table 10.1 Parameters of the model

ζ	σ	δ	α	β	ρ	κ	λ	θ	π	ν	S_0	F_0^*
0.6	1.0	0.5	0.1	0.3	0.4	1.0	1.0	0.5	2.0	0.2	1.0	1.0

147

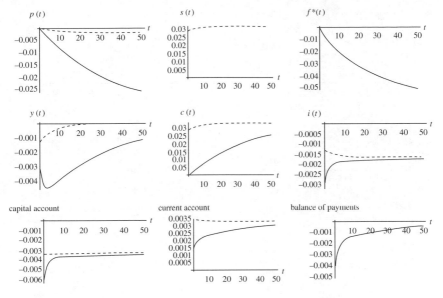

Figure 10.1 Effects of a decrease in government spending

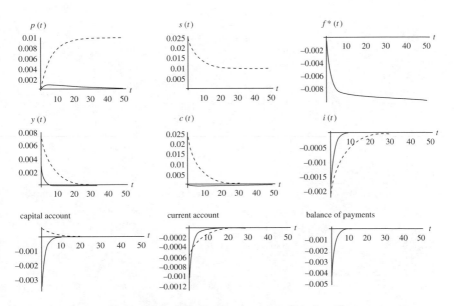

Figure 10.2 Effects of an increase of total credit

148

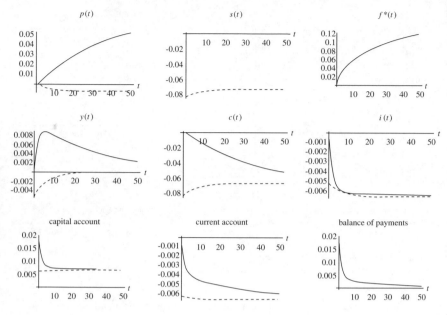

Figure 10.3   Effects of a decrease in the EU interest rate

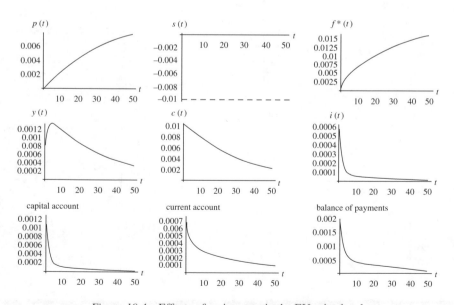

Figure 10.4   Effects of an increase in the EU price level

of percentage points. Positive (negative) values in graphs express higher (lower) states of variables in per cent or percentage points with respect to a steady-state (initial equilibrium). A similar interpretation holds for foreign reserves that are defined in terms of percentage deviations from an initial value of that variable. In the case of the following variables – the capital and current accounts as well as the balance of payments – positive (negative) values stand for a surplus (deficit) on the respective account. We assume that the time unit is a month, and that, for example, $t_0 \equiv 1999.1$ (January 1999), $t_n \equiv 2003.2$ (February 2003), $n = 50$.

In the first simulation[5] (see Figure 10.1) we trace the adjustment paths that result from an initial decrease in government spending by 1 per cent. A fiscal contraction may, for example, be required at some point of time during the convergence process to comply with budgetary criteria that are imposed for entrance into the EU. A reduced government spending also reflects the reduction in the size of the public sector as a result of the transition.

A contractionary fiscal policy impulse reduces the demand for domestic goods and lowers output. Decreasing output lowers money demand and gives rise to a decrease in the interest rate. In a system of flexible exchange rates it gives rise to the nominal and real exchange rate depreciation. The gain in competitiveness improves the current account. The decrease of the interest rate gives rise to a capital outflow and a worsening of the capital account. It can be easily seen from the adjustment paths, for example of output, that in the case of imperfect capital mobility fiscal policy may be effective in the case of the flexible exchange rate regime. Its effectiveness is lower, however, than in the system of fixed rates. In the fixed exchange rate case the effects of fiscal policy are stronger than under flexible exchange rates where there is some stabilization from exchange rate adjustment. A sharp recession is induced by the fiscal contraction and competitiveness is gained only sluggishly. In case of the fixed exchange rate, foreign reserves decline considerably as the relatively large capital outflow is only matched by a slowly improving current account. On the other hand, decreasing reserves lower the money stock that is necessary to keep the exchange rate fixed. This example indicates that a floating exchange regime reduces the adjustment burden from a fiscal consolidation. In the context of the Polish entrance into the EU one would advocate that a fiscal consolidation – if requested – is best undertaken in the transition period where exchange rate adjustment is still feasible.

Next we study the effects of a positive monetary impulse. Figure 10.2 gives the adjustment patterns that are produced by the monetary expansion, that is a growth of domestic credit by 1 per cent.

Monetary policy is an important policy instrument in our model, and therefore, we focus on its stabilizing properties. A permanent increase in the money supply is, in particular, effective in the floating exchange rate regime. It can be seen that the positive monetary shock gives rise to an interest-rate decrease. In the case of

the flexible exchange rate regime, the zloty depreciates both in nominal and real terms. The nominal and real depreciation and lower interest rates boost output in the short run. The lower interest rate, however, does not dominate the expected appreciation and a marginal capital inflow is observed, as the expected capital return is positive. In this specific example the current account goes into deficit since output growth stimulates higher imports and this dominates the increase in exports due to the increase in competitiveness. In the case of the fixed exchange rate regime it is assumed that the National Bank of Poland is committed to keep the exchange rate of zloty/euro fixed. In the case of Poland, such a policy is very likely due to the EU enlargement process criteria. It can be seen that a monetary impulse in the case of the fixed exchange rate regime results in marginal price adjustment. A lower interest rate gives rise to output growth in the short run. On the other hand, lower interest rate and lower competitiveness worsen both the capital and current accounts and thus the balance of payments. This results in a decrease of foreign exchange reserves, which at the same time protects the zloty against pressures to depreciate. Thus, in case of the fixed exchange rate regime the monetary impulse evaporates and output growth is neutralized fast. It can then be concluded that monetary policy might be more effective in the flexible exchange rate case with respect to output growth. In the fixed exchange rate regime, monetary policy retains some effectiveness, given our setting of non-perfect capital mobility.

Given the various channels of interaction of the Polish economy with the EU economy, it is interesting to study the effects on the Polish economy of macroeconomic shocks in the EU. Let us assume that there is a decrease in the EU interest rate by 1 percentage point. Figure 10.3 gives the adjustment paths of the variables.

A decrease in the EU interest rate has important implications for the Polish economy, and Figure 10.3 provides insight into the spillovers that occur in both exchange rate regimes. The principal transmission channel of the interest-rate shock in the EU occurs through international capital markets. In the floating exchange rate case the absence of full capital mobility induces some macroeconomic adjustment. The real and nominal appreciation reduces output. A current account deficit results from a drop in exports that exceed the drop in imports. The current-account deficit is matched by the capital-account surplus that arises due to the positive expected capital return. Altogether, the effect of the decrease in interest rates dominates the effect of the decrease in competitiveness and a small output recovery is observed. Under fixed exchange rates the effects are stronger. A sharp capital inflow is induced that expands reserves and thus the money supply. The reduction in interest rates that arises in due course stimulates output. The rise of output prices that follows, reduces competitiveness and contributes to a gradual worsening of the current account. However, the balance of payments is positive and the resulting build-up of reserves supports financial flows. At the same time, the resulting growth of money supply protects the exchange rate from appreciating.

Furthermore, this money-supply growth allows for a sustained drop in the interest rate. The effect on output under the fixed exchange rate regime is stronger because monetary flows support the initial drop in the interest rate. This example indicates that the choice of the exchange rate may have important implications for not only the transmission of domestic policies, but also of foreign disturbances in a transition economy like Poland that is preparing for accession into the EU. Generally speaking, the sensitivity of the domestic economy to foreign disturbances increases with the regime-switch from floating to fixed exchange rates. The effects from domestic fiscal policy become stronger while the effects from domestic monetary policy weaken. The capital market instruments and regime which may range from low to full capital mobility is also of some importance.

Now let us turn to study the effects of a boost to competitiveness that is induced by an increase in the EU price level (Figure 10.4). A rise in the foreign price level by 1 per cent gives rise to an immediate appreciation of the zloty in the flexible-system case. The exchange rate decreases by the same percentage as an initial increase of the foreign price level so that the real exchange rate remains unchanged. Clearly, the flexible exchange rate serves as an adjustment mechanism that instantaneously restores equilibrium after the foreign price shock. In the case of fixed exchange rates the shock is no longer absorbed instantaneously and a process of gradual real and nominal adjustment is initiated. We observe an increase in competitiveness that gives rise to a surplus in the current account. The interest rate rise initially decreases output and reduces money demand, which brings the money market into equilibrium. A higher interest rate gives rise to a capital-account surplus and with a current-account surplus we observe a positive balance of payments. This turns into a growth of reserves and accordingly to money-supply growth that pushes down the interest rate. A lower interest rate and a higher real exchange rate (competitiveness) both increase output. Its level, however, goes down in time since domestic prices start to increase and deteriorate the competitive position of the economy. Finally, the growth of reserves is sufficient to keep the exchange rate fixed. In the short and medium run we observe positive supply effects due to a lower interest rate and improved competitiveness.

CONCLUSIONS

The countries in Central and Eastern Europe are currently making their milestone steps on their way towards economic and political integration with the Western European economies of the European Union. Obviously, not all countries are able or willing to integrate at the same speed and intensity. Poland is among the countries whose economic performance and political determination is likely to warrant a faster integration speed than most other countries. This of course

implies that issues of policy adjustment and interaction with the EU economy become increasingly important and become an increasingly relevant constraint on macroeconomic policy design.

In this chapter we have proposed a stylized model of the Polish economy to address these issues of economic integration and convergence with the EU and the effects on economic performance and policy adjustment in Poland under transition. We focused on the effects of policy impulses and foreign disturbances under two alternative exchange rate regimes for the zloty: a floating and a fixed zloty/euro exchange rate. It was stressed that the choice of exchange rate regime is of crucial importance in the Polish case and has important implications for the transition towards a final accession to the EU. In particular, the choice between a floating or fixed exchange rate regime has considerable implications on macroeconomic policy flexibility and the transmission of macroeconomic policies and foreign disturbances. Also, the role of capital mobility (and policies towards capital market liberalization) in that respect was indicated.

In an extensive simulation example, we simulated the effects on the Polish economy of shocks to fiscal and monetary policy instruments and foreign disturbances to goods and capital markets. The model parameters were chosen to reflect the main features of transition, for example the low effectiveness of exchange rate policy in inducing demand for exports and domestic production as well as significant price rigidity in the short run. The simulation exercises provided a more detailed insight into the effects of macroeconomic policy impulses and disturbances on adjustment of the Polish economy and the role of economic integration with the EU therein. The marked differences in the adjustment dynamics that resulted, at the same time indicate that the choice between floating and fixed exchange rates is non-trivial and for that reason also has social welfare implications. As a general picture, the floating exchange rate regime has important advantages in terms of monetary policy independence, flexibility and insulation from foreign disturbances. With limited capital mobility, monetary policy retains some room for manoeuvre. In particular, it was argued that during the transition process towards accession into the EU, policy flexibility and independence could be valuable assets.

APPENDIX 10.1 SOLUTION OF THE MODEL

The model can be reduced to a linear system of first-order differential equations. The system in a matrix form can be expressed as follows:

$$\dot{\mathbf{X}}_i = \mathbf{A}_i \mathbf{X}_i + \mathbf{b}_i \quad i = \{f, l\} \tag{A10.1}$$

where $\mathbf{X}_l = p_l, s_l$ in the case of the flexible exchange rate regime and $\mathbf{X}_f = \{p_f, f_f^*\}$ for the fixed exchange rate regime. The dynamics in the floating exchange rate regime is

the following:

$$\begin{bmatrix} \dot{p}_l \\ \dot{s}_l \end{bmatrix} = \begin{bmatrix} l_{11} & l_{12} \\ l_{21} & l_{22} \end{bmatrix} \begin{bmatrix} p_l \\ s_l \end{bmatrix} + \begin{bmatrix} l_1 \\ l_2 \end{bmatrix} \tag{A10.2}$$

where

$$l_{11} = -\frac{\nu(\alpha + \sigma/\lambda)}{\Delta} \qquad l_{12} = \frac{\nu\alpha}{\Delta}$$

$$l_{21} = \frac{1}{\lambda} - \frac{\alpha}{\pi} - \frac{\kappa(\alpha\lambda + \sigma)}{\lambda^2\Delta} + \frac{\rho(\alpha + \sigma/\lambda)}{\Delta\pi}$$

$$l_{22} = \frac{\alpha}{\pi} - \frac{\rho\alpha}{\Delta\pi} + \frac{\kappa\alpha}{\lambda\Delta}$$

$$l_1 = \frac{\nu\alpha}{\Delta}p^* + \frac{\nu\beta}{\Delta}y^* + \frac{\nu\sigma}{\lambda\Delta}d + \frac{\nu\delta}{\Delta}g$$

$$l_2 = \left(\frac{\alpha}{\pi} + \frac{\kappa\alpha}{\lambda\Delta} - \frac{\rho\alpha}{\pi\Delta}\right)p^* + \frac{\beta(\lambda\Delta + \kappa\pi - \lambda\rho)}{\lambda\Delta\pi}y^*$$

$$+ \frac{\kappa\pi\sigma - \lambda\Delta\pi - \lambda\sigma\rho}{\lambda^2\Delta\pi}d + \frac{\kappa\pi - \lambda\rho}{\lambda\Delta\pi}g - i^*$$

and

$$\Delta \equiv 1 + \frac{\sigma\kappa}{\lambda} - \sigma\nu - \zeta + \rho \tag{A10.3}$$

The dynamic system in the case of the flexible exchange rate regime is saddlepoint-stable. It means that the non-predetermined variable, s, takes such an initial value that places the system upon the unique and convergent trajectory. The necessary and sufficient condition for the system to be saddlepoint-stable is that a determinant of the matrix $\mathbf{A}_l$ is negative. Then the eigenvalues must be of opposite signs. In the case of saddlepoint-stability the number of positive eigenvalues must equal the number of non-predetermined variables and the number of negative eigenvalues must equal the number of predetermined variables. The stable and unstable eigenvalues of the matrix $\mathbf{A}_l$ equal

$$h_l = \frac{1}{2}\left[Tr(\mathbf{A}_l) - \sqrt{Tr^2(\mathbf{A}_l) - 4Det(\mathbf{A}_l)}\right] \tag{A10.4}$$

$$z_l = \frac{1}{2}\left[Tr(\mathbf{A}_l) + \sqrt{Tr^2(\mathbf{A}_l) - 4Det(\mathbf{A}_l)}\right] \tag{A10.5}$$

respectively, where trace and determinant of $\mathbf{A}_l$ are given in (A10.6) and (A10.7):

$$Tr(\mathbf{A}_l) = l_{11} + l_{22} \tag{A10.6}$$

$$Det(\mathbf{A}_l) = l_{11}l_{22} - l_{12}l_{21} \tag{A10.7}$$

The analytical solution of the model in the case of the flexible exchange rate regime can be written as follows:

$$p_l(t) = p_l(0)e^{h_l t} + p_l(\infty)(1 - e^{h_l t}) \qquad (A10.8)$$

$$s_l(t) = s_l(0)e^{h_l t} + s_l(\infty)(1 - e^{h_l t}) \qquad (A10.9)$$

It can easily be seen that the solution of the system is a function of the initial values of the price index and exchange rate, the adjustment speed h_l and the steady state of variables p_l and s_l. The starting value of the price index, $p_l(0)$ is given and we assume it equals zero. As far as the exchange rate is concerned, it can take any value in response to a change in fundamentals. It was mentioned, however, that there is only one value that brings the system into a stable trajectory. In order to find the initial value of the 'jump' variable – the exchange rate – we use the procedure that was proposed by Judd (1982), in which the so-called 'singularity condition' gives the following initial value of the exchange rate s_l in a dynamic system of the flexible exchange rate regime:

$$s_l(0) = \frac{l_{22} - z_l}{l_{12}}\left(p_l(0) + \frac{l_1}{z_l}\right) - \frac{l_2}{z_l} \qquad (A10.10)$$

where z_l denotes the positive (unstable) eigenvalue of the matrix $\mathbf{A}_l$. The steady state to which the system converges is given by

$$\mathbf{X}_l = -\mathbf{A}_l^{-1}\mathbf{b}_l \qquad (A10.11)$$

which follows directly from (A10.1). According to (A10.11) we have

$$p_l(\infty) = \frac{l_{12}l_2 - l_{22}l_1}{Det(\mathbf{A}_l)} \qquad (A10.12)$$

$$s_l(\infty) = \frac{l_{21}l_1 - l_{11}l_2}{Det(\mathbf{A}_l)} \qquad (A10.13)$$

The dynamics of the system in case of the fixed exchange rate regime is the following:

$$\begin{bmatrix} \dot{p}_f \\ \dot{f}_f^* \end{bmatrix} = \begin{bmatrix} f_{11} & f_{12} \\ f_{21} & f_{22} \end{bmatrix} \begin{bmatrix} p_f \\ f_f^* \end{bmatrix} + \begin{bmatrix} f_1 \\ f_2 \end{bmatrix} \qquad (A10.14)$$

where

$$f_{11} = l_{11} \qquad f_{12} = \frac{v\sigma(1-\theta)}{\lambda\Delta},$$

$$f_{21} = \frac{\pi}{\lambda} - \frac{\kappa\pi(\alpha\lambda + \sigma)}{\lambda^2\Delta} + \frac{\rho(\alpha + \sigma/\lambda)}{\Delta} - \alpha \quad \text{and}$$

$$f_{22} = \frac{(\lambda\Delta\pi - \kappa\sigma\pi + \lambda\sigma\rho)(\theta - 1)}{\lambda^2\Delta}$$

and

$$f_1 = \frac{\nu[\alpha + \sigma/\lambda(1-\theta)]}{\Delta}\bar{s} + \frac{\nu\alpha}{\Delta}p^* + \frac{\nu\beta}{\Delta}y^* + \frac{\nu\sigma\theta}{\lambda\Delta}d + \frac{\nu\delta}{\Delta}g$$

$$f_2 = \left(\alpha - \frac{\rho(\alpha + \frac{\sigma}{\lambda}(1-\theta))}{\Delta} + \frac{\pi(\theta-1)}{\lambda} + \frac{\kappa\pi(\alpha\lambda + \sigma - \sigma\theta)}{\lambda^2\Delta}\right)\bar{s}$$

$$+ \left(\alpha + \frac{\kappa\pi\alpha}{\lambda\Delta} - \frac{\rho\alpha}{\Delta}\right)p^* + \left(\frac{\pi\kappa\beta}{\lambda\Delta} + \beta - \frac{\rho\beta}{\Delta}\right)y^*$$

$$+ \left(\frac{(\kappa\pi\sigma - \lambda\pi\Delta - \lambda\rho\sigma)\theta}{\lambda^2\Delta}\right)d + \left(\frac{\pi\kappa\delta}{\lambda\Delta} - \frac{\rho\delta}{\Delta}\right)g - \pi i^*$$

and Δ is given by (A10.3). Furthermore, we assume that $\bar{s} = 0$. In the system of the fixed exchange rate regime all variables are predetermined. This means that the matrix $\mathbf{A}_f$ has two negative eigenvalues. The system is then globally stable. The necessary and sufficient condition for the system to be globally stable is that a determinant of the matrix $\mathbf{A}_f$ was positive and a trace was negative. Its solution is the following:

$$\mathbf{X}_f = \mathbf{A}_f^{-1}\mathbf{b}_f + c_{f,1}e^{h_f t}\mathbf{v}_{f,1} + c_{f,2}e^{z_f t}\mathbf{v}_{f,2} \tag{A10.15}$$

where $\mathbf{A}_f^{-1}\mathbf{b}_f$ gives a steady state to which the system converges. The steady state is given by

$$p_f(\infty) = \frac{f_{12}f_2 - f_{22}f_1}{Det(\mathbf{A}_f)} \tag{A10.16}$$

$$f_f^*(\infty) = \frac{f_{21}f_1 - f_{11}f_2}{Det(\mathbf{A}_f)} \tag{A10.17}$$

Constants $c_{f,1}$ and $c_{f,2}$ are constants and functions of the initial conditions. Vectors $\mathbf{v}_{f,1}$ and $\mathbf{v}_{f,2}$ are eigenvectors of the matrix $\mathbf{A}_f$ which correspond to the eigenvalues h_f and z_f. The eigenvalues are easily obtained from the following expressions:

$$h_f = \frac{1}{2}\left[Tr(\mathbf{A}_f) - \sqrt{Tr^2(\mathbf{A}_f) - 4Det(\mathbf{A}_f)}\right] \tag{A10.18}$$

$$z_f = \frac{1}{2}\left[Tr(\mathbf{A}_f) + \sqrt{Tr^2(\mathbf{A}_f) - 4Det(\mathbf{A}_f)}\right] \tag{A10.19}$$

Above we have given the solution of the dynamic system in the case of flexible and fixed exchange rate regimes. Once the solution is known it is possible to give conditions of stability and carry out numerical simulations on the model that describe different scenarios of the economic policy and economic environment. This Appendix provides some details on the solution of the model and its stability conditions. Since the latter are complicated functions of respective parameters, it is more insightful to carry out the sensitivity analysis numerically. To this end we shocked *ceteris paribus* all the parameters of the transient matrices $\mathbf{A}_f$ and $\mathbf{A}_l$ by 1 per cent. Table A10.1 provides details on the response of the respective eigenvalues due to the shocks.

It can be seen that the eigenvalues in the case of the fixed exchange rate regime are the most sensitive to the parameters π, α and ν (the highest decrease of respective eigenvalues) as well as θ and ρ (the highest increase of respective eigenvalues). In the case of the

Table A10.1   The sensitivity analysis of the determinant, trace and eigenvalues (percentage change with respect to the base scenario)

Parameter	Fixed ER regime				Flexible ER regime		
	Determinant	Trace	Eigenvalue (1)	Eigenvalue (2)	Determinant	Trace	Negative eigenvalue
α	1.00	−0.02	0.03	−1.03	−1.00	2.33	−0.12
σ	−0.17	0.30	0.33	−0.16	0.17	−2.16	−0.22
ζ	0.38	0.21	0.26	−0.64	−0.38	−0.88	−0.28
ν	1.13	−0.14	−0.10	−1.03	−1.13	−3.96	−1.02
κ	−0.62	0.62	0.65	−0.03	0.62	3.11	0.69
λ	−0.37	0.35	0.37	0.00	0.37	0.21	0.19
θ	−1.00	0.78	0.81	0.19	—	—	—
π	0.67	−0.59	−0.62	−0.05	0.33	−0.99	0.01
ρ	−0.25	−0.34	−0.39	0.63	0.25	0.16	0.14
Min	−1.00	−0.59	−0.62	−1.03	−1.13	−3.96	−1.02
Max	1.13	0.78	0.81	0.63	0.62	3.11	0.69

flexible exchange rate regime, the negative eigenvalue is the most sensitive to the following parameters: ν (the highest decrease of the eigenvalue), and κ (the highest increase of the eigenvalue). For the latter case a rise in price flexibility (ν) leads to a rise in the adjustment speed h_l. On the other hand, a rise in income elasticity of money demand (κ) leads to a decrease in the adjustment speed h_l. This is not in general valid for the fixed case, since for this regime a transient matrix $\mathbf{A}_f$ has two negative eigenvalues of different values and scale. It is thus difficult to infer from the sensitivity analysis, since there are parameters (for example, α, σ, ζ or κ) for which one eigenvalue goes up and the other goes down due to a parameter shock.

Notes

1. See, for example, the analyses in Buiter and Miller (1982), Turnovsky (1986), Giavazzi and Giovannini (1989), Sheen (1992), Sutherland (1995) and Jensen (1997).
2. Of course, four EU countries (Denmark, Greece, Sweden and the UK) have not adopted the common currency in the first round. The probability that they seek to target a rather fixed euro peg and strive to adopt the common currency in the near future may render our simplifying assumption that all EU countries adopt the common currency not too problematic.
3. A dot over a variable denotes its first time derivative.
4. It is possible to analyse the stability of the system. To this end it is necessary to find relations between parameters with the use of stability conditions based on trace and determinant of the system matrix. It should be expected, however, that this will result in complicated combinations of parameters and can make it difficult to analyse feasible changes of their values. In our case, that is in the given macroeconomic framework, the system is stable. The Appendix provides some details on the solution of the model and its stability conditions.
5. The simulations were carried out in *Mathematica* software.

11 Supply and Price Effects of Monetary and Fiscal Policy in Poland under Transition: An Econometric Analysis

*Wladyslaw Milo, Urszula Ciesluk and
Aneta Zglinska-Pietrzak*

INTRODUCTION

From the end of the Second World War until the early 1970s the neo-classical synthesis dominated macroeconomics. This synthesis concluded that changes in the nominal money supply led to changes in aggregate demand, employment and output in the short run because of nominal rigidities in wages and prices, but in the longer-run changes in the money supply led to sustained changes in the price level, rather than in real output. In the early 1970s this synthesis was challenged by, among others, Lucas (1972, 1973), who argued that in a model with perfect competition anticipated monetary shocks would have no effect on output. Although unanticipated monetary shocks would have some impact on output in the short run, this was only possible to the extent that private-sector agents were deceived. An alternative line of research that overturns Lucas's argument is that based on models of imperfect competition. Fischer (1977) and Taylor (1979) show how with nominal wage and price-setting, nominal money shocks could have long-lasting effects on output and employment. More recently, since the mid-1980s, economists have been seeking the origins of these nominal rigidities. Mankiw (1985) argues that with imperfect competition in response to a change in aggregate demand the private return to each price-setter of adjusting his prices is smaller than the social returns. Thus small menu costs may lead to nominal rigidity and large output effects. Thus, despite changing theoretical fashions, in the presence of nominal rigidities it is widely expected that monetary and fiscal policy can have a sustained effect upon output and employment. This theoretical result informs the focus of this chapter, which examines the impact of monetary and fiscal policy instruments on output, employment and prices – that is the supply-side – of the Polish economy.

There are a large number of channels through which fiscal and monetary policy shocks can affect the real economy. For example, the role of monetary policy in inducing greater investment will stimulate long-term economic growth. It is also true, however, that an excessive dose of monetary expansion can lead to higher inflation, which results in a loss of competitiveness and output, so that any monetary stimulus has to be carefully judged. Alternatively, fiscal policy, by altering the tax structure, can influence the individual's supply of effort in the workplace and thus stimulate growth. This chapter, however, focuses not on the transmission mechanism of demand shocks to output, but on the empirical effects of changes in fiscal and monetary instruments on the supply-side of the Polish economy, from quasi-reduced form equations. Specifically, the chapter is concerned with two main questions:

1. To what extent has monetary policy helped to stabilize inflation, and foster growth and employment in the early stages of transition in Poland?
2. To what extent has fiscal policy been stabilizing in its effect on inflation and economic growth?

The rest of the chapter is divided into five sections. First we present empirical inflation equations to show the effect of Polish monetary and fiscal policies on inflation in the 1990s. The long-run properties of cointegration and stability are also investigated. We then investigate the effect of monetary and fiscal policies on output and economic growth, followed by an examination of the unemployment effects of these policies. Finally we offer a brief conclusion about the supply-side response to fiscal and monetary policies in Poland during the 1990s.

INFLATION EQUATIONS

Curbing inflation has been, and remains, the priority of Polish macroeconomic policy. It should therefore be possible to show the effect of monetary and fiscal policies on inflation. Before embarking on an empirical analysis of inflation it is necessary to check the time-series properties of the key macroeconomic variables used in this chapter. Table 11.1 presents a list of the variables used, and Table 11.2 reports the unit-root test results for these variables over the sample period 1992 to 1997. Table 11.2 shows that most of the variables are difference-stationary; that is, the levels are non-stationary but the difference or the rate of change is stationary. The principal exceptions are the capital to labour ratio, KN, which is non-stationary in both levels and differences, the interest rates, RL and $R3$, investment, IN, and the public-sector budget deficit, DEF, all of which are stationary in levels.

Table 11.1   Names of variables

M0	money supply M0, end of period value
M1	money supply M1, end of period value
CPI	Price index, $CPI_{1992.1} = 1$
E	zloty to $US exchange rate, quarterly average
R3	WIBOR for 3-month, quarterly average
RL	Lombard interest rate, quarterly average
GNP	Nominal GNP
RGNP	real GDP
IN	investment
PD	tax receipts, total
PDOF	household taxes
U	unemployment rate
KN	physical capital/employment ratio
DEF	public deficit

The best-fitting equation for the consumer price index (*CPI*) is

$$CPI_t = 1.177 + 0.0002M^s_{1,t-1} - 0.025RL_{t-2} + 0.741E_{t-5}$$
$$(2.705) \quad (4.105) \qquad\qquad (-2.235) \qquad (8.887) \tag{11.1}$$

where the variables are defined above in Table 11.1 and the figures in parenthesis are *t*-values. All coefficient estimates of this equation are strongly statistically significant and stable. From Table 11.2 it is clear that *CPI*, M^s_1 and *E* are all $I(1)$ process and *RL* is $I(0)$. This enables us to estimate an error-correction model (ECM) for equation (11.1). This turns out as follows:

$$DCPI_t = 0.00002DM^s_{1,t-3} - 0.025DRL_{t-4} + 0.877DE_{t-4}$$
$$(2.601) \qquad\qquad (-1.179) \qquad\quad (3.56)$$
$$- 0.911ECM_{t-3} \tag{11.2}$$
$$(-1.546)$$

$$R^2 = 0.99, \qquad DF = -5.44$$

where the error-correction coefficient estimate of -0.911 is statistically insignificant, but with the estimates of the parameters on DM^s_1 and *DE* significant and very close to their counterparts in (11.1). The model shows a very high goodness of fit and the Dickey Fuller (DF) statistic indicates that the residuals of the equation are stationary, and hence the *t*-values shown in parentheses unbiased. This result suggests that the single most important factor driving inflation over the sample period is the depreciation of the exchange rate of the zloty against the US dollar, while the growth of the money supply has had a significant but very small effect.

Supply and Price Effects in Poland

Table 11.2 Unit-root tests for stationarity

Variable Levels	Tests DF (ADF)	Intercept	Integration order	Variable *Difference*	DF	Intercept	Integration order
M_0	−4.385	—	I(1)	DM_0	−4.385	—	I(1)
				ΔM_0	−4.209	intercept	I(0)
M_1	−4.675	—	I(1)	DM_1	−4.675	—	I(0)
				ΔM_1	−6.926	intercept	I(0)
CPI	−4.421	—	I(1)	$DCPI$	−4.421	—	I(0)
				ΔCPI	−2.983	intercept	I(0)
E	−3.129	intercept	I(1)	DE	−3.129	intercept	I(0)
				ΔE	−4.107	intercept	I(0)
$R3$	−3.688	—	I(0)	$DR3$	−5.208	—	I(0)
				$\Delta R3$	−4.837	—	I(0)
RL	−3.166	—	I(0)	DRL	−3.213	—	I(0)
				ΔRL	−3.151	—	I(0)
GNP	−5.156	intercept	I(1)	$DGNP$	−5.151	intercept	I(0)
				ΔGNP	−4.928	intercept	I(0)
$RGNP$	−6.004	—	I(1)	$DRGNP$	−6.004	—	I(0)
				$\Delta RGNP$	−5.897	—	I(0)
IN	−6.313	—	I(0)	DIN	−6.313	—	I(0)
				ΔIN	−6.598	—	I(0)
PD	−5.298	—	I(1)	DPD	−5.298	—	I(0)
				ΔPD	−4.691	—	I(0)
$PDOF$	−5.100	—	I(1)	$DPDOF$	−5.100	—	I(0)
				$\Delta PDOF$	−5.471	—	I(0)
U	−5.052	trend	I(1)	DU	−5.052	trend	I(0)
				ΔU	−5.116	trend	I(0)
KN	−3.604	—	I(2)	DKN	−3.604	—	I(1)
				ΔKN	−4.399	—	I(1)
DEF	−3.922	intercept	I(0)	$DDEF$	−5.575	—	I(0)
				ΔDEF	−4.298	—	I(0)

Notes: Prefix D denotes a change, Δ denotes a rate of change. Critical values of the DF (ADF), statistic are taken from Fuller (1976). These are as follows for a sample size of 25: (without intercept): −2.66 (1%), −1.95 (5%), −1.60 (10%); (with intercept): −3.75 (1%), −3.00 (5%), −2.63; (with trend): −4.38 (1%), −3.60 (5%), −3.24 (10%).

One concern with equation (11.1) is that the monetary instruments used as regressors may be correlated. The sample pairwise correlations between $(M_{1,t-1}, RL_{t-2})$, $(M_{1,t-1}, E_{t-5})$ and (RL_{t-2}, E_{t-5}) are very strong, appropriately −0.927, 0.936 and −0.838, respectively. In view of this it was decided to estimate an alternative model for the CPI, excluding the money-supply variable since it adds little extra information. The new equation for the CPI is

$$CPI_t = 2.358 - 0.060RL_{t-2} + 1.008E_{t-5} \qquad (11.1')$$
$$(-5.18) \qquad\qquad (12.70)$$

which gives a dynamic, *ECM*-version of

$$DCPI_t = 0.036DRL_{t-4} + 0.989DE_{t-4} - 0.587ECM_{t-4} \qquad (11.2')$$
$$ (-1.67) \qquad\qquad (3.97) \qquad\qquad (-1.52)$$

where both $(11.1')$ and $(11.2')$ have significant parameter estimates. Note also that the estimates of the parameters on the monetary variables are similar to those in (11.1) and (11.2), especially for the exchange rate coefficients. Both predictors, *ex post*, give excellent fits comparable to that of equations (11.1) and (11.2). Replacing M_1^s with M_0^s does not change the *ex post CPI* predictor's qualities of stability, significance, or fit. It must be remembered that the proposed predictors have the feature that excluding one of the monetary policy variables does not significantly change the goodness of the obtained predictors, *ex post*. Thus the monetary variables used as policy instruments were, at least for our data, to some extent interchangeable in terms of their statistical features.

The significance and size of the estimates show that the inflationary effects of a rise in exchange rate of the zloty come through only after a five-quarter lag, and the effect will be equal to $0.741E_{t-5}/CPI_t$ for a given t or $0.741\bar{E}_{t-5}/\overline{CPI}$ in the whole sample, where the bars denote the mean sample values of E and CPI. From equations $(11.1')$ and $(11.2')$ it is seen that the interaction effect of $M_{1,t-1}$ with the pair (RL, E) is about -0.26 in E and 0.035 in RL. This means that the money supply M_1 (at the average level) amplifies the real inflationary effects of the exchange rate and lowers inflation, but much more weakly, if it is coordinated with the policy of RL. Since RL, M_1 and E are Central Bank tools, this means that in the 1990s Polish monetary policy was much better coordinated in the pair (M, RL) than in the pair (M, E) or in the triad (M, RL, E).

OUTPUT AND GROWTH EQUATIONS

Equation (11.3) is a nominal GNP equation for the Polish economy in the 1990s:

$$GNP_t = -52655.9 + 1.669M_{0,t} + 8.200PDOF_{t-6} + 1765.55RL_t \qquad (11.3)$$
$$ (-2.14) \quad (3.25) \qquad\quad (4.03) \qquad\qquad\qquad (2.91)$$

$$R^2 = 0.989, \qquad DF = -3.167$$

where *PDOF* denotes taxes from households. For this equation, all coefficients are significant and the equation gives a very good fit. The integration orders of $(GNP, M_0, PDOF)$ and RL are from Table 11.1, and are $I(1)$, $I(1)$, $I(1)$ and $I(0)$ and the residuals are without intercept or trend. An error-correction version of the

model was therefore estimated which is

$$DGNP_t = 1.909DM_{O,t-3} + 4.090DPDOF_{t-2} - 758.189DRL_{t-5}$$
$$\quad\quad (5.404) \quad\quad\quad\quad (4.55) \quad\quad\quad\quad (-1.32)$$
$$\quad - 0.577ECM_{t-4} \quad\quad\quad\quad\quad\quad\quad\quad\quad\quad (11.4)$$
$$\quad\quad (-1.89)$$

$$R^2 = 0.88$$

All parameter estimates, except the one corresponding to *DRL*, are significant, although the different units of measurement of the variables makes economic interpretation difficult.

An alternative equation that does not take account of fiscal effects on nominal output but replaces the fiscal instrument, *PDOF*, with the monetary policy tools, does not change the very good fit obtained. The significance of the estimate is also high, except for the interest rate, *RL*, which is insignificant. The error correction version for *GNP* is, however, a less-attractive predictor than (11.4), due to the statistically insignificant influence of DRL_{t-5} and the almost insignificant estimate of the coefficient of the error-correction term, EMC_{t-5}. This suggests that fiscal policy tools were the more stabilizing influence on output than, for example, the Lombard rate of interest.

To overcome the units of measurement problem noted above, a log-linear version of (11.3) was also estimated. This has the form:

$$LGNP_l = 8.46 + 0.177LKN_t + 0.59LT_t + 0.048LDEF_{t-2} \quad\quad (11.4')$$
$$\quad\quad (40.7) \quad (2.25) \quad\quad\quad (7.67) \quad\quad (2.63)$$

$$R^2 = 0.98$$

where the prefix *L* denotes a logarithmn of the variable. This model shows that a 1 per cent growth in the value of the logarithm of the public deficit, *ceteris paribus*, gives a 0.048 per cent growth of the value of the logarithm of output. This suggests that public deficit does not have an important influence on GNP. The elasticity of output with respect to the log of the capital/employment ratio (*LKN*) is about 0.18 per cent, and with respect to technical progress (*LT*) much greater, at about 0.6 per cent. Although this equation is good at capturing turning points in nominal GNP, dropping $LDEF_{t-2}$ (public deficit) causes instability of the *LGNP* predictor, so statistically speaking the public deficit turns out to have a stabilizing role despite its very small elasticity with respect to output. This problem also precludes the estimation of an error-correction model for this model of nominal GNP.

A more appropriate measure of the supply of output is real GDP (*RGNP*). Moreover, to address the question posed in the introduction it is the rate of growth of real output that is important rather than its level. Thus, letting Δ denote the rate of

growth of a variable, an equation for the rate of growth of real GDP is

$$\Delta RGNP_t = -0.093 - 0.467 \Delta U_t + 0.526 \Delta M_{0,t-3} - 0.445 \Delta R3_{t-3}$$
$$\quad (-4.52) \quad (-2.02) \quad\quad (3.28) \quad\quad\quad\quad (-2.51)$$
$$\quad + 0.654 \Delta E_{t-5} + 0.058 \Delta PD_{t-6} \quad\quad\quad\quad\quad (11.5)$$
$$\quad\quad (3.74) \quad\quad\quad (1.097)$$

$$R^2 = 0.86$$

where all variables are weakly stationary (see Table 11.2) and there is no need to include an error-correction term. It is interesting to find that the quarterly increment of taxes receipts (ΔPD) does not prove to be an important source of growth in real output. Equation (11.5) says that nominal rates of growth of monetary tools, the money supply M_0 (lagged 3 quarters), the three-month banking sector market rate $R3$ (lagged 3 quarters) and the exchange rate, E (lagged 5 quarters), are all significant contributors to the rate of growth in real output. Together, monetary tools contributed 41 per cent of the explanation of the growth of output. Adding the unemployment growth rate (ΔU) to the monetary instruments enhanced the explanation of the equation for the real growth rate to 59 per cent. Mixing the fiscal and monetary policy tools in the form of growth rates of the fiscal and monetary variables jointly gives almost 78 per cent of explanation of the real output growth in Poland in the 1990s. The mix of fiscal and monetary growth rates with unemployment growth explains 86 per cent of the growth in real output.

This analysis shows that for Poland over the sample period, the strongest single contribution to the explanation of real output growth comes from monetary policy (about 41 per cent), including the exchange rate.

UNEMPLOYMENT EQUATIONS

The rate of unemployment was about 12 per cent in 1991 with its peak at 16.4 per cent in 1993, since when it has slowly fallen to 10.7 per cent in 1997 and is predicted to fall further as the decade proceeds. The last linkage between monetary and fiscal policy and the supply of the Polish economy can be captured through an equation for unemployment. The rate of unemployment equation is

$$U_t = 18.92 + 0.0004 PD_{t-6} - 0.0003 M_{0,t-4} + 0.0001 IN_{t-5} \quad\quad (11.6)$$
$$\quad\quad (59.75) \quad (2.03) \quad\quad (-5.64) \quad\quad\quad (2.84)$$

$$R^2 = 0.936$$

The positive increment of taxes signifies a reduction in disposable income and hence reduces the amount of income that can be allocated to consumption expenditures, which serve to increase unemployment. The tax receipts, lagged

6 quarters, together with the intercept, contribute to 85 per cent of the variability of the unemployment rate. An increase in $M^s_{0,t-4}$ will cause a decrease in U, and the increase in investment IN_{t-5} will cause an increase in the rate of unemployment as capital is substituted for labour in the production process. Adding a monetary variable E_{t-5} does not change the explanation while spoiling the stability and significance of tax receipts and the intercept. All the coefficient estimates, except the estimate of parameter on IN, which is significant only at the 10 per cent level, are strongly significant. The error-correction version of the model is given as

$$DU_t = 0.225DU_{t-4} - 0.003DM_{0,t-5} + 0.0002DPD_{t-5}$$
$$\quad\ (1.94) \qquad\quad (-9.40) \qquad\qquad (3.71)$$

$$\qquad - 0.485ECM_{t-2} \tag{11.7}$$
$$\qquad\ (-2.57)$$

with $R^2 = 0.90$, all coefficient estimates are significant, except the lagged change in the unemployment rate, DU. Again the money supply has a significant, negative effect on the change in the unemployment rate.

CONCLUSION

The Polish economy began its transition period in 1989. In 1990–91, during the early stage of Balcerowicz's stabilization programme, industrial production was falling sharply (except for the food industry) due to a fall in domestic and COME-CON demand by households and firms. Similar trends were observed in the other former republics of the Soviet Union after its fragmentation. The most commonly exported tradables were raw materials and low-quality processed goods to western markets. Export activities were weakened due to mainly monetary policy, most especially exchange rate and interest-rate instruments. From 1994, the Polish economy begun to recover in terms of the real rate of GNP growth, from 3.34 per cent in 1994, 8.21 per cent in 1995, 5.25 per cent in 1996, to 6.6 per cent in 1997. Over the same period, inflation has been reduced from 71.1 per cent per annum in 1991 to just 13 per cent per annum in 1997.

In this chapter it has been demonstrated that appropriate fiscal and monetary policies have contributed to the fall in inflation and the rise in economic growth. In particular, exchange rate depreciation has been the most important single factor leading to the rise in growth, although this has added to inflation. The importance of fiscal policy – measured by the budget deficit or by tax receipts – has played an insignificant role in both the growth of output and the curtailment of inflation compared to monetary-policy instruments. The conclusion seems to be that appropriate interest rate and exchange rate policies are vital to the continued transformation of the Polish economy.

APPENDIX 11.1

The equations in the chapter were also used for some simple forecasting exercises for 1997, and this Appendix reports these results.

Table A11.1   Prognoses of CPI

	CPI	*DCPI*	*CPIECM**
Equation number	11.1'	11.2'	
1997.1	3.362943	0.139153	3.482701
1997.2	3.432412	0.119242	3.601943
1997.3	3.558883	0.101606	3.703549
1997.4	3.630941	0.034517	3.738066

Table A11.2   Prognoses of GNP

	DGNP	*GNPECM***	*RGNP*	*RGNP****
Equation number	11.4		11.5	
1997.1	4633.119	97446.68	0.009588	28025.1533
1997.2	1318.834	98765.51	0.022761	28663.0338
1997.3	3738.354	102503.9	−0.02562	27928.5722

Table A11.3   Prognoses of unemployment

	EU	*U*	*DU*	*UECM*****	*ERROR*	*ERRORECM*
Equation number	Empirical data	11.6	11.7		$\frac{U-EU}{EU}$	$\frac{UECM-EU}{EU}$
1997.1	*12.6*	13.49031	−0.25826	12.941744	0.07066	0.02712254
1997.2	*11.6*	12.36868	−1.37879	11.562958	0.066265	−0.0031933
1997.3	*10.6*	11.80221	−0.88595	10.677013	0.113416	0.00726538
1997.4	*10.5*	11.68467	—	—	—	—
Average error					8%	1%

Notes: **CPIECM* is the level of *CPI* calculated according to *DCPI*, equation (11.2');
***GNPECM* is the level of *GNP* calculated according to *DGNP*, equation (11.4);
****RGNP* is the level of *RGNP* calculated according to $\Delta RGNP$, equation (11.5);
*****UECM* is the level of *U* calculated according to *DU*, equation (11.7).

12 The Determination of the Real Exchange Rate and its Effects on Output and Prices in Slovenia

Boštjan Jazbec, Aleš Delakorda and Vladimir Lavrac

INTRODUCTION

The most intriguing question in defining the equilibrium real exchange rate is to determine which actual exchange rates are in line with their fundamentals. In an attempt to provide an answer to this question, two main definitions of the equilibrium exchange rate have been widely used (Clark, 1996). The first characterizes the equilibrium exchange rate as a desirable real exchange rate consistent with an ideal macroeconomic performance establishing internal and external balance. Internal balance is defined as the level of economic activity that keeps the inflation rate constant. The external position is balanced if the external current account can be regarded not only as sustainable, but also as appropriate based on desired levels of savings and investment. In this sense, the *fundamental (desirable) equilibrium real exchange rate* measure is a normative one. On the other hand, the *natural real exchange rate* is a positive concept that involves the specification and estimation of an equation that explains the actual movements of the real exchange rate in terms of changes in economic fundamentals. The most important ones are productivity and thrift. The distinctive characteristic of both definitions is, therefore, definition and characterization of the fundamentals of the real equilibrium exchange rate. While the first concept attempts to find desirable and potential economic variables, the second concept simply concentrates on the actual movements of the determinants of the real exchange rate. The concept of an equilibrium real exchange rate is especially delicate in transition economies. These economies are going through massive structural changes whose dynamics directly affect the determination of the fundamentals and, consequently, the equilibrium real exchange rate. In this sense, it would be too ambitious to define the equilibrium real exchange rate for the transition economies; therefore, hereafter we rather use the notion of the actual real exchange rate in the long run.

Although the transition and restructuring of the previously centrally-planned economies started almost ten years ago, economic theory has not provided a coherent and consistent answer to deal with most of the phenomena which are so particular to these countries. Low labour productivity, shallow financial markets and an underdeveloped non-tradable sector, an overwhelming state sector, increasing unemployment and capital inflows are just a few of the distinguishing characteristics of transition economies. Since the real exchange rate is one of the most important relative prices in developed economies, it is a key issue as to how to model transition in order to study the behaviour of the real exchange rate. Grafe and Wyplosz (1997) model the real exchange rate determination contingent upon determination of real wages. Both prices are interchangeably determined in a transition of the economy from a state to private sector with an occurrence of a new non-tradable sector. However, they make a few strong assumptions that are not consistent with reality. For example, they construct a model assuming full employment, which prevents them from fully encompassing the transition dynamics. On the other side, amongst others,[1] Aghion and Blanchard (1993) explicitly model the labour market dynamics and pay special attention to the speed of transition. However, they do not focus their analysis on evolution of the real exchange rate and other relative prices in the economy. Both models provide an excellent foundation for challenging the problem of determination of the real exchange rate in transition economies. However, at this stage we were still unable to complete the model and point out the main characteristics and determinants of the real exchange rate in these economies. The proceeding is, therefore, an alternate way of presenting the problem.

This chapter will attempt to address some of these questions. The complexity of the problem, in the sense of different fundamental characteristics of the real exchange rate determination and different responses of monetary authorities to surges in capital inflows in transition economies, requires the case-study approach from country to country. The focus of the chapter is primarily on Slovenia in the period from January 1993 to December 1996. Since its independence in late 1991, Slovenia has made remarkable progress in reducing inflation and inflationary expectations through adherence to a tight money-based stabilization programme. The inflation rate was successfully brought down from more than 200 per cent at the end of 1991 to less than 10 per cent in 1995. Targets on the money aggregates were the only possible alternative for stabilization in Slovenia because of one very simple reason: the foreign exchange reserves amounted to less than US$200 million which was only enough for four days of imports in September 1991.[2] The Bank of Slovenia had to build up international reserves and reduce inflation simultaneously. In the first two months after introducing the tolar in October 1991, the foreign exchange rate increased considerably because of high expectations and speculations on the foreign exchange market. High exchange rate levels promoted a growth of exports and prevented a rise in imports. Consequently, the net foreign

exchange reserves increased significantly. After moderating from 5.3 per cent in 1994 to 4.1 per cent in 1995, real GDP growth slowed further to 3.1 per cent in 1996. As in 1995, domestic demand was the driving force behind the expansion in 1996, but with a clear slowdown in the growth of private consumption and investment. During 1997, real GDP growth is estimated to have risen to 3.7 per cent, mostly reflecting the recovery abroad. Real wages continued to grow strongly in 1996 and early 1997. All real exchange rate indicators point to a relatively modest appreciation of some 5 to 10 per cent since 1993. The persistent capital inflows have posed a serious dilemma for monetary policy; in an effort to reduce inflation while maintaining the real exchange rate, the Bank of Slovenia continued to control base money and became heavily involved in sterilization of capital inflows.

In the second section of the chapter the reaction function of the Bank of Slovenia is modelled. It is showed that the central bank was relatively successful in steril-izing increasing inflows of foreign capital in period prior to 1997. The impact of massive sterilization on interest rates and inflation is assumed away since only the effectiveness of the Bank of Slovenia in systematic sterilization of capital inflows is empirically tested. In so doing, we were able to model the determination of the real exchange rate explicitly without direct introduction of the capital inflows in the model. The reasons for an omission of the capital inflows from the real exchange rate equations are twofold. Firstly, there has been an on-going discussion in Slovenia mainly generated by exporters who claim that the Bank of Slovenia should intervene more intensively on the foreign exchange market in order to prevent fur-ther appreciation of the real exchange rate. We deny this criticism by showing that the sterilization of the capital inflows was indeed successful during the period from January 1993 to December 1996. Secondly, we believe that capital inflows are a transitory feature of the transition process and, therefore, do not affect the determi-nation of the real exchange rate in the long run. This is especially true for Slovenia, where most of the foreign capital entered the economy in the form of short-run foreign bank loans and speculative money invested in the Slovenian stockmarket.

The model of the real exchange rate determination is presented in the third section of the chapter, which draws heavily on our conclusion that, in a sense, that capital inflows do not directly enter the real exchange rate equation. It is established that the Bank of Slovenia successfully absorbs most of the flows into the economy before they could affect the real exchange rate. In the fourth section we model the exchange rate effects on output and prices in Slovenia, before concluding in the final section.

REACTION FUNCTION OF THE BANK OF SLOVENIA

In the short run, the central bank can control the monetary base if there exists imperfect substitutability between interest-bearing assets of different currency

denomination and imperfect mobility of capital. In order to prevent appreciation of domestic currency, the central bank sterilizes capital inflows that inflate the monetary base by raising domestic assets. The offset to monetary policy gives rise to a negative correlation between the capital account surplus and the domestic monetary base. To construct a variable that would encompass the monetary policy of the central bank, Cumby and Obstfeld (1983) propose the following measure to which the central bank reacts:

$$\Delta MP_t = \Delta DA_t + \Delta B_t \tag{12.1}$$

where ΔMP represents monetary policy, ΔDA stands for the change in domestic assets of the central bank, ΔB is the change in the monetary base, and t is a time subscript. However, both variables on the right-hand side of equation (12.1) are affected by changes in reserve requirements which are a feature of monetary policy. These changes in reserve requirements are incorporated into equation (12.1) by adjusting changes in domestic assets and the monetary base in the following form:

$$\Delta MP_t = (r_0/r_{t-1})\Delta DA_t + (r_0/r_{t-1})\Delta B_t \tag{12.2}$$

where r_0 is the average ratio of reserve requirements in the base period, and r_{t-1} its counterpart in current period.

Monetary policy, ΔMP, is taken to be the dependent variable in the reaction function, and should allow for responses to a number of factors. Those factors should in general respond to real output fluctuations, to changes in international competitiveness and to seasonal fluctuations in money demand. Generally, the reaction function of the central bank can be written in a regression form as it follows:

$$\Delta MP_t = \beta_0 + \beta_1 \Delta R_t + \beta Z_t \tag{12.3}$$

where ΔR represents the change in foreign exchange reserves of the central bank. This variable is also adjusted for the changes in reserve requirements. Coefficient β_1 measures the degree of sterilization. If $\beta_1 = -1$, then the monetary authority neutralizes all reserve flows by offsetting effects on domestic credit. When $-1 < \beta < 0$, sterilization is less than perfect, and finally when $\beta_1 = 0$ the monetary authority does not engage in sterilization of capital inflows at all. Z presents the vector of other variables that influence domestic monetary policy. It includes the changes of the real exchange rate, $\Delta FXREAL$; changes of fiscal deficit, $\Delta FISCAL$; changes of industrial production, $\Delta INDU$; and the vector of dummy variables, DUM, which captures the impact of seasonality. Equation (12.3) can, therefore,

be written as follows:

$$\Delta MP_t = \beta_0 + \beta_1 \Delta R_t + \beta_2 \Delta FXREAL_t$$
$$+ \beta_3 \Delta FISCAL_t + \beta_4 \Delta INDU + \beta DUM_t \qquad (12.4)$$

We used monthly data for a period from January 1993 to December 1996 to estimate equation (12.4). All variables enter equation (12.4) as differences since they
all have unit roots in levels. Tests were performed by using both Dickey–Fuller
and Phillips–Perron tests respectively. The Slovenian fiscal deficit was relatively
balanced throughout the period. For a proxy we used the monthly net claims of the
financial sector to the government. However these manipulations did not improve
the econometric results. Since the variable *FISCAL* was statistically insignificant
at the 5 per cent level, we excluded it from further analysis. The same problem
occurred with variable *INDU* as we expected, because this variable does not include
services that represent a major part of Slovenian GDP. However, both variables had
expected positive signs. Dummy variables helped to extract the impact of December data in regression. Since most of the right-hand side variables in equation (12.4)
are endogenous, ordinary least squares (OLS) would not be the appropriate econometric technique to apply. Instead, two-stage least squares (TSLS) was used to
estimate equation (12.4). As suggested by Fair (1970), all independent variables
and their one-period lags, as well as lagged dependent variables, were used as
instruments in order to insure consistent estimates.[3]

The results are reproduced as the following (*t*-statistics in brackets):

$$\Delta MP_t = 828.506 - 0.929\Delta R_t - 19388.33\Delta FXREAL_t + \beta DUM_t \qquad (12.5)$$
$$\quad\;\; (4.142) \quad (-16.102) \quad\;\; (-1.331)$$

$$R^2 = 0.855 \qquad DW = 1.403$$

Although low Durbin–Watson statistics could reveal serial correlation in the
residuals, the Q-statistics rejects the presence of autocorrelation. The stability of
the reaction function usually poses a problem in relatively short time-series, and the
question of stability is even more problematic in cases when economies undergo
structural adjustment processes. However, the Chow test rejects the structural break
at randomly chosen dates for equation (12.5). Nonetheless, this conclusion should
not be taken for granted.

The coefficient β_1 is statistically significant at the 1 per cent level and allows
us to reject the hypothesis of being zero. Its value of close to -1 implies that the
sterilization policy of the Bank of Slovenia was complete in the observed period.
Moreover, the data suggest that the central bank attempted to control the money
stock through full neutralization of reserve flows. Although the simplicity of the

approach does not allows to make firm conclusions, the results are in line with conclusions of Bole (1994a,b) and Mencinger (1992, 1995).

The coefficient of the real exchange rate is statistically insignificant. However, it changes when we divide the observed period into sub-periods which may once again point out the problems of stability of the regression equation, and, moreover, to a different intensity of the Bank of Slovenia sterilization policies in some sub-periods from January 1993 to December 1996. Nonetheless, the coefficient β_2 is always negative which implies that the Bank of Slovenia did not get involved in targeting the real exchange rate. A positive sign of the coefficient β_2 would mean that when domestic prices rise more quickly than exchange rate adjusted foreign prices, credit policy becomes more restrictive (Cumby and Obstfeld, 1983).

Statistical insignificance and stability problems may be partly explained by the combination of a relatively short time-series and their high volatility. This seems to be a recurrent problem in transition economies. We agree that the simplicity of the regression could be overcome by an approach that would encompass dynamics of the different variables in question. However, we are not sure whether results would be substantially different. Estimates of the Bank of Slovenia reaction function provide strong evidence of sterilized intervention between 1993 and 1996, and allow us to use these results in the next section.

DETERMINATION OF THE REAL EXCHANGE RATE

The real exchange rate can be analytically defined in many different ways,[4] but it should be noted that there is no universally accepted definition. According to earlier views the real exchange rate is defined as the nominal exchange rate corrected by the rate of the foreign to the domestic price level. This is also a definition of the real exchange rate which coincides with a theoretical framework set up by the purchasing power parity (PPP) exchange rate (Froot and Rogoff, 1995). As is shown later, PPP does not completely hold in transition economies since the Law of One Price cannot be established. Slight readjustment of PPP is introduced in order to overcome this problem. Therefore, according to PPP, the real exchange rate is defined as the following:

$$e = E P_F / P_D \qquad (12.6a)$$

where e represents real exchange rate, E stands for the nominal exchange rate, P_F represents the foreign price level, and P_D the price level in the home country.[5] Foreign and domestic inflation are measured by the consumer price index (CPI) although other measures could be introduced. Edwards (1989) suggests three other price indices to be used for the construction of the real exchange rate index: firstly,

the wholesale price index; secondly, the GDP deflator; and, finally, the wage-rate index. In practice, all indices generate the same types of problems as those arising from using the CPI. These problems are mostly related to the measurement of the price index and data availability. Although none of these indices is perfect, only CPI is used in what follows since it provides the most widely used and internationally comparable measure of the inflation. This fact especially holds for the transition economies where the use of any other price index – for example the wage-rate index – would most probably lead to a distorted measure of inflation.

One of the strongest assumptions of PPP exchange rate theory is that the Law of One Price is observable. It implies that the domestic price of traded goods, P_T, is equal to the world price of traded goods, where P_F is used as a proxy, multiplied by the nominal exchange rate, E:

$$P_T = P_F E \tag{12.7}$$

Conceptually, the use of foreign CPI, P_F, as a proxy for the world price of traded goods, P_T^*, may generate the same kind of problems as the use of a favourable CPI against any other price indices used to measure the inflation. Generally, those problems are mostly ignored since the domestic prices of tradable goods are usually also neither directly observable nor available.

However, without any lack of consistency, it is assumed that the Law of One Price does not hold in transition economies. Moreover, it is assumed that there exists a coefficient, ω, for which equation (12.7) is corrected. One can define ω as a ratio between the world and domestic price of traded goods, P_T^*/P_T, which reflects poorer quality and efficiency of production of traded goods in transition economies. Moreover, it is assumed that ω represents a proxy for the terms of trade. Increased quality and efficiency of production of traded goods increases their price. Consequently, the terms of trade improve. By definition, the terms of trade are expressed as a ratio between export and import prices, so that equation (12.7) can be rewritten in the following way:

$$P_T = \omega P_F E, \quad 0 < \omega \tag{12.8a}$$

Introduction of the terms of trade into analysis of the determination of the real exchange rate follows from standard theory which suggests that an improvement in the terms of trade should induce a rise in the domestic price level relative to abroad, and lead to an appreciation of the real exchange rate. Although this direction of causation is not empirically established (see, for example, In and Menon, 1996), it provides rather intuitive evidence of the fact that the changes in the terms of trade affect determination of the real exchange rate and not vice versa (De Gregorio and Wolf, 1994). Stein and Sauernheimer (1996) provide an even stronger argument in support of the introduction of the terms of trade into a model of the real exchange

rate determination by concluding that in the case of Germany in the period from 1973 to 1994, the real exchange rate was not cointegrated with the terms of trade.

Alternatively, we could define the real exchange rate as a ratio between traded and non-traded goods:

$$e_a = EP_T/P_N \tag{12.9}$$

where P_T is a world price for traded goods expressed in foreign currency, and P_N is a domestic price of non-traded goods. Nominal and real exchange rates are defined as in equation (12.6a). However, Edwards (1989) shows that changes in the two definitions of the real exchange rate presented by equations (12.6a) and (12.9) will differ.[6] Therefore, it does not seem wrong to assume that these changes reflect the improving terms of trade in transition economies. Using the definition of the real exchange rate presented in equation (12.9) instead of that presented in equation (12.6a) would, therefore, by definition remove an opportunity to measure the effect of the changes in terms of trade on determination of the real exchange rate.

To complete the framework, we define the domestic CPI in the aggregate form as the following:

$$P_D = P_N^{\gamma} P_T^{(1-\gamma)} \tag{12.10a}$$

where P_D is the domestic price, P_N and P_T are prices of non-tradables and tradables respectively, and γ is a share of non-tradables in the economy.

By taking logarithms of equations (12.6a), (12.8a) and (12.10a), we get (for the sake of simplicity, the same symbols are used to express logarithms, that is, $e = ln(e)$, $E = ln(E)$, etc.) the system of equations as the following:

$$e = E + P_F - P_D \tag{12.6b}$$

$$P_T = \omega + P_F + E \tag{12.8b}$$

$$P_D = \gamma P_N + (1 - \gamma) P_T \tag{12.10b}$$

From equation (12.8b) we calculate $P_F = P_T - \omega - E$. Using this expression and equations (12.10b) and (12.6b) we get

$$e = P_T - \omega - [\gamma(P_N - P_T) + P_T] \tag{12.11}$$

A slight rearrangement gives us an equation of the real exchange rate:

$$e = -\omega - \gamma(P_N - P_T) \tag{12.12}$$

The expression $\gamma(P_N - P_T)$ measures the impact of tradable and non-tradable prices on the real exchange rate. However, this expression is further developed by

using equations which depict the determination of nominal wages in tradable and non-tradable sectors of the transition economy. A general formulation of nominal wages (expressed in logarithms) is presented as the following:

$$W_T = \varphi_T + P_T + A_T \tag{12.13}$$

$$W_N = \varphi_N + P_N + A_N \tag{12.14}$$

where $W_{T,N}$ represents nominal wages in tradable and non-tradable sectors of the economy respectively, $A_{T,N}$ is marginal productivity of labour in both sectors, and $\varphi_{T,N}$ is a measure of excess wages in tradable and non-tradable sectors respectively. It is assumed that wages in both sectors are higher than they would be if the economy did not undergo the process of transition. This might be a strong assumption, but the evidence in transition economies supports this way of thinking (Halpern and Wyplosz, 1996).[7]

Moreover, it is assumed that the excess of wages over the marginal productivity of labour is paid out of credits which firms are able to obtain from a domestic financial system. Therefore, the coefficient φ is a function of a market interest rate; the higher the interest rate, the lower the coefficient φ and vice versa:

$$\varphi = \varphi(r) \quad d\varphi/dr < 0 \tag{12.15}$$

From equations (12.13) and (12.14) we get

$$(P_N - P_T) = (W_N - W_T) - (\varphi_N - \varphi_T) - (A_N - A_T) \tag{12.16}$$

Equation (12.16) depicts the determination of the difference between prices in tradable and non-tradable sectors. With this notation and equation (12.12) we get a complete equation of the determination of the real exchange rate in transition economies:

$$e = -\omega + \gamma(W_T - W_N) + \gamma(\varphi_N - \varphi_T) + \gamma(A_N - A_T) \tag{12.17}$$

This theoretical framework is mostly drawn from conclusions of Halpern and Wyplosz (1997), and Stein and Sauernheimer (1996). Generally, on the basis of equation (12.17) we might illuminate four main reasons of changes of the real exchange rate in transition economies. More specifically, we might observe why the real exchange rate constantly appreciates in those countries:

- The terms of trade in transition economies improve as the quality and efficiency of production of tradable goods improve. If coefficient ω increases, the real exchange rate appreciates.
- Price liberalization and the increased power of trade unions increase nominal wages which tend to equalize across sectors. Wages in the non-tradable sector

are most likely to grow faster than wages in the tradable sector since the later are assumed to be higher at the beginning of transition. Agenor and Santaella (1998) provide an analytical argument for this statement which in general holds in developing countries. It is a rather intuitive argument which is based on the fact that the emerging non-tradable sector is offering relatively higher wages that the tradable sector which mostly consists of low productivity state-owned firms.

- The increased competition in the financial sector lowers interest rates which induces a higher demand for credits. It is to be expected that productivity of the non-tradable sector grows faster than in the tradable sector which implies that the excess of tradable wages over productivity grows faster. Again, we assume pressure of the trade unions toward equalizing wages across sectors. This conclusion is pretty much in line with the previous case. The final outcome is a real appreciation of the exchange rate.

- Productivity in the tradable sector increases faster than in the non-traded goods sector, because it is the tradable sector which is exposed to international competition. This effect is usually known as the Balassa–Samuelson effect and it predicts a real exchange rate appreciation when productivity in the tradable sector increases faster than in the non-tradable sector of the economy.

Additionally, an active fiscal policy might be one of the most important determinants of the real exchange rate determination in transition economies. According to Stein and Sauernheimer (1996), the fiscal policy variable reflects the level of social preference in the economy. This variable is usually generated as a ratio between government borrowing and GDP, a ratio which should reflect the degree of credibility of the government. Increased credibility of the government would suggest an increase of investment over savings in the economy. This would imply that some of the investment is financed abroad which would generate a non-speculative capital inflow and real exchange rate appreciation. However, it turns out that in an econometric analysis this variable is constantly insignificant which may illuminate the data problem rather than a theoretical mis-specification.

Using the aggregate variables for wages and productivity – as proposed in Halpern and Wyplosz (1996) – $W = W_N^{\gamma} W_T^{(1-\gamma)}$, and $A = A_N^{\gamma} A_T^{(1-\gamma)}$, respectively, and assuming that the weights are the same as for the construction of the price-level index, we can rewrite equation (12.17) in the form which allows us an estimation of the real exchange rate equation in the following form:

$$FXREAL_t = \beta_0 + \beta_1 TERMS_t + \beta_2 WAGES_t + \beta_3 MARGIN_t$$
$$+ \beta_4 PROD_t + \beta_5 FISCAL_t + \varepsilon_t \qquad (12.18)$$

where *FXREAL* is the real exchange rate; *TERMS* represents the terms of trade calculated on a basis of eight countries to which Slovenia exports to and imports from the most; *WAGES* are real wages calculated from nominal Tolar wages corrected

for inflation; *MARGIN* represents the arithmetic average of the difference between short-term deposits and lending interest rates; *PROD* is productivity of the Slovenian economy; and *FISCAL* represents the claims of the banking sector on the government. We use monthly Slovenian data in a period from January 1993 until December 1996. All variables except the interest rates are expressed in logarithms and observed on a monthly frequency basis.

All variables were non-stationary in levels which was checked by using the augmented Dickey–Fuller test. Equation (12.18) was, therefore, used to estimate the error-correction term:

$$ECM_t = FXREAL_t - (\beta_0 + \beta_1 TERMS_t + \beta_2 WAGES_t$$

$$+ \beta_3 MARGIN_t + \beta_4 PROD_t + \beta_5 FISCAL_t + \varepsilon_t) \tag{12.19}$$

Equation (12.18) was estimated by least-squares and produced the following result:

$$FXREAL_t = 9.631 - 1.965 TERMS_t - 0.552*WAGES_t \tag{12.20}$$
$$ (9.176) \quad (-6.010) (-5.547)$$

$$- 0.120*MARGIN_t$$
$$(-3.560)$$

$$R^2 = 0.807 \qquad SER^8 = 0.0218 \qquad DW = 0.541$$

All variables except *FISCAL* were significant at the 5 per cent level; this variable was excluded from further analysis. The unit-root test on residuals of equation (12.20) confirmed that variables were cointegrated. Although there might exist more than one cointegrating vector, this implication did not prevent us from using the single-equation error-correction model (ECM), although it might be theoretically incorrect. This problem is addressed later in the chapter. Since variables in equation (12.20) were cointegrated, we were able to proceed with the analysis by estimating the single-equation ECM of the following form:

$$\Delta FXREAL_t = \alpha_0 + \alpha_1 ECM_{t-1} + \alpha_2 \Delta FXNOM_t + \alpha_3 \Delta TERMS_t$$

$$+ \alpha_4 \Delta WAGES_t + \alpha_5 \Delta PROD_t + \alpha_6 \Delta MARGIN_t$$

$$+ \alpha_7 \Delta FISCAL_t + \varepsilon_t \tag{12.21}$$

The regression equation (12.21) represents a classical form of the ECM which enables us to distinguish between short and long-run movements of the determinants of the real exchange rate. Coefficient α_1 represents the long-run correction of the model presented by equation (12.18). According to the theory, it should be minus signed and its value gives us the speed of adjustment from the short-run actual equilibrium to the long-run equilibrium levels of the real exchange rate. It

indicates the half-life of the adjustment which is the time it takes for a discrepancy between the actual and equilibrium exchange rate to be reduced by half. It is calculated as $ln2/\alpha_1$. *ECM* is introduced to equation (12.21) as a one-period lagged variable. An additional variable in equation (12.21) is *FXNOM* which represents the nominal exchange rate. This variable is in fact a proxy for the inflation in the model. Inflation itself cannot enter the model since all variables on the right-hand side of equation (12.21) are real variables calculated by using inflation to get their real values. If inflation entered the equation directly, serious problems would have occurred related to a high correlation among variables in the model. Furthermore, if capital inflows are sterilized – which is the case in Slovenia as shown in the previous section – then monthly movements of the nominal exchange rate reflect the changes in the rate of inflation (Ross, 1997).

The model itself does not account for capital inflows since it relies on fundamental long-run determinants of the real exchange rate. A slight reformulation of the model along the lines of portfolio-based models[9] would justify the direct introduction of capital inflows in the regression equation. However, as shown in the previous section, the sterilization of capital inflows in Slovenia was complete which enabled us to estimate the equation of the real exchange rate without direct introduction of capital inflows.

Equation (12.21) was estimated by least-squares and results are produced in the following form:

$$\Delta FXREAL_t = -0.006 - 0.182ECM_{t-1} + 0.615\Delta FXNOM_t$$
$$(-5.277) \quad (-4.213) \qquad (7.344)$$

$$- \; 0.552\Delta TERMS_t - 0.055\Delta WAGES_t - 0.034\Delta MARGIN$$
$$(-3.898) \qquad\qquad (-1.267) \qquad\qquad (-2.33)$$

$$(12.22)$$

$$R^2 = 0.782 \qquad SER = 0.005 \qquad DW = 1.619$$

Because of a very high correlation between variables *PROD* and *WAGES*, we decided to run a regression using only one of the variables. Nonetheless, the results did not change substantially when either of them was used in regression. All variables in equation (12.22) were statistically significant at the 5 per cent level. There is still a problem of stability of the coefficients in the equations, but it was overcome by splitting the observed period into shorter intervals. This exercise did not affect the main results substantially. Relatively low value of the Durbin–Watson statistic could suggest problems of autoregression, but the Q-test rejected the autoregression in residuals.

All variables had expected negative signs that confirmed the theoretical framework outlined above. Real wages, terms of trade and interest margins put downward

pressure on the real exchange rate. Inflation which is measured by movements of the nominal exchange rate positively influences the real exchange rate which was expected. The error-correction term had a negative sign that led to the conclusion that there existed a long-run downward correction from actual to equilibrium levels of the real exchange rate. The speed of adjustment $\alpha_1 = -0.184$ indicates a half-life of around four months. Because of a relatively short time span the distinction between the short and long run is more or less artificial.

The results should be understood with some caution. Firstly, because of a high frequency of data there are a lot of monthly fluctuations that could skew the econometric results. Nonetheless, we used dummy variables especially for December and June. This regression is not separately presented for the sake of transparency. Secondly, the model is structured in such a way that some variables might be endogenously determined. However, the Granger causality test supports the hypothesis on exogeneity of most of the variables. Finally, the single-equation error-correction model might not be the best approach to the problem; it seems that there exists more than one cointegrating vector in the model. When there is more than one cointegrating vector, this leads to inefficiency in the sense that we can only obtain a linear combination of these vectors when estimating a single-equation model. This problem can be overcome by using the VAR approach. We ran a few VAR models which supported the concern about non-linearity of the model.

MODELLING EXCHANGE RATE EFFECTS ON OUTPUT AND PRICES IN SLOVENIA

This section presents a small *ad hoc* model of the Slovenian economy, which can be used to determine the exchange rate effects on prices and output in a small open economy like Slovenia. In the analysis, the real effective exchange rate of the Slovenian tolar was used, as it is a more suitable indicator of competitiveness and costs than the nominal exchange rate. The exchange rate regime in Slovenia is characterized as a managed floating system from the very beginning of the operation of an independent monetary policy in 1991. The initial depreciation of the tolar in the first half of 1992 was followed by appreciation in real terms and in some cases even in nominal terms.

The effects of exchange rates on prices in Slovenia were partially proven by Cufer (1997) who implemented a causality analysis, and Ross (1997) who used a VAR model. The findings of the later also point to the fact that exchange rate changes first feed into wages, which eventually cause inflation. In our model, the exchange rate was put in the wage equation; wages then impact PPI, which is followed by CPI. Gross wages are additionally influenced by government expenditures. On the other side, the exchange rate–income relation seems much more dubious and has not yet been examined for Slovenia. A direct effect is

neglected and the impact of the exchange rate on output, measured in terms of industrial production, is rather modelled through:

• the exports–export equation, although the exchange rate elasticity of exports is relatively small, but nevertheless of the right sign (a negative sign could also have been possible due to the existence of 'distressed exporters', especially in the first two years of independence when the exporters had to reorientate their trade from ex-Yugoslav towards western markets);
• the prices–CPI equation (the exchange rate as one of the most important prices in a small open economy influences the formation of CPI); and through
• the wages–wage equation (it is supposed that exchange rate depreciation improves the profitability of exporters, which are then willing to offer higher wages; obviously, it is the opposite case with importers).

Much more important in this case is the proxied foreign activity, which is quite a transparent determinant of domestic activity in the case of a small open economy. Besides that, the exchange rate also exists as a regressor in the import equation. It should be noted that the exchange rate elasticity of different component parts of imports is on average much higher than the exchange rate elasticity of exports as enterprises, and especially households, do care about imported goods prices. Anyway, imports depend very much on aggregate domestic activity.

The equations were first separately estimated by OLS for the period 1st quarter 1993 to 3rd quarter 1998. Static and dynamic simulations were performed and the results of the simulations are quite favourable. Correlation coefficients and Theil's inequality coefficients of the relation between actual data on one side and the results of static and dynamic simulation on the other side were calculated to confirm this statement. Both correlation and Theil's coefficients are presented in Table 12.1.

The equations were then entered into an Eviews System object and several methods (TSLS, weighted TSLS) of system estimation were tested. The values and significance of the coefficients were very similar to those estimated by OLS. The multi-equation model (see Appendix) was then used to examine the effect

Table 12.1   Simulation of diagnostic statistics

	Static simulation		Dynamic simulation	
	Corr. coefficient	Theil's coefficient	Corr. coefficient	Theil's coefficient
CPI	0.89	0.001	0.89	0.001
IBSCQM	0.95	0.014	0.95	0.014
IM	0.96	0.017	0.96	0.018
BTW	0.99	0.004	0.99	0.005
IND	0.82	0.013	0.81	0.014

of changes in the exchange rate on output, imports and prices. The results of the dynamic simulation in the case where the exchange rate would have continuously depreciated in the period estimated are as follows:

- Economic activity (measured by industrial production) would have risen by just under 0.4 per cent and would remain at that level after approximately nine quarters of sustained growth.
- Prices (measured by CPI) would have risen by only a small fraction (about 0.04 percentage points). As is to be expected, the rise of tradable prices would have been higher than that of non-tradable prices.
- Imports fall at the very beginning (for a marginal proportion) when the depreciation occurs, but then rise instantly and (although with minor shocks) reach the level of a 0.4 per cent change in comparison with the imports with no depreciation episode included. The rise of exports is slightly higher than that of imports with a 0.6 per cent increase, with a subsequent retreat to a 0.5 per cent increase.

The following Figures 12.1–12.3 show the percentage change of the estimated variables in the case of sustainable depreciation of the national currency.

CONCLUSIONS

Although the model was tested only on Slovenian data, it shows the directions for further research. As mentioned in the text, there are still a lot of problems

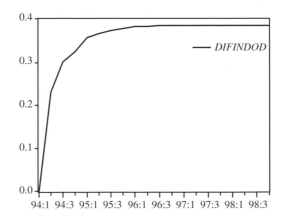

Figure 12.1   Percentage change of industrial production

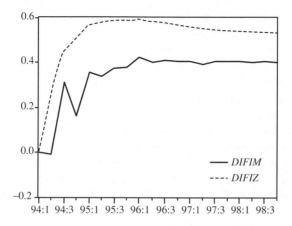

Figure 12.2 Percentage change of imports (DIFIM) and exports (DIFIZ)

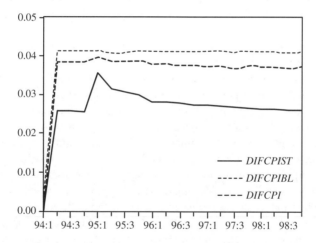

Figure 12.3 Percentage point in prices of non-tradable (DIFCPIST), tradables (DIFCPIBL) and (DIFCPI)

related to the econometric techniques as well as problems addressing the theoretical framework used, and those require further work.

It seems that most of the transition economies are going through the same set of problems which are reflected in their macroeconomic performances. Taking into consideration preliminary results on Slovenia, we see no problem in extending the analysis to other transition economies. Special attention should be paid to

five countries which are among the first to join the European Union – the Czech Republic, Hungary, Poland, Estonia and Slovenia. Differences and similarities in their macroeconomic performances should be thoroughly studied in a framework that would allow us to address the problems of the real exchange rate determination.

Further research should attempt to characterize the most suitable exchange rate policy determination in order to support the restructuring and rebuilding of the economies in transition. In this sense, the approach should be more of a normative nature that would help to define some macroeconomic equilibrium that is so desired in these economies. However, in the light of the currency crisis in East Asia, Russia and Brazil, special attention should be paid to the factors which characterize the current problems in those economies. Identification of the main determinants of the currency crisis should help to point out the degree of misbehaviour in transition economies. The main question is whether there exists some set of fundamentals that helps to explain the variation in financial crises across countries. Also, there is a question in which directions those fundamentals – if a direction exists – affect the determination of the equilibrium real exchange rate. In so doing, shocks to the equilibrium rate should be identified and empirically examined.

The first impression is that the magnitude of capital inflows to the transition economies is still small compared to other regions – especially South Asia. Also their composition has changed dramatically since the time of central planning. Most of those inflows have consisted of foreign direct investments which are understood to be 'good' for the recipient country as opposed to the 'bad' capital inflows represented mainly by short-term portfolio investment. Foreign direct investment should reflect fundamental determinants of the equilibrium real exchange rate whereas short-term portfolio investment and foreign bank loans should be understood as a short-run transitory factor affecting the real exchange rate. Moreover, the capital inflows tend to be distributed extremely unevenly across the receiving countries. When all the necessary research has been done, the direction of the influence of capital inflows on the real exchange rate should hopefully appear clearer. However, it seems that the importance of capital inflows on the determination of the real exchange rate is sometimes exaggerated as it is the case in Slovenia, because the capital flows present only one side of the coin.

The main problem is still of a conceptual issue since there seem to be problems to understand: firstly, the concept of the equilibrium real exchange rate in transition economies, and, secondly, the main forces which drive the transition of these countries towards market-structured economies. Following the rapid liberalization and privatization in the early stages of transition, most of the transition economies have started to show signs of constant growth and a tendency towards stability. There is, however, still a long way to go. After almost ten years of institutional restructuring of enterprises, financial and labour markets, many

real economic phenomena specific to transition economies are still waiting to be explained and answered. One of them is definitely the determination of the real exchange rate that seems to be different to that so far observed in developed countries (Grafe and Wyplosz, 1997). Firstly, it seems that independently of the chosen exchange rate regime, the real exchange rate steadily appreciates once the economy is liberalized. And, secondly, there is no apparent link between the evolution of the nominal and real exchange rates. The determination of the real exchange rate should, therefore, be modelled in a framework which would encompass the restructuring of the state sector, the development of a new private sector, the recurrent problem of unemployment, and the increasing importance of foreign capital in a process of transition which – it seems – will not terminate as fast as it was predicted.

The final section of the chapter has modelled the supply response of the real exchange rate changes in Slovenia. The results of the simulation show that the exchange rate in a small open economy has an important effect on prices and activity. At the same time, it defines the competitiveness of exporters through its impact on their costs, which are represented by wages in the model. The question of which effect – supply effect through wages or the demand effect through changed competitiveness in the world market – prevails, is to be answered in a separate analysis. Although the exchange rate was shown to have important effects on the national economy, there is a doubt of its high importance for exporters' activity. The exporters are namely made to sell their goods and services abroad (sometimes), no matter at what price, by the small size of the domestic market. Much more important in this sense seem to be an exogenous factor such as foreign demand (as shown in the export equation) and structural, competition-improving oriented economic policies that enable exporters to invest in new technologies and innovate and introduce new products.

APPENDIX 12.1

There are nine behavioural and three definition equations in the model as listed below (standard errors in brackets):

CPI-Tradables Equation

$\text{LOG}(CPIBLS)$

$= 4.22 - 0.04 \, \text{LOG}(REDTPPI(-1)) - 0.07 \, \text{LOG}(PIDYM(-1))$
$ (0.36) (0.02) (0.02)$

$ + 0.12 \, \text{LOG}(CPIK1) + 0.02 \, \text{LOG}(M1(-1)) + 0.005 \, D1$
$ (0.07) (0.006) (0.001)$

$R^2 = 0.81$
$DW = 2.43$
s.e. of regression $= 0.003$
25 observations

CPI-Non-Tradables Equation

LOG($CPISTS$)

$$= 4.73 + 0.08 \text{ DLOG}(BTW(-3)) + 0.03 \text{ DLOG}(M1(-3))$$
$$\quad (0.04) \quad (0.01) \qquad\qquad\qquad (0.01)$$

$$+ 0.01 \ D934 - 0.03 \text{ LOG}(REDTPPI(-1))$$
$$\quad (0.002) \qquad (0.01)$$

$R^2 = 0.95$
$DW = 1.50$
s.e. of regression $= 0.002$
25 observations

Export Equation

DLOG($IBSCQM$)

$$= 4.09 - 0.48 \text{ LOG}(IBSCQM(-1)) + 0.60 \text{ LOG}(UB\$8QM(-1))$$
$$\quad (2.35) \quad (0.18) \qquad\qquad\qquad (0.31)$$

$$- 0.27 \text{ LOG}(REDTPPI(-1)) - 0.20 \text{ LOG}(BTW(-1))$$
$$\quad (0.18) \qquad\qquad\qquad (0.10)$$

$$+ 0.50 \text{ DLOG}(UB\$8QM) + 0.30 \text{ DLOG}(PIDYM)$$
$$\quad (0.30) \qquad\qquad\qquad (0.17)$$

$$+ 0.25 \text{ LOG}(IMSKUPI)$$
$$\quad (0.16)$$

$R^2 = 0.82$
$DW = 1.58$
s.e. of regression $= 0.03$
24 observations

Imports (Intermediate Goods) Equation

DLOG($IM10\_KOL$)

$$= - 4.47 - 0.63 \text{ LOG}(IM10\_KOL(-1)) + 1.09 \text{ LOG}(IND)$$
$$\quad (1.69) \quad (0.09) \qquad\qquad\qquad (0.27)$$

$$+ 0.50 \text{ LOG}(IBSCQM) + 0.26 \text{ LOG}(REDTPPI(-1))$$
$$\quad (0.18) \qquad\qquad\qquad (0.24)$$

$R^2 = 0.79$
$DW = 2.26$
s.e. of regression $= 0.04$
24 observations

Imports (Consumer Goods) Equation

DLOG(*IM30_KOL*)

$$= 12.81 - 1.55 \text{ LOG}(IM30\_KOL(-1)) + 0.49 \text{ LOG}(BTW)$$
$$(2.06) \quad (0.17) \qquad\qquad\qquad (0.09)$$

$$+ 0.51 \text{ LOG}(REDTPPI(-1))$$
$$(0.41)$$

$R^2 = 0.80$
$DW = 2.10$
s.e. of regression $= 0.07$
24 observations

Imports (Investment Goods) Equation

DLOG(*IM20_KOL*)

$$= -8.96 + 3.04 \text{ LOG}(IND) - 0.90 \text{ LOG}(IM20\_KOL(-1))$$
$$(1.72) \quad (0.33) \qquad\qquad (0.10)$$

$$+ 1.43 \text{ LOG}(REDTPPI(-1)) - 0.30 \, D961 - 0.28 \, D951$$
$$(0.43) \qquad\qquad\qquad (0.08) \qquad\quad (0.07)$$

$R^2 = 0.91$
$DW = 2.18$
s.e. of regression $= 0.07$
24 observations

Wage Equation

LOG(*BTW*)

$$= 5.73 - 0.10 \text{ LOG}(REDTPPI(-1)) - 1.40 \text{ LOG}(CPISTS(-1))$$
$$(2.38) \quad (0.05) \qquad\qquad\qquad (0.50)$$

$$+ 0.28 \text{ LOG}(GR) + 0.11 \text{ LOG}(IND) + 0.82 \text{ LOG}(BTW(-1))$$
$$(0.03) \qquad\qquad (0.05) \qquad\qquad (0.02)$$

$$- 0.13 \text{ DLOG}(M1(-3))$$
$$(0.06)$$

$R^2 = 0.99$
$DW = 1.61$
s.e. of regression $= 0.01$
24 observations

Industrial Production Equation

LOG(*IND*)

$$= -20.64 + 0.26 \text{ LOG}(IBSCQM) + 4.25 \text{ LOG}(CPISKUPI)$$
$$\quad (8.80) \quad (0.10) \qquad\qquad\qquad (1.89)$$

$$+ 0.15 \text{ LOG}(BTW(-1)) - 0.02 \ D1$$
$$\quad (0.05) \qquad\qquad\qquad (0.01)$$

$R^2 = 0.81$
$DW = 1.75$
s.e. of regression $= 0.03$
24 observations

Identities

$$CPIEXO = K((CPWBLSM/10000 \ CPIBLS$$
$$\qquad + CPWSTSM/10000 \ CPISTS)/(CPWBLSM/10000$$
$$\qquad + CPWSTSM/10000))$$

$$CPISK = (CPIEXO \ (CPWHPPM/10000$$
$$\qquad + CPWSKKM/10000) + CPWBLSM/10000 \ CPIBLS$$
$$\qquad + CPWSTSM/10000 \ CPISTS)/(CPWHPPM/10000$$
$$\qquad + CPWSKKM/10000 + CPWBLSM/10000 + CPWSTSM/10000)$$

$$IMSKUPI = IM10\_KOL + IM20\_KOL + IM30\_KOL$$

Variables Used in the Model

CPIBLS	price index of tradables
CPISTS	price index of non-tradables
CPISK	CPI price inflation
CPIK1	CPI of controlled prices
CPIEXO	CPI of exogenously given prices (food and controlled services)
PDIYM	productivity
M1	money
IBSCQM	exports
UB\$8QM	total imports of eight important trade partners
IMSKUPI	imports
IM10_KOL	imports of intermediate goods

IM20_KOL	imports of investment goods
IM30_KOL	imports of consumer goods
BTW	gross average wage
T	time trend
D963	dummy variable for the 3rd quarter 1996
D961	dummy variable for the 1st quarter 1996
D951	dummy variable for the 1st quarter 1995
D934	dummy variable for the 4th quarter 1993
REDTPPI	real effective exchange rate
IND	industrial production
GR	government expenditure
K	indicates the adjustment process of relative prices
CPWBLSM	weight of tradables in CPI index
CPWSTSM	weight of non-tradables in CPI index
CPWHPPM	weight of food and beverages in CPI index
CPWSKKM	weight of controlled services in CPI index

Notes

1. There is an increasing number of papers concerning transition economies in recent years. However, we mention only these two since, firstly, Aghion and Blanchard (1993) provide a benchmark model for many other subsequent papers, and, secondly, Grafe and Wyplosz (1997) are believed to be the first to explicitly model the determination of the real exchange rates in transition economies.
2. All data referred to in the text are from the Bank of Slovenia *Monthly Bulletin* of various periods if not otherwise stated.
3. Cumby and Obstfeld (1983) use a two-step, two-stage least squares procedure; they also provide reasons for using it. We stick to fairly standard TSLS.
4. Extensive surveys on real exchange rate determination are provided by Edwards (1989), Froot and Rogoff (1995), Clark (1996), Stein (1990) and Stein and Sauernheimer (1996).
5. Our focus is primarily on the bilateral exchange rate. More about other approaches can be found in MacDonald (1997), Frankel and Rose (1995) and Stein (1995).
6. If aggregate price indices are defined as $P_D = P_N^{\varphi} P_T^{(1-\varphi)}$ and $P_F = P_{NF}^{\mu} P_{TF}^{(1-\mu)}$ for domestic and foreign inflation, respectively, and by further assuming that the law of one price holds for tradable goods, it is possible to show the relation between percentage changes in e and e_a:

    $$\Delta\%e = \varphi\Delta\%e_a - \mu(\Delta\%P_{TF} - \Delta\%P_{NF})$$

    Moreover, Edwards (1989) shows that the changes in the two definitions of the real exchange rate can even go in the opposite direction, depending on the behaviour of foreign relative prices (P_{TF}/P_{NF}).
7. Aghion and Blanchard (1993) conclude that the excess of wages over the marginal productivity in transition economies reflects the temporary appropriation of quasi rents by workers. Such a result is easily derived from efficiency-wage considerations.
8. Standard error of regression.
9. See Montiel and Ostry (1992), Lizondo (1993), Calvo, Reinhart and Vegh (1995), and Agenor and Santaella (1998).

References

Agenor, P.-R. (1972) 'Borrowing Risk and the Tequila Effect', *IMF Working Paper*, no. 86.

Agenor, P.-R. and Santaella, J.A. (1998) 'Efficiency Wages, Disinflation and Labour Mobility', *Journal of Economic Dynamics and Control*, vol. 22, pp. 267–91.

Aghevli, B.B., Borensztein, E. and van der Willigen, T. (1992) 'Stabilization and Structural Reform in the Czech and Slovak Federal Republic: First Stage', *IMF Occasional Paper*, no. 92, March.

Aghevli, B.B., Khan, M.S. and Montiel, P.J. (1991) 'Exchange Rate Policy in Developing Countries: Some Analytical Issues', *IMF Occasional Paper*, no. 78, March.

Aghion, P. and Blanchard, O.J. (1993) 'On the Speed of Transition in Central Europe', *EBRD Working Paper*, no. 6, July.

Aiginger, K. (1996) 'The Competitiveness of Transition Countries, Indicators of the Qualitative Competition', *WIFO Working Paper*, Vienna, April.

Aiginger, K. (1997) 'The Use of Unit Values for Discriminating between Price and Quality Competition', *Cambridge Journal of Economics*, vol. 21, pp. 571–92.

Alexander, S.S. (1952) 'Effects of a Devaluation on a Trade Balance', *IMF Staff Papers*, no. 3, pp. 263–78.

Almon, S. (1965) 'The Distributed Lag Between Capital Appropriations and Expenditures', *Econometrica*, vol. 33, pp. 178–96.

Argy, V. and Salop, J. (1983) 'Prices and Output Effects of Monetary and Fiscal Expansion in a Two-Country World under Flexible Exchange Rates', *Oxford Economic Papers*, no. 35, pp. 228–46.

Banerjee, B. (1995) 'The Transformation Path in the Czech Republic', in 'Road Maps to Transition: The Baltics, the Czech Republic, Hungary and Russia', *IMF Occasional Paper*, no. 127, September.

Begg, D. (1998) 'Disinflation in Central and Eastern Europe: The Experience to Date', in C. Cottarelli and G. Szapary (eds), *Modern Inflation: The Experience of Transition Economies*, International Monetary Fund, Washington D.C.

Benacek, V. (1999) 'Foreign Direct Investment in an Economy of Transition – The Case of the Czech Republic: Evolution, Problems and Policy Issues', *Charles University Working Paper*, Prague.

Benacek, V., Shemetilo, D. and Petrov, A. (1997) 'Efficiency under Restructuring from a Microeconomic Perspective', in S. Sarma (ed.), *Restructuring Eastern Europe*, Cheltenham: Edward Elgar.

Berg, A. and Sachs, J.D. (1992) 'Structural Adjustment and International Trade in Eastern Europe: The case of Polland,' *Economic Policy*, no.14, April, pp. 117–73.

Berg, A. and Blanchard, O.J. (1994), 'Stabilisation and Transistion: Poland, 1990–91,' in O.J. Blanchard, K.A. Frost and J.D. Sachs (eds), *The Transition in Eastern Europe Vol 1 Country Studies*, Chicago: University of Chicago Press.

Bole, V. (1994a) 'Sterilization in a Small Open Economy: The Case of Slovenia', mimeo, Ekonomski Inštitut Pravne Fakultete.

Bole, V. (1994b) 'Priliv kapitala preko sektorja prebivalstva in gospodarski dosezki', *Gospodarska gibanja*, Ekonomski Inštitut Pravne Fakultete, no. 254, October.

Bole, V. (1996) 'Kapitalska in tekoca bilanca ter obrestne mere', *Gospodarska gibanja*, Ekonomski Inštitut Pravne Fakultete, no. 272, May.

Borensztein, E. and Masson, P.R. (1993) 'Exchange Arrangements of Previously Centrally Planned Economies', in 'Financial Sector Reforms and Exchange Arrangements in Eastern Europe,' *IMF Occasional Paper*, no. 102, February.

Borensztein, E., Demekas, D.G. and Ostry, J.D. (1993) 'An Empirical Analysis of the Output Declines in Three Eastern European Countries,' *IMF Staff Papers*, vol. 48, no. 1, March, pp. 1–31.

Box, G. and Jenkins, G. (1984) *Times Series Analysis: Forecasting and Control*, 2nd edn, San Francisco: Holden Day.

Branson, W.H. (1986) 'Stabilisation, Stagflation and Investment Incentives: The Case of Kenya 1975–80', in S. Edwards and L. Ahamed (eds), *Economic Adjustment and Exchange Rates in Developing Countries*, Chicago: University of Chicago Press.

Bruno, M. (1992) 'Stabilization and Reform in Eastern Europe', *IMF Staff Papers*, vol. 39, December, pp. 741–77.

Bruno, M. and Easterly, W. (1995) 'Inflation Crises and Long-Run Growth', *NBER Working Paper*, no. 5209.

Buiter, W. and Miller, M. (1982) 'Monetary Policy and International Competitiveness: The Problems of Adjustment', *Oxford Economic Papers*, vol. 33, pp. 143–75.

Bulgarian National Bank, *Monthly Bulletin*, various issues.

Cadenillas, A. and Karatzas, I. (1995) 'The Stochastic Maximum Principle for Linear, Convex Optimal Control with Random Coefficients', *SIAM Journal of Control and Optimization*, vol. 33, no. 2, pp. 590–624.

Calvo, G.A. (1983) 'Staggered Contracts and Exchange Rate Policy', in J.A. Frenkel (ed.), *Exchange Rates and International Macroeconomics*, Chicago: NBER.

Calvo, G.A. and Coricelli, F. (1992) 'Stabilizing a Previously Centrally Planned Economy: Poland 1990', *Economic Policy*, no. 14, April, pp. 176–226.

Calvo, G.A. and Kumar, M.S. (1993) 'Financial Markets and Intermediation', in 'Financial Sector Reforms and Exchange Arrangements in Eastern Europe', *IMF Occasional Paper*, no. 102, February.

Calvo, A.G., Reinhart, C.M. and Vegh, C.A. (1995) 'Targeting the Real Exchange Rate: Theory and Evidence', *Journal of Development Economics*, vol. 47, pp. 97–133.

Capek, A. (1997) 'The Real Effective Exchange Rate: The Problems of Construction', *Czech National Bank Papers*, no. 77, Prague.

Claessens, S. (1991) 'Balance of Payments Crisis in an Optimal Portfolio Model', *European Economic Review*, vol. 35, pp. 81–101.

Clark, P.B. (1996) 'Concepts of Equilibrium Exchange Rates', *Journal of International and Comparative Economics*, vol. 20, pp. 133–40.

Clark, P.B. and MacDonald, R. (1998) 'Exchange Rates and Economic Fundamentals: A Methodological Comparison of BEERs and FEERs', *IMF Working Paper* 98/00 (Washington: IMF, March).

Corden, M.W. (1993) 'Exchange Rate Policies for Developing Countries', *The Economic Journal*, vol. 103, pp. 198–207.

Cox, J., Ingersoll, J. and Ross, S. (1985) 'An Intertemporal General Equilibrium Model of Asset Prices', *Econometrica*, vol. 53, pp. 363–84.

Cufer, U. (1997) 'Analiza strukture inflacije' [Inflation Structure Analysis], *Prikazi in analize*, vol. 3, Banka Slovenije, pp. 13–28, September.

Cumby, E.R. and Obstfeld, M. (1983) 'Capital Mobility and the Scope for Sterilization: Mexico in the 1970s', in P.A. Armerla *et al.* (eds) *Financial Policies and the World Capital Markets: The Problem of Latin American Countries*, Chicago: University of Chicago Press.

De Gregorio, J. (1993) 'Inflation, Taxation, and Long-run Growth', *Journal of Monetary Economics*, vol. 31, pp. 271–98.

Derviz, A. (1997a) 'Impact of Privatization and Capital Markets Development for the Exchange Rate of the Czech Currency', in M. Mejstrik, A. Derviz and A. Zemplinerova (eds), *Privatization in East-Central Europe: The Evolutionary Process of Czech Privatizations*, Kluwer Science Publishers.

Derviz, A. (1997b) 'Optimal Consumption and Investment under Restrictions on Portfolio Composition and Adjustment Speed', in Procedures of Quantitative Methods in Finance Conference, Sydney–Cairns–Canberra, Australia, August–September.

Derviz, A. (2001) 'Currency Options and Trade Smoothing under an Exchange Rate Regime Shift', ACE Workshop, Ljubljana, February 1998, Chapter 3 of this volume.

Drabek, Z. and Brada, J. (1998) 'Exchange Rate Regimes and the Stability of Trade Policy in Transition Economies', Geneva: WTO.

Driskill, R.A. and McCafferty, S. (1985) 'Exchange Rate Dynamics with Wealth Effects: Some Theoretical Ambiguities', *Journal of International Economics*, vol. 19, pp. 329–40.

Duffie, D. (1992) *Dynamic Asset-Pricing Theory*, Princeton, New Jersey: Princeton University Press.

Duffie, D. and Epstein, L. (1992a) 'Stochastic Differential Utility', *Econometrica*, vol. 60, no. 2, pp. 353–94.

Duffie, D. and Epstein, L. (1992b) 'Asset Pricing with Stochastic Differential Utility', *Review of Financial Studies*, vol. 5, no. 3, pp. 411–36.

Durjasz, P. and Kokoszczynski, R. (1998) 'Financial Inflows to Poland, 1990–96', *Empiricia*, vol. 25, pp. 217–42.

Easterly, W. (1996) 'When is Stabilization Expansionary? Evidence from High Inflation', *Economic Policy*, pp. 67–107, Summer.

Edwards, S. (1986) 'Are Devaluations Contractionary?', *Review of Economics and Statistics*, August, pp. 501–8.

Edwards, S. (1989) 'Real Exchange Rates in the Developing Countries: Concepts and Measurement', *NBER Working Paper*, no. 2950.

Eichengreen, B. (1988) 'RER Behaviour under Alternative International Monetary Orders', *European Economic Review*, vol. 32, no. 2/3, pp. 363–71.

Elliott, R.J. (1982) *Stochastic Calculus and Applications*, Berlin: Springer-Verlag.

Engle, R.F. and Granger, C.W. (1987) 'Cointegration and Error Correction: Representation, Estimation and Testing', *Econometrica*, vol. 55, pp. 251–76.

European Bank for Reconstruction and Development, *EBRD Transition Report*, London, various issues.

European Commission (1995) 'The Impact of Exchange Rate Movement on Trade within the Single Market', *European Economy Reports and Studies*, no. 4.

Fair, R. (1970) 'The Estimation of Simultaneous Equations Models and Lagged Endogenous Variables and First Order Serially Correlated Errors', *Econometrica*, vol. 38, pp. 507–16.

Fischer, S. (1977) 'Long-term Contracts, Rational Expectation and the Optimal Money Supply Rule', *Journal of Political Economy*, vol. 85, February, pp. 191–205.

Fischer, S. (1993) 'The Role of Macroeconomic Factors in Growth', *Journal of Monetary Economics*, Vol. 32, pp. 485–512.

Fischer, S., Sahay, R. and Vegh, C. (1996) 'Stabilization and Growth in Transition Economies: The Early Experience', *Journal of Economic Perspectives*, no. 2, pp. 45–66, Spring.

Fleming, W.H. and Rishel, R.W. (1975) *Deterministic and Stochastic Optimal Control*, Berlin: Springer-Verlag.

Fleming, W.H. and Soner, H.M. (1993) *Controlled Markov Processes and Viscosity Solutions*, Berlin: Springer-Verlag.

Fontagne, J., Freudenburg, M. and Pindy, R. (1998) 'Intra-Industry Trade and the Single Market: Quality Matters', *CEPR Working Paper*, London.

Frankel, J.A. and Rose, A.K. (1995) 'Empirical Research in Nominal Exchange Rates', *Handbook of International Economics*, Vol. III.

Frenkel, J.A. and Rodriguez, C. (1982) 'Exchange Rate Dynamics and the Overshooting Hypothesis', *IMF Staff Papers*, vol. 29, pp. 674–88.

Frenkel, J.A., Goldstein, M. and Masson, P.R. (1991) 'Characteristics of a Successful Exchange Rate System', *IMF Occasional Paper*, no. 82.

Froot, A.K. and Rogoff, K. (1995) 'Perspectives on PPP and Long-Run Real Exchange Rates', *Handbook of International Economics*, Vol. III.

Ghosh, A. (1995) 'Macroeconomic Performance under Alternative Exchange Rate Regimes', CEPR workshop on Convertibility and Exchange Rate Policy in the Context of the Economic Transformation of the Countries of the CEEC, Sofia, September.

Giavazzi, F. and Giovannini, A. (1989) 'Monetary Policy Interactions under Managed Exchange Rates', *Economica*, vol. 56, pp. 199–213.

Gomulka, S. (1998) 'Managing Capital Flows in Poland: 1995–98', *Economics of Transition*, vol. 6, pp. 389–96.

Grafe, C. and Wyplosz, C. (1997) 'The Real Exchange Rate in Transition Economies', *CEPR Working Paper*, no. 1773, December.

Greene, W.H. (1997) *Econometric Analysis*, 3rd edn, Englewood Cliffs, N.J.: Prentice-Hall.

Grinols, E. and Turnovsky, S. (1993) 'Risk, the Financial Market and Macroeconomic Equilibrium', *Journal of Economic Dynamics and Control*, vol. 17, pp. 1–36.

Halpern, L. and Wyplosz, C. (1997) 'Equilibrium Exchange Rates in Transition Economies', *IMF Staff Papers*, vol. 44, no. 4, pp. 430–61.

Halpern, L. (1996) 'Real Exchange Rate and Exchange Rate Policy in Hungary', *Economics of Transition*, vol. 4, no. 1, pp. 211–28.

Hanson, J. (1983) 'Contractionary Devaluation, Substitution in Production and Consumption and the Role of the Labour Market', *Journal of International Economics*, vol. 14, pp. 179–89.

Hausmann, U.G. (1981) 'On the Adjoint Process for Optimal Control of Diffusion Processes', *SIAM Journal of Control and Optimization*, vol. 19, no. 2, pp. 221–43.

Hošek, J. (1997) 'The Income Effect of Price Deregulation: The Czech Case', *Discussion Paper*, Cerge-El, Prague.

References

Hošek, J. (1999) 'The Exchange Rate and the Real Supply Response in the Czech Republic', Final Report of the ACE Project No. P96-6176-R.

Hrncir, M. (1994) 'Exchange Rate Regime for the Stages of Transition', paper presented at the workshop of the ACE Project: Exchange Rate Regime in Transition and Integration into the European Monetary Framework, Delphi, October.

Hrncir, M. (1995) 'Fixed Exchange Rate Regimes in the Stages of Transition', CEPR workshop on Convertibility and Exchange Rate Policy in the Context of the Economic Transformation of the Countries of the CEEC, Sofia, September.

Hsieh, D. (1982) 'The Determinants of the RER. The Productivity Approach', *Journal of International Economics*, vol. 12, pp. 355–62.

Humpage, O.F. and McIntire, J.M. (1995) 'An Introduction to Currency Boards', *Federal Reserve Bank of Cleveland Economic Review*, vol. 31, pp. 2–11.

In, F. and Menon, J. (1996) 'The Long-run Relationship Between the Real Exchange Rate and Terms of Trade in OECD Countries', *Applied Economics*, vol. 28, no. 9, September, pp. 1075–80.

Isard, P. (1977) 'How Far Can We Push the "Law of One Price"?', *American Economic Review*, vol. 67, no. 5, pp. 942.

Jensen, S. (1997) 'Wage Rigidity, Monetary Integration and Fiscal Stabilisation in Europe', *Review of International Economics*, vol. 5, Special Supplement, pp. 36–54.

Judd, K. (1982) 'An Alternative to Steady-state Comparisons in Perfect Foresight Models', *Economic Letters*, vol. 10, pp. 55–9.

Karatzas, I., Lehoczky, J.P. and Shreve S.E. (1987) 'Optimal Portfolio and Consumption Decisions for a "Small Investor" on a Finite Horizon', *SIAM Journal of Control and Optimization*, vol. 25, pp. 1557–86.

Karatzas, I., Lehoczky, J.P., Sethi, S.P. and Shreve, S.E. (1986) 'Explicit Solution of a General Consumption/Investment Problem', *Mathematics of Operations Research*, vol. 11, pp. 261–94.

Kenen, P. (1994) *The International Economy*, New York: Cambridge University Press.

Khan, M.S. and Knight, M.D. (1981) 'Stabilisation Programmes in Developing Countries', *IMF Staff Papers*, vol. 28, pp. 1–53.

Kokoszczynski, R. and Durjasz, P. (1995) 'From Fixed to Flexible Rate Regimes: The Case of Poland', CEPR workshop on Convertibility and Exchange Rate Policy in the Context of the Economic Transformation of the Countries of the CEEC, Sofia, September.

Krugman, P. and Taylor, L. (1978) 'The Contractionary Effects of Devaluation', *Journal of International Economics*, vol. 8, pp. 445–56.

Lipton, D. and Sachs, J. (1991) 'Creating a Market in Eastern Europe: The Case of Poland', *Brookings Papers on Economic Activity*, no. 1, pp. 75–147.

Lizondo, J.S. (1993) 'Real Exchange Rate Targeting under Imperfect Asset Substitutability', *IMF Working Paper*, no. 38.

Lizondo, J.S. and Montiel, P. (1989) 'Contractionary Devaluation in Developing Countries: An Analytical Overview', *IMF Staff Papers*, vol. 36, March, pp. 182–227.

Lucas, R.E. (1972) 'Expectation and the Neutrality of Money', *Journal of Economic Theory*, vol. 4, April, pp. 103–24.

Lucas, R.E. (1973) 'Some International Evidence on Output-Inflation Trade-offs', *American Economic Review*, vol. 63, June, pp. 326–34.

MacDonald, R. (1997) 'What Determines Real Exchange Rates? The Long and Short of It', *IMF Working Paper*, no. 21.

Mankiw, N.G. (1985) 'Small Menu Costs and Large Business Cycles: A Macroeconomic Model of Monopoly', *Quarterly Journal of Economics*, 100, May, pp. 529–39.

McKinnon, R.I. (1973) *Money and Capital in Economic Development*, Washington: Brookings Institute.

Mecagni, M. (1995) 'Experience with Nominal Anchors', in 'IMF Conditionality: Experience Under Stand-by and Extended Arrangements', Part II: Background Papers, *IMF Occasional Paper*, no. 129, September.

Mencinger, J. (1992) 'Oblikovanje tecaja tolarja', *Gospodarska Gibanja*, Ekonomski Inštitut Pravne Fakultete, no. 228, May.

Mencinger, J. (1995) 'Varljiva trdnost tolarja', *Gospodarska Gibanja*, Ekonomski Inštitut Pravne Fakultete, no. 257, October.

Merton, R. (1971) 'Optimum Consumption and Portfolio Rules in a Continuous Time Model', *Journal of Economic Theory*, no. 3, pp. 373–413, Erratum (1973): 6, pp. 213–14.

Merton, R. (1991) *Continuous-Time Finance*, Oxford: Basil Blackwell.

Milo, W. and Wdowinski, P. (1995) 'Economic Implications of Exchange Rate Control: The Case of Poland', Proceedings of the 5th International Conference of the Applied Econometrics Association on Exchange Rate Determination, Stuttgart, Germany, March.

Mitchell, A.J. and Pentecost, E.J. (2001) 'The Real Exchange Rate and the Output Response in Four Transition Economies: A Panel Data Study', ACE-PHARE Workshop, Prague, 1998, in this volume as Chapter 5.

Montiel, J.P. and Ostry, J.D. (1992) 'External Shocks and Inflation in Developing Countries under a Real Exchange Rate Rule', *IMF Working Paper*, no. 75.

National Bank of Slovenia, *Monetary Survey*, various issues.

Neary, P. (1988) 'Determinants of the Equilibrium Real Exchange Rate', *American Economic Review*, vol. 78, no. 1.

Nuti, M. (1995) 'Inflation, Interest and Exchange Rates in the Transition', CEPR workshop on Convertibility and Exchange Rate Policy in the Context of the Economic Transformation of the Countries of the CEEC, Sofia, September.

Oblath, G. and Csermely, A. (1994) 'Macroeconomic Developments and Dilemmas in Hungary', paper presented at the workshop of ACE project: Exchange Rate Regime in Transition and Integration into the European Monetary Framework, Delphi, October.

Obstfeld, M. and Rogoff, K. (1995) 'Exchange Rate Dynamics Redux', *Journal of Political Economy*, vol. 103, no. 3, pp.

OECD (1992b) 'Economic Survey for Czechoslovakia 1991', Paris.

OECD (1992c) 'Economic Survey for Poland', Centre for Co-operation with European Economies in Transition.

OECD (1992d) 'Bulgaria: An Economic Assessment', Centre for Co-operation with European Economies in Transition.

OECD (1997) 'Economic Surveys: 1996–97: Bulgaria', Paris.

Osband, K. and Villanueva, D. (1993) 'Independent Currency Authorities, An Analytic Primer', *IMF Staff Papers*, vol. 40, no. 1, March, pp. 202–16.

Papazoglou, C. and Pentecost, E.J. (2001) 'Output Dynamics in Transition Economies under Alternative Exchange Rate Regimes', ACE-PHARE Workshop, Prague 1998, reproduced as Chapter 2 in this volume.

Peng, S. (1990) 'A General Stochastic Maximum Principle for Optimal Control Problems', *SIAM Journal of Control and Optimization*, vol. 28, no. 4, pp. 966–79.

Pentecost, E.J. (1993) *Exchange Rate Dynamics*, Aldershot: Edward Elgar.

Pentecost, E.J. (1998) 'Criteria for Exchange Rate Policy with an Application to Ukraine', mimeo, University of Kiev-Mohyla Academy, April.

Pesaran, M.H. and Smith, R. (1995) 'Estimating Long-run Relationships from Dynamic Heterogeneous Panels', *Journal of Econometrics*, vol. 68, pp. 79–113.

Pomery, C. (1997) 'The First Czech Invest Annual Survey of FDI in the Czech Republic', *CzechInvest*, Prague.

Rhodd, R.G. (1993) 'The Effect of Real Exchange Rate Changes on Output: Jamaica's Devaluation Experience', *Journal of International Development*, vol. 5, pp. 291–303.

Rogoff, K. (1996) 'The Purchasing Power Parity Puzzle', *Journal of Economic Literature*, vol. 36, June, pp. 647–68.

Rosati, D. (1995) 'Exchange Rate Policies, the Transition from Market to Plan', CEPR workshop on Convertibility and Exchange Rate Policy in the Context of the Economic Transformation of the Countries of the CEEC, Sofia, September.

Ross, K. (1997) 'Post-Stabilization Inflation Dynamic in Slovenia', *IMF Republic of Slovenia*, selected issues, 22 December.

Saavalainen, T.O. (1995) 'Stabilisation in the Baltic Countries: Early Experience', in 'Road Maps of the Transition: The Baltics, the Czech Republic, Hungary and Russia', *IMF Occasional Paper*, no. 127, September.

Sachs, J.D. and Warner A.M. (1996) 'Achieving Rapid Growth in the Transition Economies of Central Europe', Development Discussion Paper no. 554, Harvard Institute for International Development, July.

Selowsky, M. and Martin, R. (1996) *Policy Performance and Output Growth in the Transition Economies*, Washington: The World Bank, December.

Sheen, J. (1992) 'International Monetary and Fiscal Policy Co-operation in the Presence of Wage Inflexibilities: Are Both Counterproductive?', *Journal of Economic Dynamics and Control*, vol. 16, pp. 359–87.

Stein, L.J. and Sauernheimer, K. (1996) 'The Equilibrium Real Exchange Rate of Germany', *Journal of International and Comparative Economics*, vol. 20, pp. 97–131.

Stein, L.J. (1990) 'The Real Exchange Rate', *Journal of Banking and Finance*, no. 14, pp. 1045–78.

Stein, L.J. (1995) 'The Fundamental Determinants of the Real Exchange Rate of the US Dollar Relative to the G7', *IMF Working Paper*, no. 81.

Stein, J. and Allen, P.R. (1995) *Fundamental Determinants of Exchange Rates*, Oxford: Oxford University Press.

Stulz, R. (1984) 'Currency Preferences, Purchasing Power Risks and the Determinants of Exchange Rate in an Optimizing Model', *Journal of Money, Credit and Banking*, vol. 16, pp. 302–16.

Sutherland, A. (1995) 'Monetary and Real Shocks and the Optimal Target Zone', *European Economic Review*, vol. 39, pp. 161–72.

Taylor, J.B. (1979) 'Staggered Wage Setting in a Macro Model', *American Economic Review*, vol. 69, May, pp. 108–13.

Turnovsky, S.J. (1986) 'Monetary and Fiscal Policy Under Perfect Foresight: A Symmetric Two-country Analysis', *Economica*, vol. 53, pp. 139–57.

Vanags, A. and Garry, J. (1995) 'Inflation, Exchange Rates and Central Bank Policy in a Transition Economy: An Analysis of the Latvian Experience, 1992–94', QMW Department of Economics *Discussion Paper* no. 333.

Williamson, J. (1993) 'Exchange Rate Management', *Economic Journal*, no. 103, March, pp. 188–97.

Williamson, J. (1994) *Estimating Equilibrium Exchange Rates*, Washington, D.C: Institute for International Economics.

World Bank (1995) 'Trends in Developing Economies', Washington, D.C.: The World Bank.

World Bank (1996) 'From Plan to Market', *World Bank Development Report 1996*, Washington, D.C.: The World Bank.

World Bank (1998) 'The World Report', Washington, D.C.: The World Bank.

Zapatero, F. (1995) 'Equilibrium Asset Prices and Exchange Rates, *Journal of Economic Dynamics and Control*, vol. 19, pp. 787–811.

Author Index

Author Index

Subject Index